Sacred and Secular Scriptures

ERASMUS INSTITUTE BOOKS

SACRED & SECULAR SCRIPTURES

A Catholic Approach to Literature

Nicholas Boyle

University of Notre Dame Press

Notre Dame, Indiana

Manufactured in the United States of America

Published in Great Britain by
Darton, Longman and Todd Ltd
1 Spencer Court
140–142 Wandsworth High Street
London
SW 18 4JJ

Library of Congress Cataloging-in-Publication Data

Boyle, Nicholas.
    Sacred and secular scriptures : a Catholic approach to literature / Nicholas Boyle.
        p.   cm.
    "The text of the third series of Erasmus lectures, delivered in the Erasmus
Institute of the University of Notre Dame in September 2002 and April 2003"—
Pref.
    Includes index.
    ISBN 0-268-02178-3 (cloth : alk. paper)
    ISBN 0-268-02180-5 (pbk. : alk. paper)
1. Religion and literature.   2. Bible as literature.   I. Title.
PN49.B695   2004
809'.93382—dc22

                                                              2004023681

∞ *This book is printed on acid-free paper.*

FOR ROSEMARY

"fantastically brilliant"

CONTENTS

This book is the text of the Third Series of Erasmus Lectures, delivered in the Erasmus Institute of the University of Notre Dame in September 2002 and April 2003. The lectures have been lightly revised for publication, and footnotes have been added, but their original character has not been disguised.

It is my belief that books, like lectures, should offer something to everyone, and, with a theme as broad as this series provided, that did not seem a difficult target. The complementary obligation was rather more daunting: to ensure that no one has to put up for too long with what does not interest them. I believe this book will offer something of interest to anyone who reads or wants to read either the Bible or the major (and minor) works of Western literature on which I touch—whether they do so as a matter of profession, or of study, or of private entertainment or devotion. I hope also that I have succeeded in offering nothing tedious that is not skippable. Part 1 is concerned with some influential theories about how we should read the biblical texts, given that not all we read is the Bible, part 3 with the practical business of reading the texts of secular literature, given that not all we read is secular. Part 2 attempts to link sacred and secular, theory and practice. The individual chapters should if necessary be able to stand alone, like the original lectures to which, largely, they correspond, and I hope that, read in this way, they may have the appeal of a portrait gallery of selected books and thinkers. At the same time I hope that those who are puzzled by the relation between sacred and secular scriptures, whether they would describe the source of their puzzlement as theological or philosophical, literary or hermeneutic, will find here a sustained attempt to clarify the distinction between these different kinds of writing, their common ground, and their shared inspiration.

The term "Catholic" in my subtitle is not meant as a sectarian rallying cry but as an admission of the source of my own puzzlement. In these matters above all there is no such thing as presuppositionless judgment, yet academic literary theory too often claims a neutrality for its own necessarily tendentious assumptions which is quite at odds with the perspectivism it also professes—Catholicism is bias, for example, but psychoanalysis is just one possible approach. By contrast, I would hope this study might give back to the word "Catholic" something of its original ecumenical meaning: if we can expand our minds enough to guess at the generous dimensions of our father's house, we shall not be surprised to discover that we all have mansions in it.

It was a privilege and a pleasure to join in the work of the Erasmus Institute at the interface between Catholic theology and secular culture. I am particularly grateful to Jim Turner, then director of the Institute, who first asked me to come and who was an attentive listener and genial host throughout my stay, and to Kathy Sobieralski, who assisted with every detail of the sometimes complex arrangements, from travel and housing to last-minute typing of the lecture on *Moby-Dick*. The other staff of the Institute, especially Dianne Philips, were a tower of strength, unperturbed even by the news that the lectures were to be delivered in sessions of two hours rather than one. Long after their occasion has been forgotten, the wonderful refreshments served in the intervals will surely linger in the memory of the audience. I owe special thanks to Bob Sullivan, now director of the Institute, and to Bishop John D'Arcy, bishop of Fort Wayne, South Bend, for their kindness and help in the difficult personal circumstances in which the second installment of the lectures had to be delivered. The University of Notre Dame itself, in the persons particularly of Provost Nathan Hatch, Dean Mark Roche, and Professor Robert Norton, among others, was as welcoming as I have always known it. The exchange of thoughts with Vittorio Hösle, Cyril O'Regan, and Kevin Hart was particularly valuable to me and has left its mark on the revision. I am also glad to be able to thank the Congregation of the Holy Cross for the warm hospitality they extended to me and my family, so making our visit to Notre Dame—rather surprisingly, perhaps, for its younger members—into the highlight of our summer holiday in 2002.

To Professor Charles Gordon I owe not only my introduction to Notre Dame in the first place, but counsel and assistance at every stage in the gestation of this project. If it has been successfully completed, that is in large part due to his attentive concern. Through him, too, I should like to thank the men of Old College, not least Brother Ed Luther, for their welcome and for their loyal support. I am also particularly grateful to Barbara Hanrahan, Rebecca DeBoer, and Sheila Berg for guiding the book through to publication with such discreet and sympathetic professionalism and to Brendan Walsh for his enthusiastic help with the English edition and with the cover.

There are many others to whom I owe debts of gratitude, which can be only poorly repaid here. The late and dear John O'Neill, who died during my second stay in Notre Dame, gave me help with my first chapter which is more specifically recorded in the footnotes, and Richard Francis did the same for the chapter on Melville. Barry Devlin and Mary Boyle were my guides to the life and work of Tolkien, and Michael Boyle identified a James Bond film for me. Eamon Duffy made the vital and timely suggestion that I might address the issues treated in chapter 14. Susan Few deciphered and typed nearly all the text—mostly to impossible deadlines and while juggling other elements in our domestic timetable—and so made a significant contribution to keeping me sane throughout the process. So too, in different ways, did Roger Bacon and Doran and Angela Boyle. My beloved father-in-law, Michael Devlin, cooked me many dinners. He rejoiced in the success of the lectures but alas has not lived to see them published. My wife, Rosemary, alone knows what a journey they represent and has accompanied me on every step of the way. This is her book as much as it is mine.

N. B.
Holy Saturday, 2004

PART I

The Bible as Literature

CHAPTER I

"Literature as the 'Site' of Theology"

LET ME BEGIN WITH AN ACT OF HOMAGE TO A NEGLECTED, IF NOT actually forgotten, father of the Second Vatican Council—father in a spiritual rather than a clerical sense. Though he prepared the way for the Council and for one of its most important documents, he was allowed to participate in it only behind the scenes, and though he may have enjoyed the role of éminence grise he certainly did not adopt it by choice. Marie-Dominique Chenu, O.P., who together with Yves Congar composed the Bishops' Message to the World which set the tone for *Gaudium et Spes,*[1] was, throughout a stormy career, an inspired meditator on the relation between the sacred and the secular, the church and the world, in what were for him the clearly related fields of historical thinking and moral acting. In 1969 Chenu published a short article, "La littérature comme 'lieu' de la théologie" (Literature as the "Site" of Theology),[2] which set out a twofold program for theology in the immediate aftermath of the Council. First, Catholic theology should seek to recover its roots in the Scriptures, which had permeated and given life to the writings of the church fathers and indeed of Catholic theologians until the end of the Middle Ages. Second, this recovery of contact with the Bible would bring Catholic theology back into contact with human culture in general, from which it had sadly become detached in recent centuries. How was it, for example, that French literature of the nineteenth century from Chateaubriand to Hugo was drenched in the Bible, while theological manuals of the period continued to draw exclusively on the rationalist abstractions of Wolff? (I mention in passing that one such manual

3

has been particularly commended to us by the late Cardinal von Balthasar.)[3] The answer was that the great representatives of literary Romanticism regarded the Bible as "part of the common property of humanity" ("La littérature," p. 76) and, by implication, that the theologians did not.

In his article Chenu attempts in a few lines to suggest how the Bible might be seen—and might in future theology come to function—as a divinely ordained mediation between human culture and divine truth. It could take on that role, he says, if it were to be regarded as literature. In what he explicitly calls a kenosis, a humbling incarnation of the Godhead, on the one hand, the Bible partakes of the images, histories, and universal concerns that, through literature, humanity puts into language and, on the other, the Bible raises language to a dignity for which "nature left to its own resources could never have hoped."

> The Bible, the ultimate measure of all Christian theologies and, one may say, itself theology in superabundance, is a picture book, a book of images. The revelation of Himself God made in it to the world has entered into association with a literary not with a theological type of comprehensibility. The Bible is a literature. God is revealed in it not through a system of ideas . . . but through a history, and through many stories, through men with individual faces and various destinies. . . . since God did not think it robbery to become a writer, it is only just if men recognize him in this capacity and take the Bible as, formally, literature, . . . assuming that we agree to define literature as a certain vision of the world bound together in a coherent system of images which between them betray the profound personality of an author. ("La littérature," pp. 76–77)

As it happens I do not agree, in some important respects, with that definition of literature, which anyway Chenu has taken from another thinker, but the disagreement over how we define literature, a question to which I shall return, does not affect Chenu's program itself, or its value.

It is evident that in the years since Chenu wrote his article the two elements in his program have met with unequal success. Certainly the Scriptures have been given a far more prominent role in Catholic liturgy, theology, and formation than was the case before the Vatican Council. But it is more doubtful whether the enhanced standing of the Scriptures has helped theology to "live in symbiosis with all human culture," in Chenu's phrase. That is, it is doubtful both whether the symbiosis has been achieved and what part the cultivation of the Scriptures has had in such progress as there has been. On the whole, the huge engine that is international biblical scholarship—which despite significant Catholic input still runs mainly on Protestant fuel—has pulsed away decoupled from the task of integrating theology and secular culture. There have of course been many important individual contributions to that task which in the nature of things have to some extent drawn on Scripture: in the United Kingdom the work of Brian Wicker and more recently of the Chesterton Institute or of John Milbank;[4] in the United States many of the initiatives that have been associated with the University of Notre Dame, for example, the work of Alasdair MacIntyre or the journal *Religion and Literature.* And the Erasmus Institute has devoted itself to the necessary project of demonstrating the relevance of Catholic intellectual traditions to any aspect of the academic study of culture. But I suspect it would be Chenu's view that we have all suffered from the divorce, in both Protestant and post-Reformation Catholic traditions, of the nourishing and unifying power of sacred Scripture from the theological engagement with the secular world.

Chenu's article suggests that the Bible can be the mediator between theology and secular culture, the "site" where theology takes "place," because the Bible is literature. I do not however intend here to attempt more than occasional literary exegesis of passages in the Bible. Professional exegetes, and more recently literary critics, have done a great deal of this far better than anything I could aspire to.[5] Rather than attempt to fulfill the prescription in Chenu's article, I want instead to try out two lines of investigation it suggests to me. For if literature is the site of theology, that site is occupied by both sacred and secular scriptures. In the first part of this book I discuss some earlier and some more recent writers on the Bible who have tried to treat it as literature, in the hope of identifying an approach to this task which is both productive and Catholic, even though not all of Chenu's predecessors, including some he mentions by name, have adopted such an approach, or even wished to adopt it. There is, obviously, a need for some discernment of spirits. There is also a need to develop a concept of literature that is capable of accommodating both the Bible and what we have normally understood by literature without forcing either into a costume in which they look constrained or ridiculous: Malvolio in cross-garters or Huck Finn in a suit. That I attempt in part 2. Then in part 3 I move from the Bible as literature to the converse theme which Chenu's article implies but does not elaborate because, as he admits at the outset, he is starting from the needs of theology: what one might call the theme of literature as Bible. We are used to the idea that literary criticism provides us with concepts and categories to apply to the Bible. Let us reverse the process and see if, through the Bible, theology can provide us with concepts that apply to literature and to the concerns of secular culture that literature embodies. Let us see how far the language of secular literature can lead us into the language of biblical literature. Let us see how far the secular scriptures are continuous with the sacred.

Like a figure of romance, then, I am setting out on a quest. In part 1 we are on relatively familiar ground as we try to find a Catholic way of reading the Bible. But that will lead us into the second and third parts, where we shall be in increasingly unfamiliar territory, as we seek a Catholic way of reading secular literature. I should therefore like to say something at this preliminary stage about the later stages of this quest—so as to give some sense of the direction in which its first stage is taking us. I can be encouraged to undertake this two-way journey, from the Bible to literature and from literature back to the Bible, by some advice from a perhaps improbable source, but then advice from mysterious strangers is a feature of the romantic quest. By confessing both his desire and his inability to believe, George Steiner has cast himself as one of those sorrowful seekers after truth—"ceux qui cherchent en gémissant"—to whom Pascal's apology for religion was to be directed.[6] In 1989, in his book *Real Presences,* Steiner proclaimed what he called his "Pascalian . . . wager on a reinsurance of sense" in these words:

> [T]he act of reading . . . is a metaphysical and, in the last analysis, a theological one. The ascription of beauty to truth and to meaning is . . . a piece of theology. . . . [E]verything we recognize as being of compelling stature in literature, art, music is of a religious inspiration or reference.[7]

Steiner presents this insight—which it took courage to publish in 1989—as the conclusion of his investigation. In parts 2 and 3, I try to take it further still, to try to tease out how it might apply in practice and in detail, specifically, in the realm of literature, to which, largely, I confine myself. I eventually try to determine the religious inspiration or reference of particular works, the extent to which that inspiration or reference can be grasped in the categories of a biblically based, that is, a Christian theology. I call this a Catholic approach for various reasons but in the first instance because it postulates that if a work has a religious reference at all, that reference will ultimately be definable in the terms of Catholic Christianity, and as, in those terms, to a greater or lesser extent orthodox, to a greater or lesser extent heretical (bearing in mind, of course, the principle that heresy is only a distortion or exaggeration of a truth). It is a corollary of this postulate that if we have correctly defined the nature of the Catholic reference of a work—the greater or lesser extent to which it embodies truths—that Catholic reference will prove to correspond to some fundamental feature of the work's literary character and value. Though there are manifest risks to such a Catholic approach—risks to which the world outside the Catholic academy will clamorously draw our attention[8]—it is an enormous advantage that in a Catholic institution it is possible to *begin* an intellectual investigation from such postulates. We do not have to spend our time like Steiner, arguing towards them, painfully and with some embarrassment, as the terminus of our inquiry. We do not have to argue about this (we can do, but we don't have to, and if we do argue, it is subject to the proviso that we know we don't have to). We can set out into the wide world of literature, with these postulates as our sword and our shield, and see what adventure we shall meet with. If we have any success we shall find some confirmation of my initial conviction that one light illuminates all the fields that a university is called to study. The result may even be that literature appears to us as a halo around the light, fading off into shadow—as if round the canonical books of sacred scripture are grouped innumerable other books of secular wisdom of which, with the appropriate qualifications, it may also be said in the words of St. Paul (2 Tm 3:16–17): "All scripture is given by inspiration of God, and is profitable for doctrine, for reproof, for correction, for instruction in righteousness: that the man of God may be perfect, throughly finished unto all good works."

My working hypothesis, then, in both parts of this investigation, is that literature is the site of theology because literature, biblical and nonbiblical, is a place where sacred and secular meet. A Catholic can expect to find in the words of noncanonical and even non-Christian writings something, though not of course everything, of the moral *and doctrinal* instruction to be found in sacred scripture, just as we expect the Bible to illuminate our daily and contemporary lives. Nor would common sense lead us to expect anything else: language is only language, a medium of communication, because all the words in it are secondhand. Even the language of a Christian sacred book is alive and meaningful, even for a Christian, only because it is the common property of Christian and non-Christian alike and passes through hands that—like the many hands that pass on coins—may be unclean and pagan. (And no more here than anywhere else can we make a distinction between words and the structures of meaning which they build up.) The words of Christian sacred texts are in permanent intercourse with the words of texts that are not sacred. This understanding of the potential value to biblical teaching of nonbiblical literature is far older and more venerable than the concept of the Bible itself as literature. The compilers of the Book of Proverbs recognized Egyptian writers as "sages" (22:17) and were happy to incorporate and reformulate their work for their own ends. Jesus himself, whose parables so often point to the logic of our behavior in the secular world and ask why we do not apply the same logic to our behavior in sacred things, cites what seems to be a popular song in Matthew 11:16–17:

> But whereunto shall I liken this generation? It is like unto children sitting in the markets, and calling unto their fellows, And saying, We have piped unto you and ye have not danced; we have mourned unto you, and ye have not lamented.

In the account in Acts of Paul's preaching on the Areopagus (17:28) Paul is reported as quoting one, possibly two pagan authorities, to make what he has to say more plausible to his audience, and in this way the words of Epimenides of Cnossus, Aratus, and Cleanthes the Stoic have been canonized for Christians as the word of God. In the second of these cases Paul is actually represented as citing a passage, "We are all his children," which is in direct conflict with a central theme in his message. According to Galatians 4:5, we are *not* all children of God, generated as by Jove, but thanks to our Lord Jesus Christ we are for Paul the *adopted* children of Jesus' Father, and it is only through the infusion of his Spirit—or, as the liturgy tells us, only because Jesus taught us to do so, only because we are "divina institutione formati"—that we dare to call God our Father. The narrative of Acts goes further still, showing Paul as beginning his address with the quotation of a pagan cultic inscription on, of all things, an altar "To the Unknown God," and as identifying the object of this dedication with the God who raised Jesus from the dead. Nonsacred words are therefore in intercourse with sacred from the very start of Christianity, and not only when they seem to endorse Christian assertions but even when they are clearly erroneous or inadequate and in need of further correction. Perhaps we could describe this intercourse as like the mixed marriage of Christian and non-Christian of which Paul says in 1 Corinthians 7:14: "For the unbelieving husband is sanctified by the wife, and the unbelieving wife is sanctified by the husband."

For the present, however, I will say no more about literature as—or as sanctified by—the Bible. The first stage in our quest requires us to pay closer attention to the more prominent concept in Chenu's article, the concept of the Bible as literature. It is much the more modern of these two possible ways of defining literature as the "site" of theology, and it has had much the greater influence in recent centuries. We shall see, however, that, as Chenu hints by acknowledging the one-sidedness of his own presentation, it needs to be complemented by the older, more Catholic, and more certainly scriptural notion that secular literature too has, in Steiner's phrase, a "religious . . . reference." We need a Catholic approach not only to literature but to the Bible as literature, and biblical scholarship has to a surprising extent failed to provide this. To understand why this should be we must consider the circumstances in which the concept of the Bible as literature originated.

The modern belief that categories appropriate to the description of nonbiblical literature should also be applied to the Bible in order to make its riches, including its theological riches, available to believers and nonbelievers alike arose in the middle of the eighteenth century as a response to the second stage in a two-stage crisis which threatened the foundations of Protestant and especially of Calvinist and Lutheran orthodoxy. The churches of the Reformation had exposed themselves to this crisis through the peculiar, indeed unique, position they accorded to the Bible. When Thomas Aquinas addresses the question of the nature and resources of theology (*sacra doctrina*) at the very start of the *Summa Theologica* he says only two things, as far as I can see, relevant to the trustworthiness of the Scriptures which reveal divine things to us. The first is that since Scripture is superior to all other knowledge there can be no arguing about the articles of faith it contains with those who do not believe it. We either have faith in it, in which case argument about its contents can begin, or we do not, in which case there is not and cannot be any argumentative procedure that will give us faith. The second point, added a little later, is that if there were such a procedure it would take away the merit of faith.[9]

One might think that these principles, as profound as they are laconic, say all that needs to be said—at least at this stage—in an exposition of Christian belief. However, when John Calvin in 1536 starts off his own exposition of reformed Christianity with a discussion of our knowledge of God and of ourselves he devotes four of the eighteen chapters of the first book of his *Christian Institutes* not to the relation of revelation and reason but to the authority and indubitability of a book: Holy Scripture, by which alone our feeble understanding can attain to God.[10] His conclusion may not be very different from that of Aquinas—that revelation cannot be proved to be such—but whereas Aquinas is concerned with a logical point about the structure of knowledge, Calvin is concerned with the establishment of a personal conviction about the reliability of a literary document. Convictions, and assurances of reliability, take time to establish and admit of degrees. Calvin therefore spends many pages on the topic and devotes a whole chapter to arguments for the plausibility of belief in the truthfulness of Scripture, even though he has already affirmed that this belief can ultimately be founded only on the inner witness of the Holy Spirit in our hearts. From these, more extended arguments three points in particular become clear about the Scriptures, according to Calvin: they surpass in their excellence all other writings; to trust in them is not to trust in the testimony of men, even though in them the word of God is spoken through human mouths; and their authority does not depend on the authority of the church.[11] It is this last point which arouses Calvin's fiercest and most rhetorical ire, and he denounces those who assert the authority of the church to decide, for example, which books shall be admitted to the Bible and which shall be held to be apocryphal as attempting merely to set up a tyranny under a fine name.[12] No trust is to be put in ecclesiastical pronouncements, particularly not those which actually contradict the word of Scripture. Calvin, with the clarity of a systematic thinker, sees the need to detach himself conceptually from the church from which he is already institutionally separated, and the first and fundamental certainty on which he founds his thinking is one which owes nothing to tradition—a word he abhors—nor to any person or institution, nor to any fact or conclusion about the world or indeed about the structure of his own thought: it is the certainty of the divine origin of the Scriptures sealed in his heart by the testimony of the Spirit.

Calvin saw far more clearly than Luther the systematic significance of the unique authority of Scripture for the movement rejecting the tyranny of Rome. The early Lutheran confessions contain little or nothing in the way of reflection on the methodology of the Reformation. However, as the Reformation grew and was forced by the confrontation with Rome and by internal division into defining itself institutionally, so Calvin's method imposed itself. It is an indication of a Calvinist tendency in the English church's 39 Articles of 1562, inherited from the 42 Articles of 1553, that the first article they contain, after those which rehearse the contents of the Apostles'

Creed, is the article "Of the sufficiency of the Holy Scriptures for Salvation" (no. 6). In 1576 an agreement was achieved between most, though not all, of the German Lutheran churches on a confessional formula which healed the divisions brought about by the presence of crypto-Calvinist tendencies in a number of them. The compromise with Calvinism is among other things visible in the presence of a preface to the first, summary part of this so-called Formula of Concord, which lays down the first rule of theological discussion among Protestants: the priority of Scripture, even over the Creeds, the Lutheran Confessions, and Luther's catechisms (whose consonance with Scripture is nonetheless affirmed). Only, we are told,

> [i]n this way [is] the clear distinction [*luculentum discrimen;* the German has simply *Unterschied*] between the Holy Scripture of the old and new testaments and all other writings [*omnia aliorum;* German, *allen andern*] maintained and only Holy Scripture [*sola sancta Scriptura*] remains [*agnoscitur*] the one judge, rule and guideline according to which, as the one touchstone [*Lydium lapidem*], all teachings ought to be and must be discerned [*exigenda;* German, *erkannt*] and judged as to whether they are good or evil, true or false.[13]

I believe this is the first use of the phrase *sola sancta scriptura* to identify a principle of Protestantism thought to be as fundamental as justification by faith alone—*sola fide*—or reliance only on grace—*sola gratia*—or on the mediation only of Christ—*solus Christus*. In all these cases, of course, the exclusive epithet *solus* is an explicit rejection of some feature of Roman Catholic teaching. As in those other areas of theology, the doctrine of the unique status of Holy Scripture, and its distinction from all other human writings, to the point where it is regarded as writing still, but not human, is a part of the self-definition of Protestantism as the negation of Roman Catholicism. In the seventeenth century the principle of *sola scriptura* was built into systematic theology by Lutheran Aristotelians such as Johann Gerhard and became a rallying cry in the great religious conflicts: in 1638 William Chillingworth, a convert first to and then from Catholicism, who may therefore be assumed to have known what he was talking about, made his famous declaration: "The BIBLE, I say, the BIBLE only, is the Religion of Protestants!"[14] In the more settled atmosphere of the eighteenth century this religion became a way of life and thinking, a cult in the full sense of the word, which could take on strange forms. Calvinism of course forbade the use of any images in worship, but in the Calvinist chapel of the university town of Göttingen, a simple rectangle of stalls arranged around the pulpit from which the incorporeal word of God was to be proclaimed, one statue was allowed, surmounting and dominating preacher and pulpit alike, a wooden image of the Bible. The religion of Protestants had become, literally, what Coleridge, who must have seen this chapel, called in his *Confessions* bibliolatry, a term he borrowed from Lessing to denote the worship not of God but of a book.[15]

Bibliolatry was singularly ill adapted to meet the two-stage crisis of the eighteenth century. The first stage originated in the Anglo-Dutch Enlightenment of the period 1680–1740 and in its notion of a natural or rational religion on which all, or practically all, hard-headed men of all, or practically all, times and places could and in fact did generally agree (women, admittedly, were another matter). The tenets of this natural religion usually proved to amount to not much more than belief in one God, in the immortality of the soul, in a few basic moral principles, and, sometimes, in rewards and punishments in an afterlife.[16] That these tenets bore a remarkable similarity to the minimal common ground between the various confessional groups, mostly Christian but also Jewish, in the countries where they were enunciated seems to have been noticed by nobody. Nobody even found it comical when Bishop William Warburton, a thuggish apologist for the Anglican establishment, strained the agreement on rational religion to its limits by declaring that "an established religion with a Test Law [such as the English constitution provided for the benefit of the Anglican church] is the universal voice of Nature."[17] Applied to the reading of the Scriptures, first by Spinoza and Locke and then more aggressively by that disparate collection of minor thinkers known as the Deists, the concept of natural or rational religion produced a series of uncomfortable dilemmas for Christian apologetics which in England were on the whole rather inadequately resolved.

After 1740, however, with the virtual demise of the English Enlightenment, these dilemmas were gradually exported to Germany.[18] Here, in the very different intellectual environment of university theology and philosophy, dominated by the deductive rationalist system of Wolff, in which reason was a matter not of general practical agreement but of an authoritative and ineluctable necessity, the dilemmas became acute. If indeed there was such a thing as natural religion what was the status of the truths contained in the Bible? What was its value when assessed by the tribunal of universal reason? This was not simply a problem for Calvinists. For Lutherans, too, the exegesis of Scripture, the one rule and judge of doctrine, formed an extensive part of the training of all pastors and would-be pastors, and of their preaching once they were appointed to a post, and the encounter with the words of Scripture was for the Pietist branch of Lutheranism the very stuff of the individual's spiritual and moral life. But did the Scriptures merely repeat what rational religion told us it was necessary to think and do in order to be saved? In that case they were superfluous, and reading them was at best a pious and supererogatory work. Did they contradict what rational religion claimed, imposing beliefs and practices that to a rational man might seem absurd or immoral? In that case they would have to be wrong and their readers deluded. Or did they enunciate truths and duties which were indeed necessary for salvation and could not be said to contradict reason but for which it was not possible to find rational grounds? This was hardly a flattering view of the Christian "mysteries," as they were often called, but it offered some prospects of defending such essential dogmas—or dogmas then thought to be essential—as original sin, the divine Sonship of Jesus, and the Trinitarian doctrine of God, the Incarnation and Resurrection, the authority of the church, the eternal punishment of the damned, and the observation of Sunday as a day of rest.

At this time, in the mid-eighteenth century, and to serve this purpose of defining and defending a body of doctrine thought not to be a part of rational religion, the term "revelation," which has a long history, with Jewish as well as Christian antecedents but which was not particularly prominent either in medieval or in sixteenth-century theology, advanced to the front line of apologetics where it has remained ever since, at least in the Protestant tradition and those parts of the Catholic tradition particularly influenced either by Protestantism directly or by altercation with Protestantism. Together with it we find, in Germany at least, the terms "positive" and "positivity" coming to the fore as more polite synonyms for "rationally groundless" or "imposed by authority": "positive" religion is the component of religion which could not be deduced from first principles by a Wolffian, the duties or beliefs that are "posited" by the authority of an institution, a tradition, a book, or, presumably and ultimately, God in person. But the notion of the sacred books as a reservoir of positive Revelation is not an easy one to defend against scoffers. In detail, it is open to ridicule—does God really bother about which day of the week we worship him on?—and in principle the very idea of Revelation is controversial. Maybe—we find this compromise creeping into orthodox thought in Germany around the middle of the century, though again it has a prehistory in English Latitudinarianism—maybe positive Revelation is not ultimately and always inaccessible to reason but an only apparently irrational, a pictorial or metaphorical, statement of rational truths "accommodated" to untutored minds. Maybe the Bible is a way of giving the widest popular circulation to truths which in a more philosophical or abstract form the great unwashed would be unable to grasp. Maybe even it was a way of communicating those truths in the past to human beings, such as the Jews, who for want of the culture which we, or the most intelligent among us, have now attained were unable to receive the truths in their pure form. And maybe therefore—though in future the Bible may continue to be of use until all have acquired the rational religion for which it is intended, no doubt by God, to pave the way— maybe, for some of us, the Bible has already become obsolete.

That, or something like it, is the point the argument about Revelation had reached in Germany by the 1770s, at least in its subtlest exposition in Lessing's deceptive, not to say deceitful, treatise, *The Education of the Human Race*. But by that time a second stage had begun in the long crisis of the biblical faith of German Protestantism. An even more powerful intellectual current than that of the English empiricist Enlightenment of Locke and Newton had begun to flow, a tide which was to cover every corner of the world and which is gently rising still. For the sake of simplicity one could call it the rise of "history," Vico's "new science," for by the beginning of the nineteenth century, and largely under the impact of this change, the word *history* had almost entirely lost its sense of "unsystematically accumulated knowledge"—still preserved, just, in the term "natural history"—and largely acquired its modern sense of "chronologically organized knowledge." But for the sake of clarity one needs some longer term such as "the rise of historical and cultural relativism." Let us settle on a compromise and use a term borrowed from German which is neither simple nor clear but has the advantage of brevity, and speak of the rise of "historicism." Karl S. Guthke has recently shown, in appealingly concrete detail,[19] the extraordinary expansion of intellectual horizons brought about in eighteenth-century Europe by the commercial and imperial expansion especially of Britain, Russia, and France and by the resultant explosion of geographical and anthropological knowledge. It did indeed become possible to observe mankind from China to Peru, and the consequence was, for those who chose to reflect on what they observed, a vastly increased awareness of the potential variety of human behavior, speech, and thought—in many ways, indeed, that variety was much greater then than it is now when McDonalds and Microsoft, television and the English language, and of course Kalashnikovs are to be found in every latitude. At the same time, and partly though not entirely as a consequence of the same process, there came about an expanded awareness of the human potential for variation across time.

Human civilization can take on different forms in different times as well as in different places or different climates. Strange to say, the sense that this expanded knowledge of the range of human possibilities presented a philosophical or theological challenge was much less pronounced in the European nations largely responsible for the change, particularly Britain, than it was in Germany. Perhaps speculative anxieties seemed an unprofitable distraction to nations whose confidence in their own superiority to the rest of the human race, past or present, was daily confirmed by the growth of trade and empire. In Germany, however, the shift in the shape and size of the world, possibly because it was observed from a greater distance, meant a shift in the scope and foundations of philosophy, and so of theology too. On the one hand, the new perspective made it possible to identify the complacent aspiration of the English and French Enlightenments to represent the universal consensus of all reasonable men everywhere as the limited, even blinkered vision of a particular interest group at a particular time. Their scorn for the supposedly primitive features of biblical religion could be unmasked as a failure of historical insight and empathy. On the other hand, an even more intractable version of the argument about Revelation now threatened. For it was now apparent that in different times and places human political and economic, literary and artistic, scientific and religious behavior and ideas had grown up in seamless interconnection into different and discrete systems for which the nineteenth century eventually found the word *cultures*. And so it became more difficult, first to assert that there was any such thing as a universal truth, whether philosophical or religious, valid for all humanity, and second to explain why any one of these discrete systems should be regarded as having articulated it. Why should one set of religious insights be privileged over another? Was there any single language in which all the various achievements and ideas of humanity could be compared and evaluated? Even if the Bible was or contained a Revelation how was it possible for it to be a Revelation for any time or culture other than that in which it originated?

These were among the questions that in the 1770s teemed in the mind of J. G. Herder, the man who more than any other deserves to be called the founder of "historicism" and who has the doubtful distinction of having been denominated by Karl Barth "the inaugurator of nineteenth-century theology before its actual inauguration by Schleiermacher."[20] Because the criticisms of Scripture and scriptural religion made by the English Deists were not expressed in historicist terms, their contribution to the definition of the issues facing later theology has been unfairly neglected, particularly their responsibility for the prominence of the distinction between reason and Revelation. England showed no interest in pursuing the questions raised by its Deists into the age of historicism. Instead these questions bore fruit, and began to receive answers, in Germany in the second stage of the eighteenth-century theological crisis. Herder, more painfully than anyone else, experienced the shock of the transition from the first to the second stage of the crisis, and his principal response to the shock was to seek to present the Bible to "connoisseurs of the most ancient, simple and sublime poetry" as a "book written by human beings for human beings,"[21] that is, to formulate an approach to the Bible as literature.

CHAPTER 2

History and Hermeneutics (1): Herder

THE CONCEPT OF LITERATURE UNDERWENT A PROFOUND CHANGE AS a result of the rise of historicism, and Herder was probably the main agent of that change.[1] Literature, he thought, is to be seen as one of the most important expressions of the spirit, "Geist," of a people or nation, a "Volk"—and *Volk* for Herder means no more than the human possessors of what will later be called a culture. More concretely, literature, like arts and crafts, political structure, and religious beliefs, makes up a whole with the economic and ultimately geographical factors that determine the character of a people, as the presence of the Nile determines the sedentary way of life of Egypt or the sea the adventurous commercial life of the Phoenicians. The differences between the manifestations of literature in different times are due not to the greater or lesser success of writers in following timeless rules for genres that do not vary from one culture to another but to the different circumstances from which literature emerges and which it has to address. Sophocles' dramas and Shakespeare's dramas are different because their social and religious functions, the circumstances of their performance, and the literary and cultural traditions on which they drew, were utterly different—and not just because their authors had a better or worse grasp of rules codified by Aristotle or Renaissance theorists. Herder, in short, saw literature as a historically determined cultural artefact, and he was one of the very first to do so. At the same time, however, and for the same reason, he saw literature as the product of individual and original genius. For the individual, even the individual genius, is made what he or she is by his or her time and place and nation. The medium which makes possible this sharing of the individual and the communal mind is language. The work of literature therefore, which, whether oral or written, exists only in and as language, can express at one and the same time the genius of its author and the genius of its context, of its Volk.

Herder rejoiced in cultural difference, in the wealth and variety of human genius opened up to him by increasing geographical and historical knowledge. He collected and translated folk poetry from all over the world and paid frequent homage to predecessors, whether individuals or whole cultures, who showed, in his view, the same generosity towards those different from themselves and who allowed for the flourishing of many and various human identities. He had a vision, derived, I believe, ultimately from the monadic philosophy of Leibniz, of all these individual cultural totalities as reflections or manifestations or indeed—he uses the word—as the Revelation (*Offenbarung*) of God. "Gang Gottes über die Nationen!"—God's passage over the peoples—was the exclamatory slogan into which, in 1774, he condensed the theme of the history of human culture that he hoped to write (*AP* 88). But within that project lay the seeds from which the old Deist problem of Reason-and-Revelation could reemerge, and in a peculiarly acute form for him as a Christian pastor. The problem existed, however, even for a non-Christian, for historicism put in question not only the claims of any particular religion but also those of Reason itself. It was all very well to appreciate the unique identities of different cultural and historical units, but what, Leibniz would have asked, was the principle of continuity between them? In what did God's passage over and between them consist? What was the plan, hidden or manifest, which made a coherent story of it all? Was history just a heap of windowless cultures that could not talk to each other? Herder seemed almost to admit that it was when in defending the right of Shakespeare to differ from Sophocles, he concluded both triumphantly and rather lamely that "Sophocles' drama and Shakespeare's drama are two things that in a certain respect hardly have even the name in common" (*S* 499–500). Why give any two so distinct and different things the same name? By what right are any distinct individual historical phenomena—dramas, wars, republics, religion, human beings even—linked by a common general term? Is there even such a thing as a universally shared human Reason? If every culture has its own language and every language is that of a particular culture, is there a language in which we can recount the history of all cultures?

The answer, to Herder, at any rate in his early years, was obvious: there is indeed such a language. Christianity is the unique particular Revelation destined by God to provide the language which will link all particular revelations into the one great plan. Christianity is the key to human history, he argues in *Yet Another Philosophy of History* (1776), destined from start to finish to be "the religion of the human race, the spur to love, and the bond of all nations" (*AP* 46). It was a grand and in its way a brilliant answer to the scoffers who asked why one particular faith, originating in one particular and rather obscure part of the world, should claim to be privileged above all others. This was the only faith, Herder replied, in which the ambition was articulated to be the universal principle of continuity while respecting the particular identities of the individual components of the great historical kaleidoscope. This—the essence of Christianity as he understood it—was also the essence of his personal ambition to write the history of human culture: "to link up the most disparate scenes without confounding them" in order to show the earth to be "the theatre of a guiding purpose[,] . . . the theatre of divinity" (*AP* 42). Yet Herder never realized his ambition, to his own or anyone else's satisfaction. As soon as we ask what is the particular Christian content of his all-connecting principle the grand scheme starts to unravel, and the Christianity that is to bind all ages and cultures together in a bond of love crumbles back into the rational religion of the Deists. Christianity, in his exposition of it, is detached from its roots in first-century Palestine, and even from the shadowy figure of its founder in order that it should be differentiated from all other previous religions. Those, he says, "were only narrowly national . . . religions of one people, one locality, one legislator, one time." But that, of course, was precisely what it had been his great originality to claim for them! If he now says that Christianity was "in every way the opposite" of those national religions, he is excluding it as thoroughly from everything he has so far shown human history to be as if he were writing not in 1774 but fifty years earlier. In order to trim Christianity to fit the universal function he wants it to fulfill, he has had to cut away the roots in particularity which it had been the strength of his historical vision to see as essential to the life of all phenomena of human culture.

In practice, in the working out of his grand idea, Herder's Christianity is an allotrope of the universal reason or common sense of his Deist predecessors. He admits as much when, under pressure from his argument to define what is unique about Christianity, he formulates it as "in short, if you will [the hesitation and the parenthesis betray his embarrassment as he puts off the moment when he has to utter the word], the most philanthropic form of deism" (AP 47). Herder has with great percipience formulated the most fundamental intellectual task imposed by the process of globalization, which in his day was entering on its modern phase with the establishment of the British and French colonial empires. That task was to relate the universal and the particular in a new concept of reason, under the impact of an awareness of human variety, and he rightly saw that the definition and the future of Christianity were closely bound up with it. Unfortunately, his own conception of Christianity was too limited by the categories and discussions of the earlier eighteenth century for him to be able to rise to the challenge. He was, in the end, too much of a Deist himself, too much in love with Enlightenment. You do not avoid the antithesis of Reason and Revelation by collapsing the one into the other. You need a different conception of human knowledge in the first place.

Herder therefore approached the study of the Bible armed with a concept of literature which fruitfully emphasized both the Bible's historical and social content and the unique contribution of the individual geniuses that were its various authors. But in that concept of literature there also lay dormant the old problematic of deism, ready to emerge as soon as the issue of continuity arose, the issue of the relevance of the literary products of one era or culture to another and different context. Herder was not the first to describe the Bible as literature like any other, but he was, I believe, the first to do so with a historicist concept of literature and with a view to elucidating not merely the form of the biblical writings but also their theological content. His long treatise of 1781–82, *On the Spirit of Hebrew Poetry,* acknowledges in its title its predecessor, Robert Lowth's volume of Oxford lectures on poetry, *De sacra poesi Hebraeorum,* published in 1753 and republished at Göttingen in 1770.[2] It has, however, a quite different and fully theological purpose. Herder aims, not to show the different literary forms to be found in the Bible and the parallels to other ancient writings, notably those of Greece and Rome, but to trump, or outmaneuver, the Deist exegesis of Scripture by the use of his own more sophisticated concept of literature. The reasonable or commonsense approach to Scripture of Spinoza and Locke demanded the exclusion of allegorical or figural readings of the text in favor of its plain sense, from which could be expected to emerge the truths of natural religion or, if appropriate, of a plain man's Christianity. The radicalization of this position by the more critical Deists, however, led to the conclusion that even the truths of natural religion—the unity and immateriality of God, the immortality of the soul, even basic morality—were not to be

found in the Bible, which was too crude, primitive, and possibly menda-
cious a work to deserve the attention of an enlightened age. Herder believes
that his approach can incorporate what seems to him acceptable in the Deist
critiques of Spinoza, Toland, or Voltaire while preserving the teaching authority of Christianity and its Scriptures. He can eliminate those allegorical
and figural meanings of the text which cannot have been part of the original intention of the author. But at the same time he can demonstrate that if
the cultural context of the writings is properly understood they can be seen
as works of literary genius which use the metaphorical language appropriate
to poetry and the moral categories of an ancient people in order to express
an individual understanding and experience of God which has at least as
much moral authority as any pagan text. The Bible is poetry, and neither
tedious literalism nor fanciful allegorizing can do justice to the way poets
understand and write. But the Bible is more: it is many different kinds of
poetry. The Bible's poetically expressed experiences of the divine can be appreciated in their own right by the historical observer, but they are also part
of a developing story. The Hebrew writings themselves represent several
stages of sophistication—the fierce and vivid primitive poetry of Moses and
Deborah, the more intimate lyricism of the Psalmist under King David, the
worldly wisdom of Solomon, and, developed out of these, as a consciously
literary language of intertextual allusion, the dramatic messianic imagery of
the prophets (*GEP* 1282–96)—but all of these are taken up into and sur-
passed in the New Testament. In the New Testament the concepts at work
in the naive terminology and metaphors of the Old are given a form suitable for an enlightened audience, they are "vergeistigt, aufgeklärt, schön
befestigt" (spiritualized, enlightened, beautifully confirmed) (*GEP* 842).
(Though it is important not to let this final stage of biblical literature contaminate our reading of the earlier stages.)

Let us take an example of Herder's approach, the example of immortality. From the point of view of the New Testament we may recognize that
Psalm 16, v. 11—"thou shalt not leave my soul in hell: neither shalt thou
suffer thy Holy One to see corruption"—shows David as a type (*Vorbild*) of
the Messiah and so can treat the passage as a prophecy or promise of resurrection. But when reading the Psalm itself we must dismiss this retrospective view from our minds and concentrate on "the character of the person
speaking in those days and the content of the psalm with respect to its context." We shall then see that it is neither a riddling prophecy of the resurrection of Jesus, as old-fashioned figural interpretation would make it, nor
the groanings of a sick priest hoping for recovery, as the literalist and Deist

would have it, but we shall recognize it as a personal prayer of King David himself in which every line betrays his character. In it David expresses his trust that his corpse will be protected in the grave and that God will welcome him as his friend, his Chasid, into his—as we would say, heavenly—palace. Despite the assaults of the Deists, Herder therefore believes he has shown that the doctrine of immortality *is* present in the Old Testament, not literally, as the Deists wanted, nor in figure, as Catholics would say, but in the metaphorical language of personal poetry, in the poet's expression of trust in the friendship of God (*GEP* 841).

By an extraordinary act of historical imagination and empathy, Herder, in his writings on the Bible, recovered a sense of the immediacy and urgency with which the biblical text was originally composed, a sense of what it means, in human terms, to say that the text is inspired. (I am not, by the way, raising the question of the accuracy of his particular historical and philological assertions.) His achievement is all the more remarkable for having virtually no predecessors—certainly none who could combine historical and literary insight to the same degree. It has been enormously influential, even if the influence has, as Goethe remarked,[3] been of the kind that is so effective that it is forgotten, having made commonplace the ideas that it originated. However, Herder paid a price for his historical empathy in the biblical field as in the field of general history. Here, too, and even with the help provided by the developmental schema that leads from the Old to the New Testament, Herder was unable to resolve the problem of historicism, the problem of continuity, except by recourse to deism. His sense of the unique character of the individual biblical writers, as he imagined them, and of their circumstances was so strong that he could not see how to describe their relevance to ages other than their own, nor even regard it as of any great importance. The worldwide distribution and reception of the Psalms through three millennia he regarded in the first instance as the occasion for "more misinterpretations and diversions from the original meaning" than have plagued any book other than the Song of Songs. David himself, in Herder's view, began the process by "making his feelings general and his own way of singing the predominant one in the Temple" and so provided a pattern which has made the Psalms "a song-book (*Gesangbuch*) for all epochs, all peoples and hearts, even though they had no connection with David's spirit or his affairs." But strange to say, Herder managed to make this sound a regrettable development. "Every commentator, every new rhymester" found his own domestic concerns in this book and "so went and gave it to his church to read and sing . . . as if every one of its members had wandered about on the mountains of Judah and been pursued by Saul" (*GEP* 1192–93). The animosity towards Pietist and other sectarian applications of Scripture is unmistakable, but the word on which the greatest weight of contempt lies is *church*.

Though himself the Lutheran equivalent of a bishop, and flattered to be treated as such when he toured Italy, Herder gave no role to the church in his vision of sacred history and literature, save as the locus of misinterpretation. One would have thought that it was precisely the church that through its tradition of interpretation and above all through its use of the psalms in liturgy and prayer ensured that there *was* a connection between "David's spirit and affairs" and those of men and women in later ages. But Herder explicitly rejects the use of Psalm 6 as "a general penitential prayer," finding it instead "pre-eminently beautiful . . . when regarded as an individual song of David's" (*GEP* 1210). Rather than invoke the church, and contaminate the individuality of the historical phenomenon, Herder prefers to leave our spirit and David's as isolated from each other as the dramas of Sophocles and Shakespeare, hardly deserving even a common name. It is the first of seven principles he lays down for the interpretation of the psalms that we should "forget all more recent paraphrases and commentators," who "read the text appropriately to their own time," and instead we should look to the original time, the *Urzeit,* and find in it "the heart and mind of [King] David and his [court] poets" (*GEP* 1193). It does not seem to occur to Herder that those more recent readers of David also have their own spirit, their own heart and mind, and that he has left unexamined and unexplained his own prejudice in favor of the "Urzeit." In a precisely similar way he is unable to recognize that the French seventeenth-century dramatists whom he accuses, no doubt rightly, of misunderstanding the Greeks and so producing an aesthetic that could not accommodate the genius of Shakespeare had, according to his own principles, a historical identity of their own which deserves recognition and appreciation as much as any other. Similarly again he feels uneasy with the prophetic literature of the Bible because, in his view, its language and its repertory of images are borrowed from earlier literature. Herder rejects mediation, the mediation of commentators and imitators, of the copyists who simply hand on a tradition according to their lights. He even, and above all, overlooks the mediation of the church, which has constituted and preserved the canon of the Scriptures and thereby determined what the word *Bible* means for him and his audience. In that, he is entirely a man of *his* time and place; his older contemporary J. S. Semler inaugurated modern German biblical criticism precisely through a questioning of the canonical status of the scriptural text.[4] Herder, in short, is unable to find his way to a Catholic appreciation of the role of the church and of tradition in making the Scriptures available and meaningful to us. Since he has rejected the church as the principle of continuity in sacred history, it is no surprise to find Herder turning instead to the freethinkers whose oppression by the English church he later said accounted for the backwardness of biblical scholarship in England.[5] Deism and Enlightenment are the essence of the New Testament in his view, and it is because it contains this perfection of purely humane concepts that the New Testament can lay a claim to universal allegiance, *not* because of its historical continuity with the Old Testament, which contains those concepts only in an imperfect form.

Herder's treatment of the Bible as literature, as poetry (as he understands those terms), has a threefold impact on the way the text is read and understood.

(1) Its context is historicized. Herder's second principle for the interpretation of the Psalms, after his requirement that we should discard the interpretative tradition in order to penetrate to the *Urzeit,* the point of origin, is "look first for the objects and situations about which the poem was composed," and his third is an injunction to study the personal and historical characteristics of the language in which it was composed (*GEP* 1193–94). The biblical text, seen as a poem, is a particular response to particular circumstances—to a battle, a conflict with Saul, a ceremony in the Temple, for example—it is an expression and interpretation, in the language of the time, of the feelings the circumstances aroused. The more we know about those circumstances and about that language, therefore, the better we shall understand the text. If that seems obvious, its degree of obviousness is a measure of how far we have absorbed the Herderian approach. In Christian practice, even today, however, other and older ways of starting the search for a better understanding are still widespread: meditating on the place assigned to the text in the liturgy, for example; or applying it to the circumstances of our own life; or looking for congruences between the text and other parts of canonical Scripture, an approach of which the medieval practice of typological and allegorical interpretation is one example and the modern quest for the *sensus plenior,* the fuller sense, another. The selection of Old Testament texts in the Sunday cycles of readings in the modern Catholic lectionary is determined by just such a belief in the interpretative value of the internal correspondences in Scripture, with no necessary appeal to historical context. For Herder all such interpretative devices drawn from ecclesiastical practice or tradition are unhistorical intrusions obstructing our

direct, unmediated access to the *Urzeit*. But without them he succumbs inexorably to the nemesis of historicism, the logic we have already seen at
work in his general theory of cultural history. The circumstances and linguistic facts from which Herder "first" expects elucidation of the text
belong to secular history; that is, they are, in principle at least, capable of
being documented by sources other than sacred Scripture. Our ability to
make overall sense of the Scriptures, therefore, is to some extent at least dependent on our ability to make overall sense of secular history. The more
the context of the Scriptures is historicized, and the more the Scriptures
are understood as historical artifacts, the more pressing becomes the need
for us to have an understanding of the shape and purpose of human history
altogether, of "God's passage over the peoples." So what if Moses provided
an appropriate code of life for a primitive people—what is that to men and
women living in eighteenth-century or twentieth-century cities? So what if
David wrote a fine psalm on his sickbed? So did Beethoven in the third
movement of his Opus 132. In order to explain the relevance to one age,
such as our own, of the achievements of another we need some overall
theory of historical continuity or development, and if the achievements of
Israel are to have a special place in it the overall theory will have to explain
why. You could say that if, in the name of historicization, you expel theology from the text, she will return in the form of a need for a theology of
history. Herder, we remember, had some difficulty in making out any coherent action on the stage of God's theater. In his case, therefore, and perhaps in others, the long-term result of treating the Scriptures as historically
particular responses to historically particular occasions is to turn them into
steps along the road to a goal for secular history which has to be formulated independently of the Scriptures, the establishment of the religion of
the human race, Christianity as the most philanthropic form of deism, the
natural religion that is detached from any particular historical embodiment
whatever.

(2) Authorship is individualized. If it now seems obvious that across the
scriptural landscape there should wander a troupe of unnamed supporting
characters, each of them known as "the biblical author," "the sacred writer,"
or even "the evangelist," the sources of that obviousness again certainly include Herder. If poetry is produced by geniuses and if the Bible is poetry,
then the Bible is produced by geniuses. Herder was unsympathetic to the
creation of authors-behind-authors—while admitting the distinction between Yahwist and Elohist strands in the Pentateuch, he did not on the
whole think they pointed to distinct writers[6]—and he preferred to accept

the biblical attributions to Moses, Job, David, Solomon, the prophets, and the named psalmists such as Asaph (e.g., *GEP* 933–34). But it was of the essence of poetry as he conceived it that it emerged from the direct contact between the life surging in the universe and the individual source of life within the poet (*GEP* 962): the "feelings" and "characteristics" of individual human beings are, he says, what we find in the psalms (*GEP* 1194), and the "genius" of all poetry lies originally in the putting into words of this moment of contact between the individual and the animator of the universe, a process that "can be called human and divine, since it is both" (*GEP* 962). Named or unnamed, the authors of the Scriptures have for Herder an individuality which is inseparable from their inspiration, their privileged access to divinity. When in more modern commentaries we read of the Yahwistic tradition that "though God is described in human terms the author has a deep sense of the divine,"[7] or that "the poetry of Deutero-Isaiah reveals someone pensive, earnest, optimistic and sympathetic" with a "sturdy . . . faith in God"[8] we are hearing remote echoes of Herder's theory that the Bible was written by poets.

The obvious weakness of that theory, at least in Herder's formulation of it, is that it neglects the role of the church, the community of believers whether Jewish or Christian, in using, revising, and transmitting the poet's inspiration and in providing the words for it in the first place. Herder's hostility to mediation shows itself again in his insistence that the point of contact with the divine necessarily lies in an *Urzeit,* an originary time and state beyond the reach of institutions. The giving of the Mosaic law is for Herder the supreme example of inspiration, in both the theological and the poetic sense. For though the Mosaic law expresses and forms the genius of a whole people it is also simultaneously the work of one man alone with his God. To those Deists who accused Moses of deception in passing off his own work as God's, Herder replies that we cannot distinguish God's finger from Moses' as it wrote on the tablets of stone. It is not possible for us in our later age to determine anything about a moment of insight so remote from our own. We cannot distinguish the human from the divine in Moses' mind and action because we cannot enter the "holy and solemn solitude of that age and that desert" and judge the purity and simplicity of his encounter with God. Our modern minds are too full of the thoughts and words and books of other people and other times, "our ownmost thoughts," he says, "are not ours" (*GEP* 1097).

But that surely is true of any use of language, including Moses'. If inspiration were really as individual as Herder makes out, no one could understand it, not even the inspired poets themselves. Herder does not notice that precisely because the witness of our age is that our "ownmost" thoughts come from others we need an account of authorship, including biblical authorship, which does not understand it as an individual, autonomous response to the universe. Instead authorship needs to be understood as an act within a tradition of which both the author's predecessors and the author's readers are a part. In his response to the challenge of historical variety Herder could go some of the way to providing such an account of secular literary authorship, and that is part of his great achievement. But he could not draw out the full consequences of that advance when he came to consider sacred literature because the argument for the role of tradition was in sacred matters in his day still too firmly in the hands of the Catholic church. And Herder was too attached not only to his Protestantism but also to his radical monadic individualism for him to be open to revelations from that source.

(3) Reception is aestheticized. Albert Schweitzer accused Herder of requiring us to read the Bible "not with learning but with taste."[9] Now it is true that some of Herder's comments on biblical texts seem to strike a false note. Comparing the Psalms with the "songs" of Moses and Deborah and the "imagery" of Job, Balaam, and Jotham, he concludes: "what poetry gained in liturgical, political, and lyrical sophistication it perhaps lost in natural power" (GEP 1192). The judgment grates—but not simply because it seems to condescend to a work accorded the highest authority in the liturgical practice of the church. It grates because, regardless of what it says about the relative literary merits of particular books of the Bible, it is claiming a peculiar authority for the category of literary merit itself. And not just over scholarly "learning." The judgment is implicitly offering a literary solution to the problem of revelation. Thereby—not least because the solution is plainly inadequate—it is surreptitiously maintaining the validity of the Deist expression of the problem. To the question, what does revelation give us that reason cannot? Herder returns the answer, poetry. And to the question, what unique authority attaches to the revelation to the Jews? he answers, its poetry is the best. There is "little or nothing like it in the poetry of other nations," he writes (GEP 1004), for there is nothing in it written as a mere pastime, for mere entertainment (by contrast with the frivolous works of the Greeks); the Bible is a "unique wonder of the world" (GEP 1005) with the "unmistakeable advantage over all other national literatures in the world that it is pure poetry of God, of the temple" (GEP 934). But even in this form—as an argument that draws attention to the poetry's theological content—this argument for the uniqueness of Hebrew poetry

cannot explain why reading it (rather than any other of the unique literary phenomena of human culture) should make us change our lives: get baptized, married, or ordained, emigrate to Israel, or even do so much as put sixpence in the poor box. The detachment necessary for such an aesthetic judgment seems incompatible with the claim the text makes upon us when it is read as it seems from its beginning to wish to be read: as addressed to, or the voice of, a believing community, a church for which the issue of what constitutes revelation has already been settled.

This is surely the nub of the matter, the point where we can begin to define a Catholic approach to the Bible as literature that differs from Herder's. In its constitution on divine revelation the Second Vatican Council reaffirmed the words of the First Vatican Council, asserting the principle that through revelation "those religious truths which are by their nature accessible to reason can be known by all men with ease, with solid certitude and with no trace of error."[10] This is a principle not so much of apologetics as of hermeneutics: it is telling us, not how to prove that the Bible is revealed, but how to read it. The Bible, this principle says, cannot be read with understanding except on the basis that the issue of the relation between reason and revelation, the issue which so agitated eighteenth-century Protestants and which led Herder to formulate his vision of the Bible as literature, has already been settled. The Second Vatican Council does not say that the books of the Old Testament should be read either with learning or with taste but that "Christians should receive them with reverence" (DR §15) and that all reading of the Scriptures should be accompanied by prayer (DR §25). A Catholic approach to reading the Bible as literature requires—as I am sure Chenu would have agreed—that reading is always accompanied, or is at least always capable of being accompanied, by prayer, prayer which, whether or not the metaphysical issues have been settled, is prepared to put them behind it for the sake of the address (which, however, is always to an unknown) and in the sure hope of a response (which, however, is always unexpected). In that, of course, prayer is like any venture into conversation, and it is in the end as words in a conversation, not as texts for learned study or aesthetic appreciation, that the Council says we have to read the Scriptures. To this effect it quotes St. Ambrose: "we speak to Him when we pray; we hear him when we read the divine sayings" (DR § 25). Now it might be objected that if the Bible cannot be read as a text for aesthetic appreciation, then it cannot be read as literature. On the contrary, I would reply, that objection implies a false view of the nature of literature. One thing Chenu certainly did not mean when he said that literature was the "site" of theology was that the Bible should become an object of aesthetic admiration. A Catholic approach to literature requires that we move beyond the terminology of art, aesthetics, and beauty which, as I have argued elsewhere, is a product of the same crisis in eighteenth-century German Protestantism that I have been examining here.[11] Just as a Catholic approach to the Bible as literature requires that even this reading of the Bible should be capable of being accompanied by prayer, so a Catholic approach to literature as Bible will require that even our reading of literature must be capable of being accompanied by prayer also.

CHAPTER 3

History and Hermeneutics (2):
Schleiermacher

IN FOUNDING THE MODERN PROCEDURES FOR TREATING THE BIBLE
as literature, Herder was making an honorable effort to construct a historicist perspective on Christianity that would transcend the Deist conception
of natural religion. But like many after him who have attempted to read
the Bible as written by historically conditioned individual geniuses, he was
unable, from that perspective, to give an account of Christianity's universal
claims that did anything but reduce them to deism. If Herder was indeed
the inaugurator of nineteenth-century theology before it was inaugurated
by Schleiermacher, then we need to ask how Herder's program fared at the
hands of the man who mediated it to our own time.

In Schleiermacher's lectures on hermeneutics, published posthumously
as a reconstruction from his notes in 1838, the intention to treat the Bible
like any other text is explicit. Although the lectures were intended for theologians and take most of their detailed examples from the Bible—which
for him means on the whole the New Testament—Schleiermacher presents
his hermeneutics as a general science or art of understanding: "the art of
understanding the speech of another," he says at the outset.[1] It is an investigation of the methodology of interpretation of texts of any kind, sacred or
secular, taken as the speech of another. Although there are special problems
with the New Testament because he regards its language as an artificial mix-
ture of Greek words and Hebraic thought patterns, Schleiermacher denies

that there is any specially biblical hermeneutics beyond what is necessary to deal with the different literary genres represented by the biblical books. That is a more explicit, perhaps a more radical, version of Herder's position, but it is not fundamentally different. Indeed, if we were to measure the distance that lies between this assertion by a prelate of the United Lutheran–Reformed Church of Prussia and the assertion two hundred fifty years before in the Formula of Concord that the Old and New Testaments are distinct from all other writings we would have to say that most of that distance was traversed by Herder, not by Schleiermacher.

And so we also find that the principal consequences of Herder's conviction that the Bible should be treated "as a human book full of ancient poems" (GEP 670) are perpetuated, perhaps radicalized, in Schleiermacher's more methodical and academic presentation of the Bible as literature, that is, as the object of hermeneutic investigation. With Schleiermacher too we shall find that the context of the Scriptures is historicized and their authorship is individualized, even if we can say only in a rather modified sense that their reception is aestheticized. Beneath the surface we shall find that the same problems that agitated Herder are still at work, influencing and even determining Schleiermacher's thinking: the difficulty of defending the historical and particular character of Christian sacred books when one is faced with the Deist claim that religion should be rational and reason is universal; the difficulty of claiming an exceptional, a uniquely universal, significance for those books when one is faced with the rapidly growing evidence of human cultural diversity across time and space. In their most abstract and general form these problems have continued to exercise German, and not only German, thinkers down to the present day: what is the relation between reason and history? And, if there is any such relation, what place does it assign to Christianity? I doubt whether we shall find Schleiermacher's answers wholly satisfactory, but then, given the circumstances in which the questions arose, what answers to them could be satisfactory?

The first consequence of Herder's decision to present the Scriptures as a "book written by human beings for human beings," was, I have suggested, that he had to historicize their context. They had, that is, to be seen as written by particular people at particular times in particular circumstances, as written in specific languages and in accordance with specific literary conventions. All of this it was the task of the expositor to clarify. If that seems obvious to us now it certainly was not obvious in Herder's day, and perhaps it should not now seem as obvious to us as it does. For Herder has to assert this principle against the weight of the assumption that the ancient texts should be approached through the accumulated wisdom represented by many centuries of commentary, paraphrase, and dogmatic, liturgical, and homiletic application. Away with it all, says Herder, let us get as close as possible to the original speaker and the original audience, indeed, if it may be, to the original moment of composition—of inspiration, as we may still say, if only in a secular sense. Precisely the same demand is made by Schleiermacher, if in the more measured tones of the professional scholar. Whether one is dealing with a text as a sample of the language available to its author, as a realization of a certain range of the options the language presented to him, or whether one is seeking to understand the same text from the point of view of the author, as the consequence of his attempt to express a meaning, an intention—in either case Schleiermacher is clear that the historical principle has priority. In adopting the first approach, what Schleiermacher calls the "grammatical" interpretation, one must be guided by "the language-stock common to the author and his original public" (*H* 101). In adopting the second, "psychological" approach one must "regard any given complex of thought as a moment in the life of a specific human being" (*H* 178). Indeed, not merely does this historical method have priority, Schleiermacher explicitly denies that, apart from his distinction of the grammatical and psychological approaches, there is any truth in the "strange view . . . that there are several kinds of interpretation" (*H* 85). Of course, the historical method includes understanding what is new about an utterance. It does not aim to reduce a statement to an assemblage of preexisting parts, and Schleiermacher is particularly anxious to assert the novelty of the foundational ethical statements of Christianity contained in the New Testament. But that novelty is always novelty in a particular, historically defined context. For Schleiermacher there is no real alternative to the historical method, to the method which seeks to understand what the original writer or speaker really meant. Only this is interpretation; anything else is at best misinterpretation. Of allegorical approaches to Scripture, which systematically seek to find a meaning in what is written other than what the original writer intended, or could possibly have intended, Schleiermacher simply says that they are wrong ("nicht richtig ausgelegt"), misunderstandings of what has been said. He even allows himself to caricature them as the attempt "to find everything in anything" (*H* 85). The Jewish or cabbalistic approach, which may go so far as to see a significance in the individual letters of Holy Writ, he describes as the "worst kind of deviation." Now there is a hypnotic obviousness about Schleiermacher's claims for the historicizing method. He sees it as no more than a further and wider application of the principles we follow when talking to another individual and trying to understand what he or she is saying. But the analogy of conversation is not as straightforward as it looks. For who, when I read the Bible, am I trying to understand? "We speak to Him when we pray, we hear Him when we read the divine sayings." When we read sacred Scripture it is not the original writer whose words we are trying to understand but God. We do not speak to Isaiah, or even to St. John, when we pray, even if we hear God by reading what Isaiah or St. John said or wrote. For that reason it seems to me that we do need a special biblical hermeneutic—assuming, that is, that we need a hermeneutic at all.

Schleiermacher, I should make clear, directly considers the objection that the Holy Spirit, not this or that holy man, is the author of the sacred writings. However, he is too much the inheritor of the second consequence of Herder's treatment of the Bible as literature—his individualization of the figure of the author—to appreciate the force of the objection. No doubt with an eye to that understanding of inspiration which holds that the Holy Spirit "dictated" the words of Scripture to the sacred authors—a view shared by both Calvin and the Council of Trent and reaffirmed by the First Vatican Council—Schleiermacher asks why in that case the Holy Spirit bothered to use human agents at all and did not simply bring the Bible into existence miraculously (H 87 88). The "divine Spirit," he says, could only have made use of human writers because it wished the Scriptures to be attributed to them in the usual way. In particular, it is only thanks to the first audience of the Scriptures that any later audience exists; we hear the message in our day only because it has been passed on to us by those who heard it first; and that first audience could only hear and understand a message communicated to them in accordance with the ordinary principles of understanding between human beings (H 131, 88). The Bible is not therefore to be regarded as a single work, with one author, the Holy Spirit, and addressed generally to a church which took on its institutional form long after the books were committed to writing: it is the work of individuals, in individual circumstances, addressing particular audiences. The books of the Bible are occasional writings, *Gelegenheitsschriften, pièces d'occasion*. Schleiermacher does allow that some parts of the Old Testament are what he calls myths, which have no single author, like the stories which are the basis of the works of Homer (H 86). Such myths, because their authorship is multiple, cannot be made the object of psychological interpretation. Schleiermacher fails to consider, as far as I can see, what alternative form of exegesis would be appropriate in these cases to complement the grammatical method of interpretation, but he is, as I have hinted, not very interested in the Old Testament anyway. In general, then, interpretation for Schleiermacher means interpreting utterances as the products of particular "moments" in the lives of particular people. The word *moment* is ambiguous, particularly in German, but whether it means "instant in time" or "unitary component element of a complex of forces" it is clear from Schleiermacher's use of the term "Gelegenheitsschriften" that he not only sees the Bible as broken down into individual texts by individual authors but also regards even the experience of the individual authors to which those texts give expression as broken down into individual occasions, moments, or foci of concentration. Indeed, he invents the word *speech-act*[2]—*Sprechakt*—to describe the individual units he regards a text as broken down into for the purposes of interpretation.

The same process of atomization is at work, in other words, in Schleiermacher's theory of the interpretation of texts as in Herder's theory of cultural history. Just as Shakespeare and Sophocles are so different that perhaps they should not be joined together under the general heading of drama, so the fourth gospel and the Book of Revelation, for example, are so different that perhaps they should not be joined together under the general heading of the New Testament, or of the works of somebody called John, and perhaps even there are individual speech-acts recorded in those texts that are so different that they should not be joined together under the general heading of this or that text, this or that book, and perhaps those speech-acts represent moments in life so different that they should not be joined together and attributed to the same phase in one person's career or should not be attributed to the same person at all. The problem Herder faced—of how to join up the units of history into a coherent whole—takes on a peculiarly deadly form in Schleiermacher's hermeneutics, a problem that he himself recognized. For the significance of the particular moment in life which determines the meaning of the speech-act has to be decided by reference to the context provided by the whole life. But the character of the whole life can be reconstructed only by reference to the meaning of the moments of which it is composed. So Schleiermacher has created the concepts which convert Herder's empathetic sense of the marvelous uniqueness of historical and cultural events into a mechanism for dismantling the Bible into texts and texts into moments of life, moments interpretable only in relation to a whole, which itself is interpretable only in relation to its component moments, in an endless search for a perpetually elusive meaning (the "hermeneutic circle" identified by one of Schleiermacher's contemporaries).[3] Herder shattered eighteenth-century progressive history into a constellation of cultural singularities in which it was virtually impossible to discern any reason for giving preeminence or centrality to first-century Palestine. Schleiermacher shattered the Reformation Bible, the one and only *scriptura,* into a constellation of historically contextualized speech-acts in which it is virtually impossible to discern the single central utterance that comes directly from the mouth of God. Schleiermacher sends off his successors in hectic pursuit of an unattainable goal, on a chase dubbed by one of the participants "the quest of the historical Jesus."[4] It was the search for the speech-act or set of speech-acts the meaning of which, either correctly understood in context or fatefully misinterpreted by being taken out of context, would have been the foundation of Christianity. That the search had necessarily to be fruitless was however already determined by the nature of the historicizing hermeneutic mechanism that had set it in motion. Just as the price Herder paid for his sense of historical individuality was that his understanding of the order in history could only ever be fragmentary, so Schleiermacher had to recognize that if our understanding of the meaning of a speech-act is dependent on our knowledge of its specific historical context, then, since the context is always potentially infinite, our understanding can only ever be provisional.

As Christians, however, both Herder and Schleiermacher wanted to set limits to the fragmentariness and provisionality of our understanding. Perhaps also, simply as rational human beings, they wanted to set such limits. They both wanted to find, in the endless landscape of human variety that had opened up before them, a particular unit or structure which would resist the deconstructive logic they had unleashed in order to do justice to the particularity and historicity of human self-expression. They had thought that the particularity which they recognized as intrinsic to Christianity was threatened by the universal claims of the reason to which Deists appealed, but they now found themselves, like the sorcerer's apprentice, the victims of their own stratagems, and at risk of losing any firm basis for the universal claims, rational or not, of the Christianity they had set out to defend. They both, therefore, engaged in a two-stage rearguard action, in which they rescued Christianity and through it the principle of the unity of human experience, but at a twofold cost: they compromised their original creatively critical undertakings, and they identified Christianity, in at least some central respects, with the deism which had appeared to be its enemy. Herder first allowed that there might after all be some progress visible in human history, even if only fragmentarily and in rather general terms, the manifestation of God's passage over the nations. He then, second, identified

Christianity with the principle of that progressive harmony between the cultures, the story of historical continuity itself, "deism," in his own words, "at its most philanthropic."

Schleiermacher proceeds similarly. His hermeneutics are an account of the expression in language of religious truth, an account which lays down that in understanding truth of any kind expressed in language we are understanding the speech of another. To that end, Schleiermacher also lays down, we have to know who that other is, in order that we may judge his or her intention; we must know when and in what circumstances they spoke and in what language, in the broadest sense and including the repertoire of rhetorical and literary conventions open to them. Applied to the particular body of texts which constitute the New Testament, as the nineteenth-century quest for the historical Jesus has shown, these principles are capable of leading us into a void in which no meaning can be established for certain and interpretation is endless. Schleiermacher, however, in his own theology cut off this possibility of infinite regress and consequent loss of the meaning he set out to ground historically. At the start of his theological career he rescued himself from the eighteenth-century crisis of biblical Protestantism by appealing to another form of religious truth, a truth not expressed in language and so not dependent, for our understanding of it, on our understanding of another. This is a truth known with certainty by our inner feeling (*Gefühl*), the truth, to put it into language, that we are dependent, without qualification, on something outside ourselves.[5] This certainty of unqualified dependence is for Schleiermacher the basic certainty in all religions; it is a universal certainty of what, in the language of most religions, is called God, and it remained throughout his life the cornerstone of Christian faith as he understood it. To explicate this certainty, to draw out its implications in language and in the life we lead, he quickly concluded that we need—and the need is fully consistent with the original certainty—the assistance, that is, the mediation, of others. We need a priest. This original certainty of our unqualified dependence on God and of our need for a mediating priest so that we may know and serve God came to constitute for Schleiermacher a universal religious certainty that is itself unmediated, not given to us by others, and prior to all language. It is a universal natural religion beyond the reach of hermeneutics and history. The content of this natural religion is somewhat different from the content of eighteenth-century natural religion. (And the difference is largely due to the intervention of the philosophy of German Idealism.) Since, however, its central feature remains the knowledge of an otherwise undifferentiated God we may properly call it a form of deism. Schleiermacher, like Herder, called in the natural religion of deism to police the chaos created by individualism and historicism. His second step was also similar to Herder's: he identified his police officer with Christianity. We all need a mediator with God, Schleiermacher believes, and we all may at some time in our lives function as mediator, as priest, for someone else. Religious communities, major or minor, group themselves round an individual whose mediation is accessible to many and constitutes the revelation of God to them. The mediating ability, the capacity both for revelatory insight into God and for passing that revelation on in words which give it textual expression, is so great in some individuals as to amount to religious genius. Moses and Mohammed, Jesus and the Buddha, are some of the greatest such religious geniuses, the priests of humanity. What makes for the unique universality of Christianity is that the need for mediation was itself the central insight of its founder, Jesus. Jesus preached the need for the priest that he himself was. Christianity thus became for Schleiermacher, so to speak, the religion of religions, the pure expression of the principle which all religions differently exemplify. It is the most philanthropic form of deism.

Schleiermacher therefore grounds his faith in a natural and allegedly universal religious apprehension of dependence on God and the need for mediation, of which Christianity is recognized to be the purest expression. Understanding the Bible, which is anyway a potentially infinite task, contributes nothing to the establishment of this faith. We have here a paradox. Schleiermacher's principle of mediation, which played so crucial and original a role in his philosophical theology, seems to be disconnected from his hermeneutics. He has an innovative and influential theory of how to study the Bible, but the Bible is not the source of his Christianity. He has an equally novel and influential understanding of the essential part played by a religious community—a church—in formulating the expression even of the foundations of individual belief and practice, but that understanding is not transferred to his treatment of the biblical texts.

As far as Schleiermacher is concerned, in his lectures on hermeneutics, the church can assist neither in psychological nor in grammatical interpretation. The church has no role to play, for example, in helping us to understand such statements in the New Testament as "This is my Son," or "God was in Christ" by reference to its own later doctrinal formulations; no role in helping us to interpret what John's gospel says about eating Christ's flesh by reference to the practice of the Eucharist; nor, to take an Old Testament example, can the church's incorporation of the Exodus story into the Easter liturgy shed any light on the concepts of liberation and redemption to be found in the Hebrew narrative. The church contributes nothing to our understanding of the meaning of a biblical utterance insofar as that meaning is determined by the intention of the original writer, and that alone is the object of what Schleiermacher calls psychological interpretation. Moreover, and even more significantly, the church—to judge by Schleiermacher's silence on the matter—contributes nothing either to understanding the only other kind of meaning that he allows, the meaning that is the object of what he calls grammatical interpretation. The linguistic corpus that Schleiermacher is seeking to understand is virtually a creation of the church. However, he gives no attention to the church's involvement in the selection of the books that make up the Bible, though this had been a matter of contention as recently as the sixteenth century, when the Reformers excluded from the Old Testament the so-called deuterocanonical books—such as Maccabees, Ecclesiasticus, Tobit, and Wisdom—and Luther considered excluding the Letter of James from the New Testament since it did not accord with his doctrine of justification. Schleiermacher is inexplicit about his own reasons for neglecting the Old Testament to the point where he virtually reduces the Bible to the New. He does not consider that choices—which are not simply scholarly decisions about authorship and authenticity—have to be made about the detail of the biblical text if a generally agreed version is to be available for purposes of teaching, prayer, and worship: choices about whether or not to include as Holy Scripture the long ending of Mark or the story of the woman taken in adultery, or entire sections of the Books of Daniel and Esther, and about the enormous range of longer and shorter variants to every verse. Of particular significance, however, is Schleiermacher's failure to respond to the omnipresence of translation in the Bible itself and in the history of the use of the Bible by the church community which mediates to Christians their faith in God. Translation is after all the principal form of mediation. What original words could matter more to a Christian than those of Jesus? Yet his discourses, presumably originally pronounced in Aramaic, are known to us at best as Greek résumés or translations. The work of translation has gone on ever since. The gospel was for a thousand years in the West a Latin text and since the sixteenth century has been preached in all European vernaculars. Whatever kind of a meaning it has that can be approached only through its first surviving written version in Greek can hardly lay claim to exclusive authority in matters of doctrine or practice. Moreover, the New Testament world itself, whether of Palestine or the eastern Mediterranean generally, was a polyglot, interlingual world. To the New Testament writers and to many other Jews of the time, the Hebrew Scriptures were as likely to be known in the Greek translations, the Septuagint, or in the Aramaic Targums, as in the original. We are told by John that the charge against Jesus, nailed to his cross and in a sense the distillation of his perceived public ministry, the gospel in four or five words, was written in Hebrew, Latin, and Greek. Christian truth, it seems, spills out over the limitations of any one language, any one textual formulation. Schleiermacher, however, remains grimly attached to the notion of the original words in the original language even though the Christian biblical tradition cannot, it seems, unequivocally offer us either, and does not need to.

I return to the paradox, to Schleiermacher's inability to link the understanding of the church originally shown and developed in what we might call his rational argument, or his argument from natural religion, for the special truth of Christianity, with his later rules for the interpretation of the Christian Scriptures. Christians are called on by Schleiermacher to rely, indeed he says they cannot avoid relying, on the church for their faith, but they must not rely on her for their understanding of the sacred writings. How are we to explain this paradox? We see here, I believe, the ultimate consequence—let us be unkind and call it the nemesis—of the Reformation concept of Scripture, the concept which was tried and found wanting in the fires of the Deist controversy of the eighteenth century. The dilemmas imposed on Christians by that controversy still mark Schleiermacher's presentation of the Christian fundamentals. In the last analysis he has failed to resolve them, and so he has no choice but to perpetuate them. Not even Herder's concept of the Bible as literature can help him: in the last analysis Schleiermacher is forced to let the Bible lie where the Deist controversy had left it, for he has not developed the new concept of reason which would have enabled him to put that controversy behind him.

The assertion that the church has no part in determining the meaning, or even the text, of Scripture is, we have seen, one of the founding principles of the Reformation. Schleiermacher is simply staying true to his Calvinist roots in giving the church no role in biblical exegesis. However, by the beginning of the nineteenth century the Bible is not what it was at the beginning of the sixteenth. It may still be fenced off from ecclesiastical trespassers, but the monolith dropped from heaven, out of which spoke the unmistakable voice of God, has fallen silent. How has this come about? Precisely because they held the Bible to be the unique and fully adequate source and rule of Christian doctrine and Christian faith, the Deist assault on it was particularly damaging to the Reformed and Lutheran confessions: any questioning of the Bible's textual, intellectual, or moral integrity was a questioning of Christianity itself. For bibliolaters there were two alternative forms of defence to arguments that the Bible was unreliable, incredible, or immoral.[6] Unfortunately, both had serious concomitant disadvantages. You could, first, rely on what were called the "external" evidences for Christianity's divine origin: the miracles reported in the Bible, the unique antiquity of the Jewish people and their sacred books, the miraculous preservation of them and their Christian successors through the vicissitudes of history. If you thought these arguments strong enough, you did not have to concern yourself with the rationality or attractiveness of the biblical message. However nonsensical or repugnant it might seem to eighteenth-century man, it was evidenced as the word of God and had to be accepted. However, the "external" arguments were unfortunately wide open to skeptical or satirical attack and had the disadvantage of multiplicity: if any one of them was discredited—if the Bible could be proved wrong or self-contradictory on any point of ancient history, for example—then the principle of scriptural infallibility seemed to have been surrendered.

Alternatively, then, you could have recourse to the "internal" evidences of Christianity: the perfection, usually the moral perfection, of the Christian scheme. Because Christianity—and usually but not necessarily that meant the teaching of the Bible—was so good, therefore it must be true. This was more dangerous ground, though in Germany it proved exceptionally fertile. Christianity was good and reasonable, perhaps even more reasonable than anything reason alone could achieve, and if you felt that argument strong enough you did not have to concern yourself with the rickety structure of biblical history or with rationally indefensible claims to miraculous support. However, these internal arguments carried the risk that such rational Christianity would evaporate into natural religion, any distinctively Christian features being superfluous, and they had the particular disadvantage that they actively encouraged the assumption that the external, or biblical and historical, arguments for Christianity were inadequate. In one of the last original English contributions to the Deist controversy, Soame Jenyns's *A View of the Internal Evidence of the Christian Religion,* published in 1776 and immediately translated into German, we read:

> [I]f any one could prove . . . that there are errors in geography, chronology and philosophy, in every page of the Bible; that the prophecies therein delivered are all but fortunate guesses, or artful ap-

plications, and the miracles there recorded no better than legendary tales: if any one could shew, that these books were never written by their pretended authors, but were posterior impositions on illiterate and credulous ages . . . [nonetheless it would still be true that] if in these books a religion superior to all human imagination actually exists, it is of no consequence to the proof of its divine origin, by what means it was there introduced, or with what human errors and imperfections it is blended.[7]

With friends like this, one asks, what need has Christianity of Deists? And indeed virtually every element in Jenyns's catalogue of errors was to figure in the charge sheet against the New Testament drawn up just after Schleiermacher's death by his younger contemporary D. F. Strauß.

Schleiermacher's theology of dependency on God and on the mediation of the faith community can be regarded as an extreme form of the argument from internal evidences. It sets up a rational argument for all religions and demonstrates the unique position of Christianity among them while reducing to a minimum the need for historical appeal to Christianity's supposed founding documents. Those documents need demonstrate no more than that Jesus existed and that he claimed for himself, or was recognized as having taken on himself, the role of mediator between God and Man. For the rest the documents can safely be turned over to professional exegetes, even if these have put themselves outside the Christian faith community as decisively as Strauß. There is no need for the faith community to mediate the Scriptures to the individual believer, and Schleiermacher could not allow for the possibility that it should, without repudiating the Reformation at its source and handing Christianity back to the care of the Catholic church. His refusal to take that step, however, is what exposed him to the Deist dilemmas in the first place. In Schleiermacher's scheme the Bible continues to have the exceptional status conferred on it by the original Reformers, but that exceptionality now consists in the Bible's being the one aspect of Christian life and faith that is not in the hands of the community. The gulf yawns open between ecclesiology and hermeneutics as an ineradicable sign that here is a Reformation thinker who has escaped from the Deist crisis by the route of the internal evidences and has left the Bible behind him for the Deists, or their successors, to do their worst on—as, in the course of the nineteenth century, they did. The gulf could be closed only by a return to Catholic principles or by the development of a new concept of reason, a concept that resolved the opposition between rational and positive religion, between external and internal evidences, and indeed the antithesis of reason and revelation itself, at least insofar as it was applied to the Scriptures. If, however, I say that in the end those two possible solutions come down to the same thing, I have to add I do not think that we have reached that end even now.

In any event, Schleiermacher could not develop that new concept of reason and close the gulf in his system. Even to Herder's conception of the Bible as literature he gives a form which maintains the division between religion and the Bible, between faith and history. That conception was developed by Herder in the first place as an acknowledgment that the broadening scope of anthropological and historical science was showing the world to be full of non-Christian revelations and non-Christian sacred poetry. This acknowledgment, however, was also an attempt to exploit the new and wider sense of humanity as a counter to the narrow rationalism of the Deists: in poetry, any poetry, and in poetic genius, there was a human power far greater than the petty reason they invoked, and in the Bible, he somewhat lamely argued, that power, at least in its religious employment, was shown to its best effect. Lame though the formulation may have been, the intent of the argument was clear—to find a form of faith that encompassed the exciting new riches of history. From the full scope of that ambition, Schleiermacher cautiously retreats. Schleiermacher's religious geniuses, like Herder's poetic geniuses, enjoy a unique and unfathomable moment of relationship with the divine mystery that sustains the universe, but Schleiermacher shrinks from the final step of identifying the two forms of genius. He thereby avoids the aestheticization of the response to the sacred writings which was the final consequence of Herder's literary approach to the Bible, but he substitutes for it not the reverence which the Second Vatican Council required, not the setting of the Scriptures in a prayerful conversation between the church and God, but what Schweitzer called scholarly "learning." In Schleiermacher's hands the concept of the Bible as literature leads not to an aestheticization of our response but to an academicization. Understanding the Bible becomes a matter of following the rules for a school exercise in *explication de texte*. It becomes the affair not of the whole church but of an academic caste of hermeneuts for whom the biblical texts are, emphatically, texts like any other: literature with its own particular problems no doubt but simply literature—the distinction between sacred and secular is, for Schleiermacher's hermeneutics, simply irrelevant.

Yet for the church at large, at least according to the Vatican Council, reading the Bible is precisely the activity in which sacred and secular converse. It is an activity not only in which we find out something about the Bible but also in which we are told something about ourselves. Schleiermacher defined the task of hermeneutics as "understanding an utterance firstly as well as, and then better than, its author" (*H* 94). He forgot that, in the case of the Bible at least, it is also true that the utterance understands its interpreters better than they do themselves. But then that is part of what we mean by the proposition that the author of the Bible is the Holy Spirit, whose utterances presumably we cannot expect to understand better than their author—which of course is why Schleiermacher rejects the proposition. Schleiermacher also forgot that, no more than an author, an interpreter is never singular. He emphasizes the importance of understanding the writer as in dialogue with an audience, as having an intention and being situated in and momentarily embodying a whole language. He overlooks that the interpreter is a whole language too, both a whole person with their own intentions as well as their own understanding and the totality of social, linguistic, and other factors that a person temporarily integrates. Interpreters have their audience too, for the sake of whom they are interpreting the text—as indeed is apparent at the moment—and the act of reading is not just a collision between a person and a text, or between a reader and an author, but between two spirits, the spirits of two worlds, the spirit in which the text was written and the spirit in which it is read. For all the ecclesial dimension of his account of faith, Schleiermacher's account of reading is intensely individualistic: he sees the reader as a solitary, male, all-powerful interrogator of the text, of the prisoner and victim to which the instruments of "scholarship" are applied. For one reason or another this conception of reading appealed to the churchmen, particularly the academic churchmen, of the nineteenth century. Schleiermacher's academic and interrogatory hermeneutics provided a justification for a quest for the historical Jesus which went on for nearly a hundred years and was seen while it lasted as one of the greatest triumphs of "scholarship." In this way both the antithesis of reason and revelation inherited from the Deist controversy and the antithesis of the universal and particular characteristic of eighteenth-century historicism were kept alive as a price worth paying to maintain the original impulse of the Reformation. Evidently it is not here that we must look for a Catholic approach to the Bible as literature.

In 1922, Ernst Troeltsch published an article, "The Crisis of Historicism," summarizing the intended thesis of his unfinished work of eight hundred pages on that subject (in which incidentally, Herder is scarcely mentioned).[8] The problem of historicism, according to Troeltsch, consisted essentially in the impossibility of deriving permanent and universal values from the changing particularities of history, and was still unsolved. Unsolved, that is, he remarked in passing, unless one swallowed Hegel whole. In the 1920s, of course, that was a joke, or at any rate a reductio ad absurdum. No one in the 1920s thought of swallowing Hegel—whole, or even in bite-sized chunks. Besides, Troeltsch was in the end a disciple of Schleiermacher, and at the University of Berlin in the 1820s the hostility between Hegel and Schleiermacher was legendary. Troeltsch was in effect continuing that battle by suppressing the roles of Herder and Hegel in setting up the conceptual structure within which Schleiermacher operated: Herder in formulating the "problem of historicism" as a religious problem, Hegel in seeking to resolve the problem by synthesizing Herder's historicism with Kant's critical rationalism. But, like most great developments in intellectual history, Schleiermacher's theories of faith and reading need to be understood as responses to the difficulties and dilemmas of his time and place rather than as contributions to some timeless or very long term debate between disembodied ideas. And in Schleiermacher's time and place the urgent questions were on the whole rather better answered by Hegel than they were by Schleiermacher. Troeltsch's "crisis of historicism"—the dramatic formula tells us that the Nietzschean sun is still high in the sky—was perhaps only a crisis, or a passing fluctuation, in the reception of Hegel.

For Hegel produced the new concept of reason which the nineteenth century needed in order to be released from the dilemmas of the eighteenth, whether those dilemmas were Deist or historicist in origin. Reason itself, he saw, had to be historicized. This meant not only understanding reason as changing with time and circumstances, but understanding those changes themselves as rational—as following an internal logic even as they appeared to be produced by a submission of reason to external factors. Understanding the past, however remote, is always a form of self-understanding. This cannot be the place to try to follow through Hegel's entire grand project in its depth and complexity, or to try to determine how successful it was. It must at once be evident, though, that far more fundamental and difficult issues are raised by this project and by its dual nature—both rational and historical—than by anything in Schleiermacher. Perhaps for that reason, nineteenth-century theology, in Germany at least, preferred to proceed down the road indicated by Schleiermacher: with the aid of the science, or supposed science, of hermeneutics, the past was to be understood in its own terms, while as a consequence the self-understanding of the present was detached from any control or support by the past, or any responsibility to it.

Condescension to the past and complacency in the present continued to re-produce in German Protestant theology the attitudes and problems of the pre-Kantian Enlightenment, under a pious veneer of biblical historicism, until the catastrophe of the First World War. Meanwhile Hegel's conception of history as reason—our own reason—at work was allowed to continue to be productive only in the realms of political and social theory, notably in Marxism.[9]

CHAPTER 4

Revelation and Reason: Hegel

IN THE MIDDLE OF THE EIGHTEENTH CENTURY A CRISIS AROSE FOR the Protestant affirmation that divine truth is known through Scripture alone, *sola scriptura,* as a result of the convergence of two kinds of critique: deism, which accentuated the antithesis of reason and revelation to the point where the Bible could in the extreme case have no rational content of its own; and historicism, which through its accentuation of human variety through space and time challenged the biblical claim that a particular place and time had been the scene of a revelation valid for and in all human cultures. Both Herder and Schleiermacher sought to disarm these criticisms by surrendering initially any special status for the Bible and allowing that it was literature, poetry, written by human beings for human beings. They then sought to expand our understanding of the nature of literature so that Christian faith could survive this act of self-abnegation, and in both cases, though in different ways, the Bible was then restored to a special if subordinate position, as the object respectively of aesthetic admiration or academic research. In neither case, however, were the traces of that original dual critique eliminated; indeed, the systems of Christian thought that resulted continued to be vehicles of deism and historicism. This was, in the last analysis, a consequence of their holding fast to the Reformation's rejection of tradition as a component of Revelation inseparable from Scripture, and that link to the central negative assertion of the Reformation showed itself in their refusal to give an ecclesiological dimension to hermeneutics—their refusal to allow the church to meddle in the interpretation of the Scriptures. My analysis so far has, inevitably, been rather negative too. It is time to strike a more positive note and turn to thinkers whose attempts to overcome the crisis of the mid-eighteenth century have met with a degree of success. More than Herder or Schleiermacher, they can contribute to a recovery and even development of that Catholic understanding of the Scriptures which the Reformation made problematic. I start with Hegel's philosophy of religion, and with some of its features which have the potential to be fruitful in a Catholic approach to biblical literature.

In the first place, then, there is Hegel's rejection of a purely historicist hermeneutics, and so his rejection of the Deist antithesis of reason and revelation which that hermeneutics implies—an antithesis which readily leads, as we have seen, to the complete erosion of the idea of revelation. There cannot be, Hegel argues, an interpretation of a text that is not an importation into the text of the ideas and the way of thinking of the interpreter. "Commentaries on the Bible," he says, "do not so much acquaint us with the content of Scripture as themselves contain the attitudes (*Vorstellungsweise*) of their time."[1] That does not matter. What matters is that the ideas and attitudes which the commentaries contain should be the right ones, the doctrines affirmed in the Creeds, the triune nature of the Godhead, the divinity of Christ, the eternal judgment to come (*W* xvii, 200; xvi, 46). The criterion for the interpretation of Scripture has to be dogmatic, Hegel asserts: anything else turns Scripture, he says, into a wax nose that can be given any shape you like (*W* xvi, 37). In the words of Lichtenberg, written before Hegelian Idealism was thought of, "A book is a mirror: if a monkey looks into it, an apostle is certainly not going to look out."[2] When Schleiermacher's disciples, academic churchmen of a deistical disposition, looked into the New Testament they could not track down an apostle anywhere. The Bible, according to Hegel, is Revelation only if it is read with the right theological categories in mind. But if we have faith in the Trinity, if we have a Trinitarian understanding of God, then God will reveal himself to us, in the words of Scripture, as triune. How those theological categories of Trinity and Unity themselves arose is for this purpose irrelevant (*W* xvii, 318). The history of ecclesiastical decrees, of machinations at general councils and narrowly won votes, to which skeptics tried to reduce the most important Christian dogmas, all that is insignificant compared with the revelation that occurs when the Bible is rightly read. For God is always revealing himself, just as he is always creating and sustaining the world, and that activity is misunderstood—God's nature as permanently active Spirit is misunderstood—if his activity is locked away in a past event to which only specialists have access. It is of course possible to read the Bible as a specialist in ancient history, to read it as one would read Livy, but then all that one will find in it is Livy—not the Spirit of God.

Hegel therefore rejects not only the historicist hermeneutic approach to the Bible as the source of truth about God but also the antithesis of Reason and Revelation which sustained the entire dispute out of which the historicist hermeneutic approach arose (*W* xvi, 35–40). The belief that there is a rational theology as opposed to a biblical theology—whichever of the two is thought to be more reliable—is a belief Hegel wishes to supersede. There are not two spirits, a divine and a human spirit, any more than there are two reasons, or two revelations, one positive—imposed from outside—and one rational and internal. There is one divine Spirit which operates in us particular human beings, and the truth which comes to us in the form of a positive—that is, a historically specific—revelation is a rational truth. "That it is positive," Hegel says, "in no way detracts from its quality of being rational, of being our own" (*W* xvii, 195). On the contrary, anything rational is met by us in sensuous experience in a positive form: the laws of our own country are positive, they are historical accidents, but we recognize in them a higher rationality than accident; we recognize them as an expression of our own freedom. Fundamental to Hegel's entire system, and so to his understanding of the Bible, is his belief—subject to certain qualifications to which we shall come in a moment—that God can be known by human reason, a belief which is also asserted by the Second Vatican Council in its Constitution on Revelation (DR §6).

In the second place, Hegel has a fully developed conception of the role of the church in the process of revelation. For Reason and Revelation must not be opposed, just as the universal and the particular must not be opposed, in our understanding of how the Scriptures came to be written (which for Hegel, as exclusively as for Schleiermacher, means the Scriptures of the New Testament). If the one Spirit of God, at once rational and positive, operates in our reading of the Scriptures it also operated in the writing of them. "The story of Christ," Hegel says, "has been narrated by those on whom the Spirit had already been poured out. The miracles were received and narrated in this Spirit and the death of Christ was understood by that Spirit as meaning that in Christ God was revealed, as was the unity of the divine and human natures" (*W* xvii, 289). The Scriptures must be read in the light of the dogmatic categories, for in that light they were written. The

Christian Scriptures are from the start part of the outpouring of the Spirit that first constituted the Christian community. Christianity is called by Hegel "the religion of the Spirit," and the Spirit, the Holy Spirit of love, is God real, present, and active in the community (*Gemeinde*), that is, the church (*W* xvii, 305; cp. 193). The antithesis between written Scripture and oral tradition—so essential to Calvin's understanding of the Reformation—is said explicitly by Hegel to be an irrelevance (*W* xvii, 321), for both Scripture and tradition are subordinate to the activity of the Spirit and manifestations of it: tradition must of its nature be grounded in an authority which only the Spirit can provide, Scripture must of its nature be interpreted, and interpretation is the Spirit in action. Scripture and tradition, then, are equally expressions of the identity of the community which comes into being with its recognition of Christ as both God and man and which is given full power by the Spirit to define and refine its teaching (*W* xvii, 298, 321). In the words of the Constitution on Divine Revelation: "Sacred tradition, sacred Scripture, and the teaching authority of the Church . . . are so linked and joined together that one cannot stand without the others and that all together and each in its own way under the action of the one Holy Spirit contribute effectively to the salvation of souls" (DR §10). Hegel therefore maintains one of the favorite distinctions of the deist Enlightenment but uses it for a purpose diametrically opposed to that which it previously served: he distinguishes the religion of Jesus from the religion about Jesus, but he does so in order to assert the necessary supersession of Jesus' own teachings by the teachings of the church. Both Lessing and Herder, for example, praise what they call the pure morality of Jesus' teaching in order to contrast it with the teaching of the church which has allegedly corrupted Jesus' legacy by turning it into a theology, a cult of Jesus' person (as God), not of Jesus' teachings. According to Hegel, the teachings of the church *cannot* be identical with those of Jesus, for they are based on the full experience of his life, death, and resurrection, and so on the necessarily posthumous recognition of who he was. Jesus' teachings during his life—such commands as "Leave the dead to bury their dead," "Sell all you have and give to the poor"—were a part, and only a part, of who he was. They were determined by his particular personal and historical situation: he taught as one man, not as the community, while the community, the church, has to address all nations and all times. That in no way detracts from his uniqueness. Jesus' teachings are an element in his historical particularity, but the particularity, the unique individuality, of Jesus, in whom God becomes

Man, is the glory, "der schönste Punkt," Hegel says (*W* xvii, 276), of the Christian religion—for the Christian religion is the "transfiguration," the glorification of our finitude. The universal significance of the fact that God becomes *one* man, and no other, is, then, for the community, the innumerably many individuals who make up the church, to proclaim in their own and later way.

This is Hegel's answer to the challenge offered by historicism to the universal claim of Christianity. Historicism objected that an individual event in a particular culture could not possibly have a universal significance for all cultures; Hegel replies that after the outpouring of the spirit at Pentecost, Christianity speaks in as many tongues as world history provides of the absolute and universal significance of particular and finite individuality. Christianity is not a set of documents about one past event among many others—so many dead letters—but the life of the spirit in a potentially universal community, the church, which has expressed its self-understanding in various ways, including by the composition of documents about its founding events. The price paid for this truly brilliant answer to the Enlightenment critique of Christianity—and to a Catholic it must I think seem too high a price—is the radical separation of Jesus and the church. The compliment thus paid to the church is really too fulsome: at moments it can look as if Jesus is little more than the creation of the church, a back-projection from the founding moment of Pentecost, a necessary fiction. Equally, the church itself is allowed no existence prior to Pentecost: at moments it can look as if Hegel is suggesting that it came into existence out of nothing, perhaps with the destruction of the Jewish Temple in A.D. 70, and as if the particularity in which God became incarnate was the particularity not of Jesus but of the early church.[3] I shall have to return to these reservations.

The third feature of Hegel's account of Christianity to which I wish to draw attention is really only a particular aspect of the second: his exposition of the centrality to Revelation of the doctrine of the Incarnation. Part of the problem of Revelation, both for Deists and for their opponents, had been the apparent claim that there was a list, of uncertain length, of discrete truths which had revealed status—the immortality of the soul, observance of the Sabbath, not marrying one's wife's grandmother, and so on. These were linked only by their appearing, or perhaps appearing, in Holy Scripture, and only by showing that Holy Scripture had a divine origin could the special status of these truths be secured. Hegel renders that entire debate obsolete by arguing that there is only one revealed truth—that God has become Man in Jesus Christ. The recognition of this one truth is the primal act of the Spirit which constitutes the community of the church, sends it out on its worldwide mission, and empowers it to develop all other doctrine from this single central fact. But Hegel's analysis goes one step further. God reveals himself in the moment in which the community recognizes the dead Jesus as God and Man (*W* xvii, 298). In Christ the divine nature is revealed (*W* xvii, 287). But what God reveals is simply that his nature is to reveal himself and that this nature is united with human nature (*W* xvii, 194, 204). The Incarnation is the supreme moment in the unending process of God's self-revelation as the one who reveals himself. Incarnation is inseparable from Revelation, if not identical with it. This means that not only has Hegel reduced the untidy accumulation of revealed truths argued over by the eighteenth century to one, he has shown that the basis of all that argument, its conception of Revelation, was flawed. For that argument proceeded on the assumption that it was necessary somehow to demonstrate the revealed, that is, supernatural, status of the Scriptures in order, as a second stage, to prove the truth of certain otherwise indemonstrable assertions which were therefore called revealed. But Hegel has shown that the Incarnation is not revealed in the sense that it is known and vouched for only by the revealed status of the Scriptures. It is not necessary to prove the peculiar status of the Scriptures in order to prove that God has become Man, as if nothing else could prove such an assertion. Rather, the assertion of the Incarnation is itself synonymous with the assertion of the revealed status of the Scriptures, in which the recognition of Christ's divinity is first given expression by the believing community, the church (see *W* xvii, 312–20). That the Scriptures are Divine Revelation is no more open to demonstration than that Jesus is the Son of God; that Scripture is the Word of God is no more open to demonstration than that Jesus is. Both are grounded only in the testimony of the spirit to itself, that is to say, in the faith of believers, both individually and collectively, as the church—a faith to which the nature of God as the one who reveals himself is self-evident, manifest, revealed. Hegel, in short, has shown that the original claim that God can be known by reason needs to be made more precise: we can know by reason that only by faith can we know the God who has revealed himself, and that if he has revealed himself he has done so as the one who reveals himself to faith. Hegel has, I think, seen the conceptual misapprehension at the basis of bibliolatry as clearly as Aquinas did before the problem arose: there cannot be a proof of Revelation, or it would not be Revelation. Hegel's Reformed inheritance, both Lutheran and Calvinist, is evident in his insistence on the testimony of the Spirit, but in his exposition of the way in which Revelation and Incarnation mutually imply each other we have, I think, another pointer to a Catholic way of reading the Scriptures as both human documents and inspired.

Fourth and finally, there is an extraordinarily original feature of Hegel's account of the origins of Christianity which is as profound as it is ambiguous, and which is of a certain obvious relevance to our quest. I mean what he has to say about Rome. Hegel is no doubt building on the work of skeptical eighteenth-century historians—Gibbon, for example—who explained the supposedly miraculous rise of Christianity by the existence of the Roman Empire, which provided a structure to diffuse it throughout the known world.[4] But he makes the relationship between Christianity and Rome far more intimate than a mere distribution opportunity. In his lectures both on the philosophy of world history and on the philosophy of religion Hegel presents Christianity as a reaction not against Judaism but against the religion of the Roman state. In the lectures on religion he deals, under the heading "Religion of Spiritual Individuality," first with Judaism as the religion of sublimity, then with Greek religion as the religion of beauty, and finally with Roman religion as the religion of utility, before making the transition to Christianity, which as "absolute religion" has a section of its own. In this sequence Rome represents not so much a culmination as a low point: the empire, so to speak, pillages the religious treasuries of all its subject nations and drags them to Rome to display them in its Pantheon, where, deprived of all substance, they are trampled beneath the feet of the emperor, the only truly divine being. The emperor, in Hegel's presentation, is a kind of negative Christ, enthroned in a court of death (*W* xvii, 177–78)—that is, the circuses, with their murderous games—a death which he imposes but in which he does not share, and as the ruler over life and death and the law itself, as the source of all power and status, he is "divinity expressed and revealed (*geoffenbart*) in the uniqueness of the individual" (*W* xvii, 181–82). Against *this* religion—against the enforced subservience of all particular religions to the monolithic State—Christianity is the revolution. And just as Hegel does not represent Christianity as a revolt against Judaism, so he represents Jesus' death as an act not of the Jews but of the Roman imperium. Crucifixion, the penalty not only of death but also of degradation, demonstrates precisely the nature of the emperor's absolute power, manifest in the reduction of all other powers and values to impotence and dishonor. When, therefore, Christianity raises crucifixion to the place of highest honor, makes it the bearer of the supreme good, namely, the Kingdom of God, and when its followers lose their fear of the empire's only weapon, the power of death, the entire tyrannical structure is brought crashing down (*W* xvii, 290–91). With extraordinary ingenuity Hegel has reinterpreted Gibbon's view of Christianity as the agent of the destruction of the empire (which Gibbon regarded as having once secured the height of human felicity) and has made that view essential to his understanding of Christianity itself. Hegel has seen something about Christianity so blindingly obvious that no one else in his time seems to have noticed it: the central icon of Christianity, the cross, has nothing Judaic about it but is a sign of Rome, Roman law, Roman power. By exploiting this insight, Hegel opens the way for an understanding of the political and world historical significance of Christianity: he has established the relevance of Christianity to his philosophy of right, that is, of the state and of history. And a Catholic cannot but be gratified to note that he has also established the centrality to Christianity of its relations with Rome—even if in a negative sense and even if the result is not so much Roman Catholicism as Roman Lutheranism.[5]

It is a manifest advantage of Hegel's account of Christian origins not only that it provides Christianity from the start with a political dimension but also that it reduces to marginality the hints of anti-Semitism in the New Testament which in recent years have been a cause of increasing concern.[6] It is, however, a major disadvantage that it cuts Christianity off completely from its Jewish roots. To some extent this is a result of Hegel's fidelity to a Lutheran tradition as old as Luther himself: a suspicion of Judaism as a religion of the Law from which Christ has liberated us, and so as a foreshadowing of Catholicism; a concentration also on the doctrine of the fall and of original sin which, after the first two chapters of Genesis, was seen as playing little or no role in the Old Testament but which was elevated in the Lutheran confessions to the first article of Christian belief. To some extent also this detachment of Christianity from its Jewish roots is a result of the renovation and intensification of Lutheran concepts in the moral and religious philosophy of Kant, for whom Judaism is an image of life lived in obedience to externally imposed laws, rather than the self-imposed law of autonomous rational beings, and so an image of immorality and servitude. Hegel is at one with Schleiermacher and Kant in seeing in Christianity an ethical revolution which breaks completely with Judaism (even if his conception of the nature of the revolution is very different from theirs), and like Schleiermacher he has little to say about the Old Testament, apart from some memorable if uncomplimentary pages about Abraham.[7] Even in his lectures on aesthetics he dismisses Herder's attempt to recover the Old Testament for the connoisseur of primitive poetry. The Old Testament is not a work of art, he says (*W* xv, 331), and the religious intention is too dominant even for those parts of it which have some of the qualities of ancient epics to amount to more than "religio-poetical legends" or "didactic-religious stories" (*W* xv, 398). If anything, the separation of Christianity from the Old Testament goes even deeper in Hegel than it does in Schleiermacher. The separation of Jesus' teachings from the teachings of the community, the *Gemeinde,* insulates the nascent Church from Jesus' Jewish setting and all but consigns Jesus himself to the Old Dispensation. There is no attempt to see the church as continuous with Israel or even—as Catholic and Calvinist traditions allowed—as prefigured by it, nor does Hegel raise the question of the relation between the community constituted by Pentecost and the Jews who remained outside it. There are, it is true, one or two hints that Hegel was prepared to contemplate a historical and conceptual continuity between Judaism and Christianity: a note added to the lectures on religion in 1821 seems to envisage using Psalm 16:10, in direct contradiction of Herder's principles, as a precursor, in some sense, of belief in the resurrection (*W* xvii, 291). More significantly, Hegel identifies the moment of Jesus' appearance with a moment of crisis for Judaism caused by its absorption into the Roman Empire and its confrontation, as a result, with a bigger world, "a generality of humanity . . . whose existence it could no longer deny [as exclusive nationalist Judaism had in Hegel's view done hitherto] but which was as yet wholly untouched by the spirit" (*W* xvii, 283–84). Judaism, that is, for all its sublime claims about its God, found it had nothing to say about him to the world at large. The community that learned at Pentecost to believe that God was in Jesus did however find that it had something to say to all the world, a faith and a love stronger than the death with which Caesar surrounded himself. And in his lectures on the philosophy of history Hegel identifies the moment of that discovery with the moment of "infinite pain" for the Jewish people as a whole, the destruction of their state and their Temple by the future emperor Titus in A.D. 70 (*W* xii, 390–91). As far as I can tell, Hegel has nothing to say about the gap of about forty years separating these two crucial moments—the ministry of Jesus and Rome's Final Solution to its Jewish problem. That gap holds apart two extremely suggestive and potentially fruitful ideas: Jesus' ministry as a point when Jewish tradition collides with the wider world created by the Roman Empire; and the destruction of the Temple as the moment when a Christian community starts the spiritual revolution which through the empire, which it will long outlast, reaches out to the whole world. Hegel keeps these moments apart even at the cost of making the historical circumstances of Jesus' life and teaching seem almost irrelevant to the revolution brought about in his name. I suspect, though I cannot prove, that he does so because to bring the two moments together would require him to establish a continuity between the Old and New Testaments, between Judaism, as he calls it, and Christianity, and so to reassess completely his account of both. He would have to see Christianity as both growing out of Judaism and—there is no need to assume the two processes are incompatible—as reacting against the Caesarism of Rome. And he would have to see in Judaism, or perhaps it would be better to say, in the religion of the Old Testament, the roots of the universalism which in Christianity he attributes to the impact of historical circumstance and the ubiquity of Roman power. For such a reading of the Judeo-Christian Scriptures he did not in the end, perhaps as a result of his own loyal Lutheranism, possess the necessary theological categories.

Hegel, alone among Germany's great thinkers of the Idealist period, responds directly to the dual challenge to Christianity from deism and from historicism, which Herder had thought he could avoid by relying on the poetic appeal and intrinsic persuasive power of the Bible regarded simply as literature, simply as the product of poetic and perhaps also narrative and moral genius. In the course of his direct confrontation of both Deist critique and historical relativism Hegel took up a number of positions which promise more assistance to a Catholic reading of Scripture than does the hermeneutic school represented by Schleiermacher and German academic biblical scholarship of the nineteenth and early twentieth century. These positions include the following:

i)   God can be known by reason, properly understood, and operating in conjunction with faith, and there is no true antithesis between reason and revelation (the Bible therefore is to be read as Aquinas read it, as extending our knowledge of God's work, not as founding it);

ii) the faith of the individual is inseparable from the faith of the church, the *Gemeinde;* the Bible is the book of faith, written in the spirit of the church and to be read in that spirit; there is therefore no true antithesis between Scripture and tradition;

iii) it follows that in the interpretation of Scripture by the church the dogmatic interest is always ultimately decisive;

iv) the Incarnation is central to the content of Revelation because Incarnation and Revelation are formally the same process: the making manifest, and making man, of the Word of God;

v) as the church has of its nature both a spiritual and a worldly existence, the history of the church as recorded in Scripture is the point of connection between the philosophy of religion and the philosophy of history;

vi) if the New Testament is the witness to a spiritual revolution that revolution is to be understood as directed not against the religion of Judaism but against the religion of Caesarism—against the kingdom which is of this world and which contemptuously turns into its tools all partial and specific faiths.

In explication of the last two points we can add two more, which are certainly not to be found in Hegel. My reflection on Hegel, however, has suggested that these may be crucial to a specifically Catholic reading of the Scriptures, a reading, that is, which is specifically different from that required by the German Idealist reinterpretation of the Reformation tradition:

vii) the Scriptures must not be read in a way which posits a radical distinction between the spirit of Jesus and the Spirit of the church;

viii) nor must they be read in a way which posits a radical distinction between the Old and New Testaments, between Christianity and pre-Christian Judaism.

With the formulation of these eight points our consideration of the early stages of modern biblical hermeneutics has, I think, taken us as far as it can towards solving the first part of the puzzle Chenu bequeathed us when he designated literature as the "site" of theology. That was the question: what would be a Catholic approach to reading the Bible as literature, as part of the common literary treasury of humanity? I posed that question not because I wanted to attempt such a reading but as a preliminary to another question, the second part of Chenu's puzzle: what would be a Catholic approach to reading profane literature as a partial or inadequate statement of the truths we see more fully revealed in Holy Scripture, a propaedeutic, if you like, to the reading of the Bible? The provisional answer to the first question seems to be that certain theological elements cannot be eliminated from any coherent, and certainly from any Catholic, reading of the Bible.

That does not imply that Chenu was misguided when he set up his puzzle. But it does imply that if the Bible is to be read as literature, literature itself must be understood as at least capable, in its nonbiblical varieties, of containing theological elements. The first question—how far can the Bible be read as literature?—requires the second—how far can literature be read as Bible? As the next stage in our search I wish to get closer to answering that second question by drawing not on the tradition of biblical exegesis derived from Schleiermacher but on three more recent thinkers about the Bible whose notions of the nature of reading are altogether different from his.

CHAPTER 5

Revelation and Realism:
Frei and Ricoeur

HANS W. FREI WAS A HUMANE AND LEARNED THEOLOGIAN WHO
reflected deeply, and at much greater length than is possible here, on the
German figures I have considered so far. In *The Eclipse of Biblical Narrative:
A Study in Eighteenth- and Nineteenth-Century Hermeneutics,*[1] Frei set himself
a task which had several elements in common with my own, though their
rather different combination produced different results. Starting with a particular conception of the Bible as literature, which he believed had been
held, at least unconsciously, both in the medieval period and in the first two
centuries of Reformation thinking, he tried to show that the rise of hermeneutics in eighteenth- and nineteenth-century Germany destabilized the
sense of the truth of biblical utterances which that age-old conception had
protected. Eighteenth- and nineteenth-century German theologians were
unable to maintain or update or even replace that conception of the Bible as
literature because their culture lacked the requisite understanding of literature; indeed, it lacked literature of the kind which could have produced
such an understanding. This impressively wide-ranging argument is intriguing and infuriating in almost equal measure. It is intriguing because
certain elements in the argument have a natural rightness about them; it is
infuriating because it is impossible to work out how they are supposed to fit
together.

The literary concept Frei deploys in order to link the Bible and other literature is that of realistic narrative, in the sense in which that term is used by Erich Auerbach. In his great book *Mimesis* and his almost equally important essay, "Figura," [2] Auerbach takes as his subject the whole of Western literature from late antiquity and medieval romance to the nineteenth- and twentieth-century novel and aims to show how the ability of that literature to give a realistic depiction of an individual in relation to the large-scale historical and social categories of his or her time derives ultimately from a particular feature of biblical narrative. The feature in question is the combination of typology, the principle that earlier events and characters in the biblical story prefigure later, with the use of a plain, unelevated style for the narration of events of great seriousness. This model, perfected in the Gospels, makes possible, according to Auerbach, the development of a literature able to represent physical and social reality in a direct but noncomic way, and as something interpretable, indeed as something capable of bearing the fullest and deepest meanings words can express. Frei rightly sees that this thesis of Auerbach's has great theological potential. I wonder, though, whether he is also right to try to exploit that potential by using Auerbach directly in the study of the Bible and of the history of hermeneutics, rather than indirectly, in the study of the theological content of secular literature.

Frei argues that an instinctive understanding of the Bible, or at any rate of the Book of Genesis and of the Gospels, as "realistic narrative" was eclipsed in the course of the eighteenth century and replaced by a view of these texts as (reliable or very unreliable) documentary evidence for historical propositions. I think we may agree that, particularly in the Protestant churches, a shift in the understanding of the Bible's literary form took place from the early eighteenth century onwards. We may also fully endorse the suggestion that an impoverished conception of secular literature, a conception less broad and deep than Auerbach's, for example, will necessarily lead to an impoverished conception of biblical literature, and it may well be that German nineteenth-century hermeneutics in particular suffered from such an impoverishment, in the general German culture, of the understanding of what literature, any literature, can be and do. Frei, however, muddles the issue by trying to argue too many different things at once. He seems sometimes to be suggesting that we in the twentieth or twenty-first century could avoid some of the dilemmas and anxieties we have inherited from the rise of hermeneutics two hundred years ago by learning to read the Bible as if it were a nineteenth-century novel—perhaps even a nineteenth-century novel that not merely happened to be true but that, given what it was saying, could not be anything other than true. This is a defensible view, though ultimately a rather limited one, and it has had some influence.[3] But Frei also wants to make a historical claim about what happened in the eighteenth century, whereupon two kinds of absurdity threaten him. First, he can seem to be arguing that eighteenth-century biblical hermeneuts all failed to consider the possibility that the Bible ought to be read like a nineteenth-century novel. Second, he can seem to be arguing that before the rise of eighteenth-century hermeneutics the Bible *was* read like a nineteenth-century novel. It is difficult to take seriously the suggestion that belief in the literal divine inspiration of the Scriptures such as was enjoined on a sixteenth- and seventeenth-century Lutheran is tantamount to treating them as realistic narrative. Belief in literal divine inspiration certainly implies belief that everything the Scriptures say is true, but telling the truth is not at all what Auerbach, or I think anybody else, means by realism. If it were, then saying a story is true to life would mean the same as saying that it is true—and usually it means that it is not.

Frei is on stronger ground in his analysis of eighteenth-century literary history, but here once again the issue is muddled because the historical analysis does not bear out the hermeneutical theory. Frei rightly puts great stress on the strangely divergent paths of English and German culture in the eighteenth century, and he again rightly points out that the English at this time had lots of novels and not much in the way of biblical criticism, while the Germans had lots of biblical criticism and not many novels. But neither England nor Germany, he notes with sorrow and some bewilderment, succeeded in developing anything like a respectable theory of the Bible as novel. However, far from being evidence of the eclipse of what he calls the realistic narrative option, this failure of two cultures, starting from opposite but complementary premises, to come up with what he wants surely suggests that what he wants is a mare's nest, a chimera. Whatever might be meant by saying that the Bible is literature, or even poetry, saying that does *not* mean that the Bible is a novel. Frei's fundamental mistake, I think, is to assume that if, as Auerbach claims, a certain feature of the Bible makes realism possible in secular narrative written by Christians, or within the framework of a Christian culture, then it follows that the Bible itself must also be an example of realistic narrative. On the contrary, I would say, the Bible may contain examples of realistic narrative, but if it is to found the possibility of the entire genre it must itself and as a whole be something more, more than a mere collection of examples: it must at least show us the special character and importance of a realistic literary text by giving us some notion of what such a text is not; it must contain more literary genres than narrative and more literary modes than realism; and it must itself be more than simply a text—it must be animated by the living Spirit of the church in which and for which it is the Word of God.

Realism in Auerbach's sense, we must remember, is not merely representation of reality in a low but noncomic style. It is also representation that is meaningful and serious; that is to say, it represents things as if they mattered. What makes things matter? Not—emphatically not—how they are represented but—so the Bible tells us—how they are related to the Incarnate Word of God. And the Bible does not and probably could not tell us this simply by its use of literary realism. From the first chapter of Genesis, which can hardly be accused of realism, things are shown to us as things that matter, as good, indeed very good, because God has made them by his Word. Even the life and death of Jesus is shown to matter by its relation to something other than its own story—and not just to other stories, but to the prophecies, psalms, genealogies, events, laws, and liturgies that precede it (and to which Jesus' own words make appeal) and to the events and reflections and expectations and liturgies that follow it, in virtue of all of which it is manifested as the story of the Incarnation. Hegel would even say more, and probably rightly: the story of Jesus is not finally and definitively manifested as the story of the Incarnate Word until it has been proclaimed as such by the Spirit, that is, by a church now living and active. The text alone, however elaborated and multiple, however full of typological echoes and pre-echoes, will not suffice to interpret the story of Jesus as something that matters. Mattering comes from the Spirit. In the realistic narrative of the Gospels—and realistic narrative is not the whole even of them, as is shown by the Prologue to St. John—the incarnate Word of God is spoken in its absolutely unique particularity, Hegel would say; but even that utterance is possible only because the Word is spoken elsewhere in the Bible, and elsewhere in the church, in preincarnate and postresurrection forms, that is, in modes other than realistic narrative and other than literature altogether, in the prior history of the Jewish people and the posterior history of the Christian church, in obedience to the Old Law and to Christ's new commandment, in sacrament and in good works, and so, to use Hegel's vocabulary, with the moments of universality or specificity rather than of particularity.

The necessary implication of Auerbach's argument, then, it seems to me, is that realism, in his sense, is made possible not by the Bible but by the Christian church—as Hegel would say, by the spirit of Christianity—which gives the Bible its meaning, its interpretability, its seriousness. Frei is unable fully to appropriate Auerbach because, like Schleiermacher before him, and like a long line of Protestant Reformers before Schleiermacher, he is unwilling to allow the church a role in biblical hermeneutics. In the end he too wants to be able to say that the Bible stands alone and that we know God and ourselves *sola scriptura*. His use of Auerbach is an up-to-date version of an old error: the Bible is said to have a unique natural quality—in this case the quality of being a realistic story which is so true to life that it must be true—as a consequence of which it can claim a supernatural function. This is bibliolatry in a new guise: a uniqueness and transcendence is given to the biblical text that belongs properly only to God. Frei's conception of the Bible is far too narrow. Interpretation of it simply as realistic narrative would anyway be inadequate to the theological, indeed to the pneumatological, complexity of realism itself. But this conception of the Bible is also, and very obviously, too narrow in a purely quantitative sense. Frei concentrates on a corpus of texts—the Gospels and Genesis—even smaller than Schleiermacher's; he says nothing of poetic and non-narrative forms; and it is difficult, for example, to see how his preferred category of realistic narrative could be applied at all to such central texts as Isaiah or Romans. By his appeal to Auerbach he has done something very important for us which I suspect lies very far indeed from his original intention: he has shown that the issues in German eighteenth-century biblical interpretation with which we began are linked to general issues in the understanding of secular literature. But in order to exploit this opening up of our field of enquiry we need help from other sources.

Now an obvious possible alternative source would be Hans-Georg Gadamer's great work *Wahrheit und Methode* (*Truth and Method*), of which Frei takes little notice, though it was published in 1960.[4] Gadamer offers a serious critique of what he calls Romantic hermeneutics, which he takes to originate in Schleiermacher, but which he sees as rooted in the Enlightenment. He criticizes the "prejudice against prejudices" which is inherent in Herder's and Schleiermacher's aim to achieve completely dispassionate understanding of a text's original meaning for its original audience. "Prejudice" (*Vorurteil*) is, both etymologically and really, a "prejudgment," a presupposition of judgment, and no act of interpretative judgment is possible without presuppositions. We are not infinite, immortal, and godlike judges when we try to understand a text; we speak and listen out of a network of prejudgments provided for example by our family, our society, and our state (*WM* 261), and these will usually contribute more to our interpretation than our individual, personal, judgments. The passage of time, which for Herder and Schleiermacher separated us from the original utterance and made its meaning more difficult of access, should be understood not as an abyss but as a bridge, as the process of tradition or handing-on (*Überlieferung*) which makes meanings accessible at all. For the very notion of an original meaning is suspect. It is in the nature of an utterance that it always potentially means *more* than the original speaker intended—"the meaning of a text always outdoes (*übertrifft*) its author" (*WM* 280)—and in the course of time and changing circumstances more, not less, of the text's potential is revealed. Interpretation, for Gadamer, is conversation, a conversation between the limitations and presuppositions of a text and those of its readers, and, the point is crucial, it is a conversation *about* something known to both parties. Interpretation involves not just finding out more about the text, but finding out more about what the text is about. This process is made possible by the writtenness (*Schriftlichkeit*) of the text, for only "what has been fixed in writing has detached itself from the contingency of its origins and its author and freed itself, in a positive sense, for new relationships" (*WM* 373). Gadamer therefore makes hermeneutics an open adventure rather than a closed discipline. Openness towards the new, the acceptance of limitation—learned in part no doubt from Heidegger—and so the expectation that one's limits will one day be transcended—will indeed be transcended in the very next text one reads—all this amounts to a remarkably fruitful act of intellectual humility.

If I choose nevertheless not to ask Gadamer to join in the present quest it is because, in comparison with some who have come after him, he is surprisingly reticent about the topic that particularly concerns me: the hermeneutics of the Bible. This is perhaps a consequence of his own "prejudices," his own historicity. Gadamer speaks as a member of the early-twentieth-century German academic Lutheran class. The "application" of biblical texts that seems to him intrinsic to the process of understanding them is their use in the proclamation (*kerygma*) to individual souls of the saving message. His preferred theologian is not, as for Frei, Karl Barth but Rudolf Bultmann. Despite the importance he assigns to "family, society, and state" as the source of our prejudgments, he has surprisingly little to say about the institutional forms, or even the historical tradition, of biblical interpretation. His cultural presuppositions angle his perspective on history. He is reluctant to locate the origins of Schleiermacher's hermeneutics in the eighteenth-century crisis I have outlined, and while he acknowledges Herder's role he also underestimates it. In particular, while he grasps, of course, the intimate relation between hermeneutics and nineteenth-century historicism, he largely overlooks the vitally important convergence of historicist and Deist critiques of Christianity in the middle of the eighteenth century. For that alliance, which provoked Herder to try to safeguard Christianity by demanding that the Bible be read as literature, was above all effective, not against the witness of Catholic church tradition, but against a conception of the uniquely authoritative Scriptures which had its roots in the sixteenth-century Reformation. Gadamer implausibly makes Schleiermacher into the fountainhead of "Romantic" hermeneutics,[5] because to investigate the crisis to which Schleiermacher was responding would be to uncover its origins in the thought of Luther and Calvin.[6]

Many of Gadamer's themes can be found productively varied, and adapted to a specifically theological context, in the thought of Paul Ricoeur. It is no criticism of the general hermeneutic achievement of Gadamer or, in a narrower field, of Frei to say that those who want to understand the relation between sacred and secular scriptures and who turn to Ricoeur will find themselves breathing more easily and in a freer air. The exegetical traditions of Bultmann and Barth, on which Gadamer and Frei respectively rely, are still too much prisoners of the problematic of revelation created by the collision in eighteenth-century Germany of bibliolatry and deism. With Ricoeur the horizons widen and the problematic evaporates as the concepts regain something of the generosity they were given by Thomas. In two respects invoking the help of Ricoeur brings us significantly nearer to our goal. First, he is open to the full range of the material of the Old Testament and has a relatively untroubled sense of its continuity with the New. Second, he has cleared out channels of communication between sacred and profane literature which look capable of bearing heavy traffic.

First, then, Ricoeur releases us from the constricting, even asphyxiating, antithesis of Judaism and Christianity, Law and Freedom, whose grip can be felt through the velvet gloves of German Idealism in all its many styles—even of Hegel's extraordinary attempt to dissociate Christianity from Judaism completely. When Ricoeur writes, "the Sermon on the Mount proclaims the same intention of perfection and holiness that runs through the ancient Law,"[7] his assertion of the continuity between the Old and New Dispensations overturns the founding principle—I am tempted to say the Lutheran principle—of every variant on the Idealist reinterpretation of Christianity from Herder to Feuerbach—the asserted discontinuity, namely, between Old and New, between, in Kant's terms, statutory and moral religion, between Jewish "heteronomy" and Christian "autonomy."[8] Hegel's secondary discontinuity, between the teaching of Jesus and the teaching of the early church, is also subverted by Ricoeur in his interpretation of the parable as the characteristic literary form of the synoptic gospels,[9] though I find this less persuasive. Ricoeur has no qualms about incorporating into his biblical hermeneutics the entire range of Scriptures to which the church has given the collective name of Bible. In specific contradistinction to Frei, and inspired by Northrop Frye rather than by Auerbach, he treats narrative as only one of several forms of biblical discourse. Each of these forms of discourse is characterized by a different relation to the name of God. This in itself is an important advance on Frei's position, for Ricoeur recognizes the necessity of a theological component in the literary categories that are to be applied to the Bible. The weakness in Frei's position was that he did not recognize the need to define the theological—specifically the ecclesiological—element in the concept of narrative realism he wished to deploy. Ricoeur's approach produces not only a more comprehensive account of biblical literature than Frei's, but an account in which the Bible's relation to nonbiblical literature becomes clearer, as does the concept of Revelation itself.

In an outstanding summary analysis, first presented to the symposium "The Idea of Revelation" in Brussels in 1976 and translated into English under the title "Toward a Hermeneutic of the Idea of Revelation," Ricoeur distinguishes five forms of biblical discourse, some originally spoken but all now written.

First, there is prophetic discourse in which, preeminently, God speaks in the first person, through the person of the prophet: "Thus saith the Lord, thy Redeemer, the Holy One of Israel; I am the Lord thy God" (Is 48:17). This form of discourse is plainly fundamental in Holy Scripture and equally plainly deserves a special position in any analysis. However, according to Ricoeur, prophetic discourse has two features which, precisely because they are the most immediate sources of the concept of revelation, can be misleading if they are assumed to apply to all other forms of biblical writing: the necessary doubling of the role of the speaker—"I" is said equally by Isaiah and by the Lord—so that revelation is understood as God's voice whispering in the ear of the prophet, who then passes on what he has heard; and the specific form of prophecy known as revelation, or apocalypse, which consists in the making public of hidden things, secrets about the end of time. These are legitimate, indeed essential features of prophecy, Ricoeur thinks, but should not be extended to furnish a concept of revelation for all the other literary forms to be found in the Bible (as they have been in the literalist-supernaturalist tradition which is the basis of bibliolatry).

Second, then, there is narrative discourse, to which Ricoeur is prepared to give perhaps the most important role in constituting Jewish and Christian religious identity, and to that extent he accommodates Frei's perspective. In narrative God is referred to in the third person, and whereas in prophecy we had a double speaker, the "I" of the prophet and the "I" of God, in narrative we have what Ricoeur calls a double "actant" (TH 5), in that all the deeds of individual men and women, the hes and shes of the stories of Genesis and Exodus, Judges and Mark, are also the deeds of God, the second or ultimate "He." And the Jewish or Christian community identifies itself as constituted by a series of such history-making events, recounted as the work of both Man and God, whether in the Pentateuch, the synoptic gospels, or the Acts of the Apostles. In narrative of this kind the narrator has effectively no part in the story told. We must guard against the tendency to treat histories as if they were simply an indirect expression of a narrator's worldview, and so a subset of prophecy—with Yahwist or Elohist narrators, for example, or, for that matter, with Evangelists, as unnamed prophets behind whose third-person narrative lurks always a first person's theology. What matters in history is the event, not the act of recounting it. This defense by Ricoeur of what he calls "the realism of the event of history" seems to me both a justification of Frei's use of the term "realism" and a much clearer explanation of what it might mean in the biblical context—clearer because it is restricted to one particular genre.

The third form of biblical discourse identified by Ricoeur is prescriptive discourse, in which God speaks not in the first person of a finite mood but in the imperative, so providing what Ricoeur calls "the ethical dimension of revelation" (TH 10). Here I have to confess to some doubts. Not only does this account of the Old and New Covenants, the Law, whether of the Decalogue and Leviticus or of the Sermon on the Mount and the Pastoral Epistles, seem rather understated, Ricoeur seems to contravene his own strongly expressed principle that one should not overextend individual genres, or confuse their boundaries, when he states that "the Legislative genre is in a way included in the narrative genre" (TH 9). That presumably means that the different phases of the Law—the Covenants with Abraham, on Sinai, and in Ezekiel, the second legislation of Ezra and Deuteronomy, the new Covenant in Christ—are to be understood as different stages in the story of the people of God, and that comes perilously close to evacuating the claim of prescriptive discourse to independent status. We shall have to return to this point.

Fourth, there is wisdom discourse. It is of course evident that the reflections on human life of Proverbs, Ecclesiastes, or Job constitute a wholly different kind of biblical writing from the prophetic or narrative books, and they have long been separately grouped as such. Ricoeur's special contribution is to understand these books as characterized, in formal terms, by their referring to God, not through the use of the first or third person, or of the imperative mood, but as absent. On the one hand, no reference to any special revelation, whether as prophecy, narrative, or law, is necessary as a foundation for the universal precepts of prudence which make up much of Proverbs. On the other hand, the existentialist's "limit-situations" of solitude, guilt, unjust suffering, and death are in Job or Ecclesiastes given a divine dimension or content through being interpreted as manifestations of the incomprehensibility and silence of God and the emptiness of all humanly constructed meaning. The importance of this insight for us is obvious. It suggests that wisdom discourse is the closest point of contact between sacred and secular scripture. It is the point where the Bible looks most like profane literature, and profane literature looks most like the Bible. But exploiting this point of contact is not simply a matter of identifying the theme of the hiddenness and silence of God as a sacred theme in apparently secular literature. It is also a matter of understanding the relationship—the dialectical relationship, Ricoeur would say—between the different forms of biblical discourse and specifically between wisdom discourse and other biblical genres. For if we can explain something of how the biblical presentation of God's incomprehensibility is related to the equally biblical revelation of his words, deeds, and laws we shall have come a long way towards understanding how secular presentations of the hidden God can also be related to the fullness of revelation, and so towards understanding the specific nature of the theological underpinning that George Steiner thinks is essential to all literary creation. Ricoeur says little about the works of biblical wisdom in which the tragic themes of the limit-situations are muted or modified by the opening up of a transition to other biblical genres—notably the deuterocanonical works such as Ecclesiasticus or the Wisdom of Solomon but also universally canonical works such as Jonah, Ruth, or the particularly challenging case of the Song of Songs. But it is perhaps in these that we shall find the traffic from sacred to secular, from secular to sacred, that will enable us to move from treating the Bible as literature to treating literature as at any rate a prolegomenon to the Bible.

I must however mention Ricoeur's fifth category of biblical discourse, and not just for the sake of completeness. The fifth category, hymnic discourse, is above all represented by the Book of Psalms, which for Herder was the supreme, even if not the most vigorous, example of Hebrew poetry.

For Ricoeur too hymnic discourse is a kind of culmination, though one whose exceptional character must not be exaggerated. In hymnic discourse God is referred to in the second person, as "you," "thou"—whether in praise, or prayer, or thanksgiving—and the general significance of this structural feature of a particular genre was overstated by Martin Buber, much, I might add, as the significance of the narrative mode was overstated by Frei. Ricoeur sees the general significance of the Psalms as lying in their relation to wisdom literature. If wisdom literature, in Ricoeur's words, "transforms suffering into knowing how to suffer" (TH 15), the Psalms transform that knowledge into revelation of God. For the Psalms turn our knowledge, whether of the absence of God from our suffering or of the deeds of God in nature and history or of the words of God in the Law and the Prophets, into the expression of our feelings towards God addressed as "you." And, as Ricoeur nicely puts it, "the sentiments expressed [in the Psalms] are formed by and conformed to their object. . . . The word forms our feeling in the process of expressing it" (TH 15). Since, moreover, the ultimate object of those feelings is the person to whom their expression is addressed, namely God—so, at any rate, I interpret Ricoeur's argument—the conformation to their object which their expression in words brings about is a conformation to God. Saying or singing the Psalms, therefore, is a revelation of God which consists not in knowledge communicated but in the process of the expression of feeling in words, in "the raising up of the heart and mind to God," as the Catechism used to define prayer. I am perhaps overinterpreting what Ricoeur says here. It is possible to read his words as claiming no more than that any verbal expression of our feelings constitutes a transcendence, as he puts it, of "their ordinary, everyday modalities," and as such is tantamount to a revelation. He would then be arguing that the Psalms do as much as, but no more than, any other specimen of lyric poetry, which is little different from Herder's view. I do not think that Ricoeur really means to say anything so pseudoreligious, so derivative from aestheticist Idealism. That he may appear to do so is a consequence of the great strength of his general concept of revelation, of which I now want to say a little more. However, it is worth remembering that such misinterpretation is possible if Ricoeur's hermeneutics are not firmly anchored, as he obviously intends them to be, in reference to God.

The great strength of Ricoeur's general concept of revelation is that it is a direct response to the two-stage crisis for Christian biblical faith that emerged in the course of the eighteenth century, but it puts the crisis in a new systematic framework provided largely by twentieth-century literary and linguistic theory. The first, or Deist, stage of the critical challenge to what we may, with Ricoeur, call biblical faith was a challenge to the concept of revelation itself. Revelation was either impossible or unnecessary, the knowledge the Bible supposedly imparted being either incompatible with knowledge acquired through the usual processes of reasoning or superfluous to it. Ricoeur's response might at first sight seem very similar to Herder's: the Bible is not reasoning, it is poetry. "Poetic discourse," Ricoeur says, "does not directly augment our knowledge of objects [as does "everyday language and . . . scientific discourse"]." And he goes on "to place the originary expressions of biblical faith under the sign of the poetic function of language . . . the Bible is one of the great poems of existence" (TH 23–26). However, these remarks are not just Herder dressed up in twentieth-century terminology; they are a genuine development and strengthening of Herder's position.[10] Written language, Ricoeur believes like Gadamer, is not simply speech fixed in material form. A written text has from the start a life of its own: it is from the start a thing, an artifact, that exists independently of the context which produced it and which it will outlast. A written work is a structure of meanings independent both of its author's intentions and of the expectations of the audience for which it is written (TH 22). These principles of course imply a radical critique of Schleiermacher's translation of Herder into the formalities of hermeneutics and of the nineteenth-century biblical scholarship Schleiermacher inspired—and Ricoeur acknowledges his debt to Gadamer (TH 22). Ricoeur is, I believe, recovering the literary theory which Herder intended but could not sustain with any consistency (which is one reason for thinking, despite Ricoeur, that "the author's intention" is not an entirely outdated conceptual tool). For Ricoeur develops Gadamer's recognition that utterance is always *about* something. He substitutes for the notion of what the author intended by the work the notion of what the text itself implies—we might almost say "intends"—about the way the world is in order for the text to have meaning,—about "the sort of world intended [that word here probably has a technical sense derived from Husserl] beyond the text as its reference" (TH 23). This, his substitute for the notion of the author's intention, Ricoeur calls "the world of the text." Written texts do not merely say things (and it is noteworthy that we cannot in practice do without the metaphor of speech)—they do not merely provide information about states of affairs—they also imply the existence of the whole system in which those states of affairs occur about which things are said. The annual report of a company to its shareholders does not merely make explicit statements about the results from different branches of its operations; it also implies a world of money and law, capital and work, countable units and a system of international trade, about which perhaps nothing may be said explicitly at all but which makes possible everything that is said explicitly; and without understanding, as we might say, the world that the report is talking about, we will not understand the report at all. In the case of poetic texts, of any fictional texts, the element of communicating instrumentally, descriptively, or factually about things falls away entirely and we are left only with "the world of the text"—the world of the report without the report—and so we are left with a sense of our presence to what is, independently of the utilitarian relationship with it that our normal, nonfictional way of talking about it implies and enables. When we read Homer, or a novel, we are not being told something verifiable or useful about objects, rather, Ricoeur says, a whole world—the world of the text—is being "proposed" or "manifested" to us as something to which we belong or in which we are rooted before we start the business of reasoning, verifying, using, and exploiting, to which functional language is devoted. A lost continent, an Atlantis, of sheer being, the ground of our existence, rises up, he says, out of the ocean of our everyday or scientific preoccupations (TH 25). "In this sense of manifestation," he goes on, "language in its poetic function is a vehicle of revelation," though of course in this sense, in which it is a universal feature of all poetry (meaning by "poetry" all literary fictions), revelation "is to be understood in a non-religious, non-theistic and non-biblical sense of the word" (TH 24). There is nothing odd or exceptional about revelation, then: the manifestation to us of something that utilitarian reason could not possibly predict or infer or construct is as commonplace as the reading of a poem or a story. We have only to pick up a new volume of Seamus Heaney, or for that matter an old volume of Dickens, or even Pope, to have revealed to us a truth at which the reason of the Deists could not arrive before the end of the world. Herder's conviction that the appeal to poetry is the answer, or part of the answer, to the Deist critique of revelation is thus triumphantly vindicated by Ricoeur.

However, Ricoeur is emphatically clear that although it is no argument against biblical truth to say that it is revealed rather than rational, revealed truth in this sense is "non-religious" and "non-theistic." This definition of revelation as common to all poetic utterance can prove no more than that at best the Bible is one of the great poems of existence. What makes the

Bible's truth into religious truth, according to Ricoeur, is not the fact that the Bible's truth is revealed rather than rational but what the Bible is about. Unlike other revelations, other poems, indeed unlike other great poems of existence, the Bible, as we have seen in Ricoeur's formal analysis, is in all its different forms of discourse directed towards a single vanishing point, the Name of the Unnameable. What makes the Bible unique is that the world of the text that it proposes to us, the Atlantis of being that it reveals, is, Ricoeur says, the new Creation, the Kingdom of God—the world, we might say, centered on God. With this demonstration of the Bible's uniqueness Ricoeur can move on to respond to the second stage in the eighteenth-century crisis of biblical faith.

That second-stage crisis was occasioned by the rise of historicism. Given the variety of the forms and expressions of human culture in the present and in the past, why should any special, let alone unique, authority attach to any one of them? Ricoeur is brought to consider this question by his analysis of the concept of revelation in his response to the first stage of the crisis. For there is something in us that resists the idea that things that our reason could not construct can be, and very frequently are, revealed to us. The source of that resistance is the belief that we are masters of our selves, of our consciousness, and of the way we organize its content, the belief in our "autonomy," that is, the belief that we make the laws of our own way of being. "The pretension of consciousness to constitute itself," he writes, "is the most formidable obstacle to the idea of revelation" (TH 30). This pretension is most outraged by the idea that consciousness might be constituted not just by something else but by something else that is itself a mere historical accident, an arbitrary event in the past that happened to happen but could perfectly well not have happened at all. "This refusal of historical contingency," in Ricoeur's words again, "constitutes one of the most dug-in defenses of the claim to autonomy" (TH 31), and the resistance is naturally fiercest when what is revealed by a historically contingent utterance is said to be of absolute importance. When we open a book of poetry—Chapman's Homer, for example—we not only discover that there is such a thing as revelation, we also have the experience of being constituted, in Ricoeur's terms, by the world of the text. In that moment of revelation what we are is determined by the world—the Pacific Ocean—of possibilities that the text contains and communicates. That in itself is a hard enough blow for our pretension to autonomy. But there is a worse "paradox" or "scandal"—Ricoeur's words—yet: the scandal that this new ocean, which for the moment has made us, was, like our discovery of it, not a necessary and eternal fact of nature or reason but something made by a human and historical person who did and made what he might not have done or made and who himself might not have been—Homer, who was perhaps many people who might not have composed what they did or whose works might have been put together in a different way, Chapman, who might have translated something else, or Cortés, who was really Balboa, or Keats, who might have died even younger and never written the sonnet. Seamus Heaney might have died like his younger brother at the age of four, but here we are opening *Death of a Naturalist*—and had he died that "we" would never have been. The refusal to admit the historical contingency of revelation, biblical and nonbiblical, is a refusal to admit the historical contingency of our selves, our historicity, as Gadamer calls it. In the language of the eighteenth-century discussion we have pursued—though Ricoeur does not explicitly mention this source for his terminology—it is the refusal to admit, alongside the evidence of reason, the evidence of testimony. Testimony, Ricoeur says, is "the most appropriate concept for making us understand what a thinking subject formed by and conforming to poetic discourse might be" (TH 27). Ricoeur's analysis shows that the Deist and historicist stages of the eighteenth-century argument about revelation were simply the objective and subjective aspects of the same problem. The Deist criticism that reason and revelation were conceptually incompatible was met in objective terms by Ricoeur's hermeneutics of poetic discourse, his demonstration that all poetry is revelation. The historicist criticism that particular and contingent events cannot, except by arbitrary decision, be invested with absolute authority is a claim about what is or is not authority for a subject which claims to be autonomous. The theory of testimony is Ricoeur's weapon against this subjective aspect of the eighteenth-century argument.

Testimony is the communication of truth not through the statement of a rule of reason, or even through the furnishing of examples or symbols of such a rule, but through events, through singular, real instances of the overcoming of evil, of that which is unjustifiable by any rational rule. Testimony is the nonrational defense of reason against the nonrational assault on it, against the absolutely unjustifiable that we call evil, and testimony comes to us in the form of meaningful events. Whether those events are reported to us or are lived out before our eyes—the word *testimony* has both senses—they are revelation, they are, or are like, a text which constitutes us, its readers and interpreters. "We exist because we are seized by those events that happen to us in the strong sense of the word[,] . . . that, as one says, have completely changed the course of our existence. . . . In themselves they are event-signs. To understand ourselves is to continue to attest and to testify to them" (TH 34). Testimony thus has a moral element which is lacking in Gadamer's concept of tradition. Our birth from one pair of individuals, our marriage to and generation of others, our historic, economic, and cultural dependence on other events, collective or personal, recent or remote, wars and worse, movements and migrations as far back perhaps as Cortés or Homer, these are the texts, the external signs offered to us by a generous Absolute, which it is our task to interpret as signs of the overcoming of evil in the same process by which we interpret ourselves. Interpretation is necessary and inevitable, for the coincidence of the event and its meaning is never, or only momentarily, immediate. At best only momentarily do we see with clarity and beyond peradventure the hand of God in history or in our lives; the event and its meaning shift apart and have to be reconnected, mediated to each other, by institutional or personal memory or symbolic embodiment, by signs enacted and by words spoken and written. And where there is mediation and interpretation there is also the sifting of the true and the false, the distinguishing of the authentic memory from the inauthentic gloss that speaks not out of the event but out of the pretension of consciousness to be self-constituting, to be independent, to be absolute.

The conclusion from all this looks very positive. The Bible, as poetry, has been shown by Ricoeur to be, in a nonreligious sense, revelation; it has also been shown by him to be formally unique in virtue of its religious, its theological, structure. Our self understanding has been shown to be necessarily dependent on unique revelations, historically contingent event-signs given to us from an external source. We seem to have come as near as philosophy can bring us to resolving the eighteenth-century crisis and demonstrating the reasonableness of biblical faith, its ability to withstand both Deist and historicist critique. There can be no doubt that Ricoeur's argument that poetry is revelation and that, historically speaking, revelation comes to us as testimony greatly enriches the concepts both of the Bible as literature and of secular literature as capable of revealing sacred things. But all is not entirely well. Ricoeur's avowed aim of establishing a "post-Hegelian Kantianism"[11] seems in a certain sense to be right and to be achieved, above all when he recognizes that interpretation is a never-ending dialectic between event and meaning, true and false exegesis, the report given and the life lived. But in a certain sense too his position looks like a regression to a pre-Hegelian stance: he shies away from accounting for the church's role in establishing and interpreting texts, and the Incarnation is not as central to either his biblical or his nonbiblical hermeneutics as ought to be the case, whether for Christians or for post-Hegelians. The life of Jesus cannot be assimilated simply to testimony, whether that is testimony to higher things seen or testimony given by a life in martyrdom. Hegel has already shown as much in his magisterial dismissal of that eighteenth-century commonplace, the comparison of Jesus and Socrates. The essential difference between the two, Hegel says, lies in theology, in the Resurrection, however that is understood.[12] Moreover, Ricoeur has a tendency to overvalue the fact that the Bible is a written text, a tendency which leads him to join many others in describing Judaism, Christianity, and Islam as, explicitly, "religions of the book" (TH 22). Equally explicitly, the new Catholic Catechism states that "the Christian faith is not a 'religion of the book.'"[13] Now the Catechism is not Scripture; it is not even, shall we say, infallible, but as a hermeneutical instance it must be allowed a certain authority. Let us merely say: there is something fishy here. Just as there is something fishy when Ricoeur suggests that revelation operates on the imagination rather than on the will, making a "non-violent appeal" to us to open ourselves, rather than issuing an "unacceptable" claim (or "pretension") to obedience (TH 37). There seems here to be a confusion of the Holy Office and Holy Writ, a confusion encouraged equally by the Holy Office itself and by its Protestant adversaries. When, however, Ricoeur chooses to conclude his argument with his demonstration of what he calls "the non-heteronomous dependence of conscious reflection on external testimonies" (TH 37), the question positively bursts from the page: have we not been here before? And of course we have. Ricoeur is not the first systematizer of Herder's discovery that the Bible is literature to find in the notion of nonheteronomous dependence a counter to the claims of self-constituting consciousness which permits reason to coexist with the historical and anthropological reality of specific and differing religious beliefs. But whereas Schleiermacher used the concept of dependence to found an ecclesiology that had virtually no contact with his biblical hermeneutics, Ricoeur uses it to found a biblical hermeneutics that is virtually divorced from an ecclesiology. Let us hope this is not because the authority of the church has become as embarrassing a subject in the twentieth and twenty-first century as the authority of the Bible had become in the eighteenth century. For it is too readily forgotten that the authority of the church, like the authority of the Bible, is derivative— given, as it was given to Pilate, from above—and that the church, like the

Bible, may be the object of idolatry. But that is not to argue that the concept of authority is void, merely that we must locate it where it belongs, in the Word of God. It is not from a Christian tradition at all that I have been able to draw that sense of the authority of revelation which alone can furnish us with the full sense of what it could mean to treat the Bible as literature or literature as Bible. Rather I have found it in a Jewish thinker, Emmanuel Lévinas.

CHAPTER 6

Lévinas (1): Beyond Bibliolatry?

IT IS TIME FOR A RECAPITULATION, AT LEAST OF THE MORE RECENT stages in this quest. Hegel offered us an alternative way of reading the Scriptures largely independent of the historical hermeneutic method that emerged from Herder and Schleiermacher. However, he did so at the cost of severing, or appearing to sever, Christianity almost entirely from its Jewish roots. Frei acknowledged Hegel's exceptional position but did not build on it, and his own attempt to escape from the Protestant and Idealist hermeneutic tradition of nineteenth- and early-twentieth-century German biblical scholarship was doubly flawed: his attempt to bring together sacred and secular methods of reading texts reposed first on too narrow a conception of literature—literature is more than the nineteenth-century novel, however great an achievement that may be—and second on too narrow a conception of the Bible—the Bible is more than narrative, and one consequence of concentrating too exclusively on its narrative texts is that a great deal, in particular of the Old Testament, is ignored. Ricoeur provides a far broader and more balanced conception of what the Bible is, and his fivefold division of its forms of discourse is particularly valuable in giving us a sense of the variety-in-unity of the Old Testament. Welcome though his emphasis on the continuity between New Testament and Old Testament forms of discourse may be, it does however constitute an elision of an issue: the question is not addressed, why there is a Bible at all, why this set of texts is held to constitute a unity, and why in particular it includes the writings of the New Testament, and the division into Old and New. Ricoeur seems reluctant to discuss the ecclesiology of the Bible: the institution that uses the text, that safeguards it and that determines its scope and content. There are issues here not only between Catholic and Protestant but also between Christian and Jewish traditions. Two questions seemed to call for further consideration in Ricoeur's account of the types of biblical text: the status of prescriptive discourse, which he seemed ready to absorb into narrative discourse, and the nature of the link between wisdom discourse and the remainder of the Bible. Lévinas can take our discussion further, and not only because he is a major philosopher of the generation immediately subsequent to Heidegger's, who proposes a way of dealing with some of the most obvious weaknesses in Heidegger's system and who therefore comes as close as anyone to answering the question, where, or even who, are we now? He also offers a Jewish perspective on my topic which has been notably absent from the authorities I have called on so far, with the doubtful exception of Spinoza. We must of course remember that Lévinas represents a particularly strict, Lithuanian Judaism, opposed to mysticism, messianism, and any compromise with Christianity or secular Enlightenment. Just beneath the surface of his texts, and sometimes not even beneath it, there is a systematic rejection of Christian claims. However, this strictness makes for a welcome clarity and seriousness in the positions he adopts.

Lévinas also contributed to the 1976 Brussels symposium on revelation at which Ricoeur first presented his analysis of biblical discourse and of the concept of revelation. Lévinas's contribution, translated under the title "Revelation in the Jewish Tradition,"[1] came after Ricoeur's and included some responses to it. Much the most important of these is a fundamental modification—perhaps really a fundamental objection—to Ricoeur's system of biblical genres.[2] Far from allowing that prescriptive discourse might in the end be absorbed into narrative discourse, Lévinas asserts that from a Jewish point of view prescriptive discourse is primary: for a Jew, everything in the Bible is law, and the art of interpretation, an intrinsic part of Jewish tradition for over two thousand years, consists in demonstrating the relevance to the law of every last detail of the text, including even, for some authorities, the shape of the letters. (Even that extreme position, denounced by Schleiermacher as the ultimate absurdity [H 87], is treated by Lévinas with affectionate respect [R 59; LR 194].) Lévinas comes close to hinting that the generic distinctions, so carefully organized by Ricoeur, are irrelevant. The Psalms, for example, are not merely lyrical but include allusions to the material of history and meditations on the law. Wisdom literature, far from being detached from the rest of the Bible, is shot through with prophetic, narrative, and prescriptive elements. But anyway—even if we think that distinctions do not cease to exist simply because they are fuzzy at the edges and even if we note that we have to wait until Exodus 12:2 before the Bible utters an imperative—we have to recognize that in the Jewish tradition the genre that comes first is prescription: "It is commandment," Lévinas says, "rather than narration which marks the first step towards human understanding and is, therefore, the beginning of language. . . . Our model of revelation must be an ethical one"(R 70–72; *LR* 204–6). In full accordance with this principle, the contents of biblical revelation are described by Lévinas in terms which keep them very close to the formal structure of the primal commandment, as that is defined by him in his other major writings, including those which make very little reference to the Bible. Revelation, he tells us, with the full authority of Exodus and Deuteronomy behind him, enjoins "of course" that anyone who hears it must follow the Most High with exclusive fidelity—excluding particularly any worship of the state which corrupts morality with its *raison d'état* (R 68; *LR* 202). But there is a parallel commandment—and, unlike the New Testament which he seems to be echoing here, Lévinas suggests that this second commandment is analytically identical to or fully implied in the first. This second commandment is to approach one's neighbor, "the widow and orphan, the stranger and the poor man" with full hands, not empty. Lévinas elsewhere makes even knowledge of or prayer to God derivative from this fundamental ethical principle (*LR* 179, 231–33), and here he clearly relates to it the other elements which make up the content of Revelation: to hear the command, the ethical imperative, is to be detached from nature, from the way things are, by that awareness of how things ought to be; it is to be made different from mere things, to be made responsible, and in that sense it is to be chosen. If the Bible reveals that there is a chosen people, what constitutes their being chosen is simply that to them the supreme commandment that is their responsibility is revealed: their responsibility for their neighbor, their responsibility to work and wait for the messianic kingdom, which will always be different from the present world and can never be contained in it. And finally the Bible commands that life be led as a ritual, formed and marked by ritual observance, because thereby that difference is maintained between the ethical and the natural, between what ought to be and what is, which keeps alive the hope for the messianic kingdom and is in a sense the tangible, visible, physical waiting for it. "*Next* year in Jerusalem" is the conclusion to the Passover ritual.

"It is as an ethical kerygma," Lévinas says, "that the Bible is Revelation" (R 75; *LR* 207). No amount of ratiocination about the way things are can generate the imperative that tells us what we ought to do, tells us that we are responsible. There is, however, nothing irrational about the Revelation once it is there: its contents and implications can be rationally, and endlessly, discussed, and a rational account of the disruption and discontinuity in experience that we call Revelation is also perfectly possible, once the Revelation has happened. The rationality involved, Lévinas says, is that of what Kant calls practical reason, though he does not wholly accept what he takes to be Kant's deduction of the categorical imperative. It seems to me that the Catholic Christian can have no fundamental quarrel with this way of asserting that there is no antithesis between reason and revelation; indeed, it could have a powerful unifying and systematizing role in a Catholic hermeneutics of Revelation. Equally, because in Lévinas's account of the Bible a rational ethical theology is combined with the highest possible respect for the text, it seems directly relevant to the task of constructing the conceptual foundation for a Catholic way of reading secular literature. It need hardly be said, however, that any attempt to use Lévinas for either of these tasks will very quickly arrive at decisive points of difference between Catholic and Jewish traditions. But to define difference is also to clarify what is common, and if I now attempt to say what a Lévinas-inspired Catholic approach to reading sacred Scripture might be, I shall do so in a spirit not of controversy but of gratitude for what a Jewish thinker, by talking about his religion, has told us about ours.

In my discussion of Hegel I drew out a total of eight points which gave us a first, provisional definition of a Catholic way of reading Scripture—a hermeneutic that escaped the dilemmas created by the collision of the Reformation faith in *sola scriptura* with Deist and historicist critique. I shall now take these points more or less in turn in order to set up a dialogue with the interpretative method of Lévinas from which I hope that a fully Catholic way of reading will at last emerge.

The first of the Hegelian principles was that God can be known by reason in conjunction with faith. The reason which Hegel believes capable of achieving this knowledge is a reason realized in history, the reason Lévinas invokes in his metaphysical writings is practical, that is, moral, reason, but both philosophers offer us different ways of eliminating the antithesis of reason and revelation. Ricoeur in his analysis of the revelatory nature of reading has offered us a third. Let us attempt to bring these approaches together, if not precisely to synthesize them. As a first step, I have to concede that of the three thinkers Lévinas seems to have most difficulty with a problem all too familiar to us from our discussion of the eighteenth-century crisis: if the Bible—that is, the Old Testament—is Revelation because it is an ethical kerygma, how does it differ from other proclamations of the fundamental commandment to be responsible for one's neighbor—in the New Testament or the Koran, for example, or in Kant, or indeed in Lévinas's own nonexegetical writings? Why is it more revelatory than they are? If the proclamation can be expressed—as by Lévinas and to a great extent by Kant it is expressed—in the terms of rational metaphysics, is the Bible necessary at all? Lévinas, I think, offers two answers to this question neither of which seems to me wholly satisfactory and both of which tend to lead us back to the bibliolatry which remains in fruitless and static antithesis to Deist and historicist critique instead of rising above it. At the same time, however, they also contain an element which is precisely capable of taking us beyond deism and historicism and so beyond bibliolatry too.

The first answer to the question, is the Bible necessary? is one that Lévinas, to some extent, shares with Ricoeur. The Bible—the Old Testament— is simply there. In a process of confluence over centuries, if not millennia, these texts have, by writing, rewriting, reading, and interpretation, been brought together into a unity-in-variety whose cohesion and persistence are as miraculous as that of the Jewish people itself, and certainly are as great a miracle as any asserted by claims about the Bible's divine origin. The trouble, though, with the argument that the Bible is simply there is not just that it looks too like the Reformation assertion that the Bible is a supernatural artifact. It is that other books are simply there too. Indeed, for Ricoeur all books are simply there, and that is why all books offer revelation. Moreover, the Old Testament is not unique in being the product of a process of confluence. Most obviously, there is the New Testament as well, and there are sacred books, and corpora of sacred books, outside the Judeo-Christian tradition, and secular works too, from Homer to the Arthurian cycles, which have come into existence in this way. Ricoeur seems on stronger ground than Lévinas when he argues that although the Bible is like any book in offering us a revelation independent of any intention of its author (if indeed it had one), it is a unique book because it contains a multiplicity of generically varied texts, all oriented towards the single vanishing point, the Name of the Unnameable. The Bible in Ricoeur's view calls for our attention, not because it is a revelation, indeed many coordinated revelations, but because those revelations are about God. Ricoeur, I think, has rightly seen that any claim for the Bible's uniqueness, for its being a miracle, must include a reference, however abstract and formal, to its content. Equally, Lévinas has rightly seen that Ricoeur understates the importance of the Bible's ethical, or prescriptive, content, its imperative mode. Lévinas's claim that the Bible is, historically speaking, a miracle can be made more plausible, and Ricoeur's claim that the Bible is, formally speaking, unique can be made more compelling, if we combine both authors' approaches and redefine the argument that the Bible is simply there as follows: the Bible is a revelation with miraculously unique authority because it is an ethical kerygma proclaimed in the name of the Unnameable, which both comes into existence by a process of confluence and understands itself as coming into existence in this way. This redefined argument, however, we should note, applies as much to the New Testament as to the Old.

The second answer offered by Lévinas to the question, is the Bible necessary? indirectly addresses—perhaps I mean indirectly excludes—the question of the relation between the Old Testament and the New. The answer is, the Bible—that is, the Old Testament—is necessary to the Jews. "The people of Israel are the people of the Book, whose relationship to the Revelation is unique" (R 56; LR 192). The meaning of this sentence is far from clear. Conceivably, what it means is that the Bible is an ethical kerygma which calls and constitutes a people—"Listen Israel"—who read, study, and interpret this book, and for that people the Bible is a unique revelation, practical reason speaking these specific words. The problem with this view— if it is indeed that of Lévinas—is that it does not tell us who the people of Israel are, the people who have the unique relationship with the biblical revelation. Who are the Jews? Oddly enough, Lévinas returns no very clear answer to this question. He explicitly rejects the view that Jewish self-identification with the land of Israel might owe anything "to any organic attachment to a particular piece of soil" (R 56; LR 192), that is, that it might be a matter of physical descent from inhabitants of a particular region; Jewish nostalgia for the land of Israel is, he says, a nostalgia entirely nourished by texts, it is a matter of holding to a particular interpretation of the Book. "The Holy Land is a land which spits out unworthy occupants"— those, that is, who do not make it a kingdom of justice in which the primacy of the ethical is respected.[3] As for the notion that Jews are the chosen people, we have already seen that for Lévinas being chosen means having heard the ethical kerygma, the commandment to responsibility to one's neighbor. It would seem, therefore, that for Lévinas the chosen people are "those who hear the Word of God and keep it" (Lk 11:28). Lévinas seeks to exclude all extrabiblical considerations from the definition of the "people of the Book." He criticizes Ricoeur for using Emil Fackenheim's idea of "history-making events" because events such as the Exodus or Exile or the building or rebuilding of the Temple only become history making through being interpreted as such in the Bible. Belonging to the people of the Book is not a matter of having such events as part of your personal or national past, of being descended from people to whom these events happened; it is a matter of reading about them and interpreting them as part of the book of the Law of God. But since the people of the Book are therefore so exclusively defined as those who read and respond to the Bible, it is difficult to see why the term should not include Christians. After all, Lévinas's description of the various forms of the relationship to Revelation of the people of the Book—"reading the Bible, forgetting it, or harbouring memories or feelings of remorse even after it is forgotten" (*LR* 191)—applies equally to those usually called Christians and those usually called Jews, once we allow that they may have different ways of reading.

It might seem absurd to attribute such a position to Lévinas, and indeed he does not hold it. But it is a position which a Christian could properly hold as a conclusion from Lévinas's premises, and the belief that Christians, as the people, or part of the people, of the Book have a unique relationship to the biblical Revelation seems to me not very far from the position of St. Thomas: if by faith we have heard in the Bible the voice and commandments of God, there will be for us no conflict in sacred theology between revelation and reason but only an extension by revelation of the field over which reason can operate.

Lévinas's reasons for not holding that Christians are people of the Book—or what he calls Jews—his reasons for not drawing from his premises the conclusion I have just drawn, are implicit, rather than explicit, in his definition of the Book. What he has to say on this matter is of particular relevance to the second hermeneutic principle I extracted from Hegel's philosophy of religion. It is this element in what Lévinas says that can, I believe, definitively take us beyond bibliolatry even while we maintain the utmost respect for the biblical text. It can also, I believe, remedy a major deficiency in Ricoeur's hermeneutics—their detachment from an ecclesiology. My second Hegelian principle ran, the faith of the individual is inseparable from the faith of the Church, the *Gemeinde;* the Bible is the book of faith, written in the spirit of the church and to be read in that spirit; there is therefore no true antithesis between Scripture and tradition. Lévinas too thinks the Bible a book of faith written in the spirit of a community, a

Gemeinde—produced over centuries by the confluence of individuals and schools living within that spirit—and he too thinks there is no antithesis between Scripture and tradition. On the contrary, the Bible is not merely written by tradition, it is read by tradition too. A book, and this book above all, exists in the tradition of reading it, in the process of interpreting it. "I was recently able to read," Lévinas says, "in a very remarkable book written by a rabbinical doctor at the end of the eighteenth century, that the slightest question put to the schoolmaster by a novice constitutes an ineluctable articulation of the Revelation which was heard at Sinai" (R 61; *LR* 195). Reading the text with the intention to interpret it, hearing the word with understanding, that—and Ricoeur would surely agree—is the process of Revelation. But Lévinas, unlike Ricoeur, understands that we cannot ultimately distinguish between the written and the spoken word. The written text lives in an atmosphere of its oral interpretation: without that atmosphere it cannot breathe, cannot live and be active and so perform its work of revelation. The letter cannot be separated from the spirit. For the Jew there is an oral law parallel to the written law, interpreting, applying, and completing it, an oral Torah which has an authority in Lévinas's phrase "at least equal" to that of the written Torah. This oral law has itself been written down as the Mishnah and the expansive commentary on the Mishnah that is the Talmud, and the Talmud, "for the Jews . . . constitutes a Revelation which completes that of the Old Testament" (R 62; *LR* 197).

The reason, I presume, therefore, why for Lévinas Christians are not Jews, not part of the people of the Book—those who read, study, and interpret the Old Testament, who hear its ethical proclamation and seek to live by its laws—is that they are not part of the process of interpretation given written form in the Talmud, a process which has "at least equal authority" with the Law of Moses which is being interpreted. For Christians, however, the Old Testament also lives in and by an atmosphere, a Spirit, of interpretation, and that spirit is the spirit of what Hegel calls the *Gemeinde,* the church. Christians too are constituted as a people—as the "people of God" we say nowadays—not by physical descent but by their response to and application of the Old Testament call to love God and neighbor. And for Christians too the oral interpretation of the original written text has itself been written down as a text, or law, with "at least equal authority" with the Law of Moses, which it completes, namely the New Testament. The question of the relation between Judaism and Christianity, of the origins of the cruel division between those now called Jews and those now called Christians, is a question about the relation of the Talmud to the New Testament.

That is to say, it is a question about two schools of interpretation of the Old Testament that arose in the centuries immediately before and after the beginning of the Christian era—from the first emergence of clearly proto-Christian thought in the late deuterocanonical and so-called intertestamental works, roughly at the time when the oral law began to be committed to writing, to about A.D. 200, when the compilation of the Mishnah was completed, shortly after the final formation of the New Testament canon and the definitive establishment by Christians and Jews, probably in response and reaction to each other, of their respective canons of the Old Testament.

As Christians we are probably not used to thinking of the New Testament as essentially an interpretation of, or gloss on, the Old. We think of it, rather more expressly than Lévinas does of the Talmud, as of higher authority than the original on which it comments. That, formally speaking, it is dependent on an original is, however, manifest in the name we give it: it is a new, that is, a second covenant, and what a covenant is we must find out from the first. We think of it (Hans Frei certainly thinks of it) as a narrative of events, but in fact it is mostly discursive material in constant dialogue with the law, prophecy, narrative, poetry, and wisdom literature of the Old Testament: the Gospels and Acts together make up only 60 percent of the whole, half of them are discourses, and many of the events recorded in what remains are actions performed or recounted as allusions to or commentaries on stories told in the Old Testament. We think of it as Revelation, but if it is, as Hegel says, a book written out of the faith of the community it is necessarily in its entirety an act of interpretation and response, and what it is responding to and interpreting are events, traditions, and writings. That does not make it any less Revelation: on the contrary, it is precisely Revelation in the sense that Lévinas means, and that I think Ricoeur understands too, when Lévinas says that the process of exegesis, of interpretation, of the novice asking questions of the schoolmaster, is the process of Revelation on Mount Sinai.

Everywhere in the Old Testament the process of confluent exegesis is at work: the conscious interpretation or recollection or application of one part of the tradition in another, which itself constitutes a new, even essential moment in the Revelation. As early as Leviticus 10:3 we find Moses interpreting an event, the death of Nadab and Abihu, in the light of a preceding word of God, even though it is a word not otherwise recorded in Scripture; the exhortations of the prophets to the people to repent and observe the Law, like the Psalmists' meditations on it, give rise to expressions of the Lord's anger, justice, love, or intention of redemption, which are themselves

authoritative revelations; in the Book of Nehemiah Ezra reads out the Book
of the Law, and in different traditions either he or the Levites renarrate the
Exodus, and the rituals of the Day of Atonement and the Feast of Tabernacles are renewed; Jesus ben Sirach characterizes the prophets individually
and cites some of their best-known phrases as part of a codification of a distinctive religious tradition. In the Christians' written down oral law, in the
New Testament, we read both how our Master three times rejects the temptations of Satan with an appeal to what is written in the Law and how he
repeatedly explicates the provisions of the Law with the words "Ye have
heard that it was said by them of old time. . . . But I say unto you. . . ."
Not merely then does the Bible come into existence through a process of
confluence—a gathering together of different texts and traditions—but that
process is self-conscious. It is a part of the revelation which the texts and
traditions contain that they belong in a process of collecting, remembering,
renewing, and interpreting a revelation derived from many sources, including even sources not part of the texts collected themselves. This self-
consciousness—the fact that the fact that it is a tradition is a part of the
tradition—is intrinsic to the Bible, the Book of the Law, whether narrowly
understood as the Jewish Old Testament or more broadly understood as the
written Law, together with the deuterocanonical writings, and the oral Law
of the New Testament or of the Mishnah and the Talmud. The principle of
self-conscious confluence is the element in the Jewish-Christian Revelation
which preserves it from bibliolatry, from the separation of the Book from
the spirit of the community which has written it, now reads it, and thereby
rewrites it for the future. It is also incidentally the principle which makes
the Jewish-Christian books unacceptable to Islam, which therefore has a book
of its own, regarded in much the same way as Calvin regarded his Bible, as
directly dictated by God.

My third Hegelian principle was a deduction from the first two: in interpretation of the Scriptures by the church the dogmatic interest is always
decisive. What a text means is to be determined in the end not by historical
investigation of what its author or—more probably—its successive authors
and rewriters may have meant by it but by its role in the entire body of
written Revelation, taken as a unity. That unity is itself defined by the
church, the *Gemeinde,* which has determined which texts have ultimate
authority—that is, belong to the canon—and which do not. Theology and
hermeneutics cannot in the end be separated, and the rule of faith and the
rule of reading are in the end identical. The church determines not only
what the totality of Scripture is—what is the whole Bible—but also what

the whole Bible is about. The dogmatic interest is decisive because dogmatic issues are those that relate to the question how Scripture, taken as a whole, is to be read. Our answer to the question whether God is a Trinity-in-Unity will determine our entire understanding of the entire Bible, Old Testament and New. Knowing that God is Three-in-One will not tell us whether 1 John 5:7–8 is an interpolated gloss, but knowing that will tell us that even if the passage is—as it plainly is—an interpolation, the Trinitarian doctrine it teaches is sound, is to be found everywhere in the Bible, and is not shaken by the fact that this formulation of it is relatively late; just as, conversely, the doctrine itself rests on much firmer and broader foundations than this one passage even if this one passage were to prove authentic. The eighteenth-century scholars who thought they had shaken the foundations of Christian belief by showing that this reference in 1 John to Father, Son, and Spirit is a later insertion overlooked, since their secular literary criticism was insufficiently developed to notice it, that the gospel of St. Mark begins, in 1:10–11, with an emphatically Trinitarian statement, a tableau of Father, Son, and Spirit, in the scene of Jesus' baptism. Similarly, the question whether the Christ comes as the fulfillment of prophecy cannot be determined by trying to work out whether Isaiah really meant to prophesy that a virgin would conceive, or what he meant by saying whatever he said. The question is a dogmatic one—is the Nicene Creed right to say that Jesus the Christ lived, died, and rose again *secundum Scripturas?*—and if the answer is yes, then the Scriptures have to be read from beginning to end as one long "Maranatha—Come Lord Jesus"—and that means that in some way or other that cry is certainly contained in Isaiah 7:14. The task of hermeneutics is to discover how it is contained there, not whether it is. Historical exegesis of what Isaiah originally meant, of what his Greek translators thought he meant, and of what St. Matthew thought whatever text he used meant, is legitimate, even necessary. But it is necessary only as a means to establishing how the ultimate truths that Scripture as a whole contains are expressed in certain of its particular parts—what is the precise network of channels through which the different rivers of revelation flow, in Lévinas's terms, to their confluence. Unlike Lévinas, but like Herder, I see no reason why historical hermeneutics—interpretation of particular biblical texts and genres in the light of their development—should not be one of the methods used to find dogmatic meaning in every corner of the written Law. Such historical discussion is, like the question of the novice to the schoolmaster, as much a part of the process of Revelation as the self-conscious discussion which, as we have seen, is already to be found in the written down oral Law and indeed in the written Law itself. That does not of course commit us to any exclusive claims for the historical method; it remains simply one of several possibilities. In the words of Luke Timothy Johnson, "We can affirm the need to learn history in order to understand the text, without agreeing that we should deconstruct the text in order to reconstruct history."[4]

Historical hermeneutics are not, in their origin, the academic discipline formulated by Schleiermacher but a creative, even a poetic response by Herder to an eighteenth-century crisis of faith. Nevertheless, Lévinas is reluctant to allow them a role in the interpretation of the sacred text, even in the modified form represented by Ricoeur's taxonomy of biblical genres. This is partly because he lacks a theory of the means for controlling them, for maintaining institutionally the priority of the dogmatic interest, such as is provided for Hegel by his developed concept of the *Gemeinde,* the community of faith or church. For Lévinas the interpretative tradition embodied in the Talmud is self-regulating and requires no control or reinforcement by external credal formulations or digests of essential, non-negotiable teaching. (I suspect, incidentally, though it is very far from being my field, that this is a somewhat romanticized view of Judaism, and Lévinas of course acknowledges the existence of authoritative post-Talmudic summaries of the Law.) Lévinas is, as we have noticed, more generally reluctant to allow a role in hermeneutics to any concept of extrabiblical history—as the space, for example, in which history-making events occur—and prefers to maintain that any such historical structure is purely an internal feature of the biblical text. Now while this may be an acceptable way to treat the Exodus itself, or even, outside the Pentateuch, the biblical accounts of David and Solomon, it is clearly unacceptable in respect of the later analogue of the Exodus, the return from Exile, which is accompanied, even in the Hebrew Old Testament, by meditation on the role of Cyrus, the Gentile Messiah, unaware of what he is doing, and on the collision of biblical and nonbiblical history. Here I think we run up against the limits on the reading of Lévinas's Jewish hermeneutics as Hegelian (and so as Catholic, if only provisionally such). For while Lévinas can certainly be said to understand the sacred books as written and read in and by the spirit of a faith community, a *Gemeinde,* he cannot—the whole of Jewish history after the destruction of the Temple requires that he cannot—describe that *Gemeinde* as a church in a dialectical relation with the state, as the Christian church is described by Hegel. And therefore he cannot define that *Gemeinde*—the Jewish people—as in any significant relation to a secular history external to them, or their sacred books even as talking about such a secular history, let alone being formed by their interaction with it.[5] Yet already in Second Isaiah, and obviously in Ezra-Nehemiah, there is a historical perspective on the mission of Israel, as manifested in contemporary events, which makes it difficult to take these books, as Lévinas requires they should be taken, as timeless contemporaries of the events of the Exodus to which they allude. Such an approach is manifestly unnatural in the case of works outside the Hebrew canon such as Maccabees or Ecclesiasticus, which may be one reason why Lévinas prefers not to deal with them.

There is a further reason why Lévinas prefers to exclude historical understanding from biblical hermeneutics altogether rather than define it as always ultimately subordinate to the dogmatic interest. The dogmatic, non-historical interest which for Lévinas is exclusively dominant, universally present, is, he would say, something beyond dogma altogether: the ethical kerygma, the announcement of the imperative to responsibility. That in the end is the one thing the Bible is always announcing: the unfulfillable obligation to our neighbor (and not least because it is unfulfillable it is always to be reiterated). That ethical kerygma is, according to him, what gives the Bible its transcendent status, for the Bible is the place where our human status as different from the rest of nature, as different from all things that merely "are," is announced. *We* are transcendent because we hear the voice that submits us to an obligation: we not merely *are* something; we *ought to* be and do something, namely, approach our neighbor with full hands. The other who is our neighbor is made present to us, Lévinas says in an essay on the work of Michel Leiris (*LR* 144–49), by the transcendent word that formulates our relationship of responsibility for him or her. And that transcendence is essential if the other is not to sink back into being a mere object that we contemplate as if it were some aesthetic artifact. The other person can only be really present to us, in a social relation, if we are quickened by the word of command which is no part of the world of objects and artifacts, just as sound and spoken words are no part of the world manifest to mere vision. "It is to the extent," Lévinas says, "that the word refuses to become flesh that it assures a presence among us" (*LR* 148). This sentence, uttered in the context of a rather marginal piece of secular literary criticism, is obviously of central importance for Lévinas's biblical hermeneutics. The Word of God is present among us as a transcendent reality, and makes present to us the other as the locus of a transcendent obligation—the Bible, in other words, is ethical kerygma and Revelation—only if the word does not become flesh. Only on that condition does the Bible reveal its meaning. Only if the word spoken in the Bible remains transcendent, equally insis-

tent, equally ineluctable, equally unchanging in pronouncing the unfulfillable obligation whatever the circumstances in which its audience and its
instruments—those who hear it and those who write it down—may find
themselves, only then will it do the work it was appointed to do. The Bible's
essential meaning—the kerygma in virtue of which it *is* Revelation and the
utterance of the Word of God—must remain disembodied, invisible, and
outside history.[6] It must never become an object involved in all the natural
and social and historical relations in which objects of human interest are
always involved; it must remain the voice which comes from no mouth but
from an impossible object, the bush that burns but is not consumed. (Indeed, of the arts it is only music, the opening of Schoenberg's *Moses und
Aron,* that can give us an idea of the sublime authority Lévinas attributes to
the disembodied voice that speaks the ethical imperative.) Of this Word there
can be no history, and historical hermeneutics cannot explain it. They can
neither interpret it nor account for it.

It is plain, therefore, that Lévinas would flatly contradict the fourth
principle of my Hegelian-Catholic hermeneutics: the Incarnation is central
to the content of Revelation because Incarnation and Revelation are formally the same process: the making manifest, and making man, of the Word
of God. The gulf separating Lévinas's position from the Catholic position
must seem broader and deeper still if we recall the words of the new Catechism: Christianity is not a religion of the Book. Lévinas, by contrast, seems
to be treading a path to a new bibliolatry, reducing the Bible to pure text,
necessarily detached from any context. Yet it may be that the completeness
of the opposition opens up a certain area of agreement. Christianity is not a
religion of the Book because it is the religion of Christ, the Word of God
made flesh, Who is the meaning of the Book. As exegesis of the Old Testament, the New Testament is diminutive by comparison with the Talmud
because its task is not to attempt to capture in further words the infinite
meanings of the written Law but to direct all interpretations of the Law to
a single focus from which may spring, by the working of the Spirit, the infinite applications of the Law in individual human lives. That one focus—
the center towards which both Testaments face, as Pascal has it[7]—is not a
word but a person, *the* Word, born a man, born a subject of the Law. If any
words have a meaning, the New Testament tells us, they are the words of
the Old Testament whose meaning is Christ; if any signifiers have a signified, here it is—not more words, more textuality, but a man. If an act of
faith is necessary, as Steiner thought, to ground our belief that words refer
to something that is not mere words, here is the original and primary object

of that faith. Jesus is what the Law means: that is what the New Testament tells us everywhere, most concisely in the words of St. John: "the Word became flesh . . . and we saw. . . ." That which for Lévinas can only be heard became something, someone, to be seen. But Lévinas says the word can quicken what we see into life, into presence to us as a person and not merely as an object of our gaze, only if it remains transcendent. The Old Testament is Revelation only insofar as it is the announcement of an obligation whose fulfillment is unimaginable and whose origin is unnameable. But the good news—"good if false news," says Lévinas (*LR* 259)—is that the requirement of the Law has been met, the unfulfillable obligation has been fulfilled, and the invisible and transcendent Law, and so its unnameable source, has been made visible in the death of a man born subject to it. ("He that hath seen me hath seen the Father," says Jesus in John 14:9, and in the same gospel the glory that we see, as of the only-begotten of the Father, is that of the Word's flesh lifted high on the instrument of execution.) The New Testament therefore changes the sense in which we can say that the Old Testament is Revelation. No longer is the Old Testament Revelation, simply because in its pure textuality, its being purely words, and purely words of command, it utters the transcendent "ought" to and against a world of visible things and artifacts that merely "are." The Old Testament now appears as a Revelation that has already begun to bridge the gulf between the "ought" and the "is," a command that has already begun to bring about its own fulfillment, a word and a prophecy that have already begun to determine the features of what or who they will turn out to have been pointing to. The Old Testament now appears, not just to mean something, but to be beginning to form someone. It now appears to be beginning to provide the ethical, religious, emotional, narrative, and intellectual context for the man born subject to its Laws who will also be, in what he does and says, in his life and death, the embodiment of what it has for centuries been trying to put into words, the love of God. The obligation of the Law does not cease to apply once the Word has become flesh: the Old Covenant is not abolished in the New, and the voice imposing absolute responsibility to the neighbor continues to be heard, insistently and unchangingly, by the subjects of the new Law as of the old. But the good news is that in a world in which the proclamation has become visible—the Word has become flesh—the one commandment has a new form: "That ye love one another, *as I have loved you*" (Jn 15:12). "As I have loved you": the commandment now relates to a specific, personal and historical, event. And it says that thanks to that event the nature of the obligation has changed. It has changed in two ways. First, under the Old Covenant, God promised his love to Israel on the condition that Israel listened to the ethical kerygma and undertook to observe the unfulfillable obligation. Under the New Dispensation the obligation has not ceased, and it has not ceased to be unfulfillable, but God has revealed that his love for us is unaffected by our failure to keep his commandment; he will maintain his half of the covenant though we have—as was inevitable—failed to keep ours. In the words of St. John again: "Herein is love, not that we loved God, but that he loved us, and sent his Son to be the propitiation for our sins" (1 Jn 4:10). It is God himself—God the Son, we say—who is the propitiation, he through whom the Law that makes us sinners was first announced. When we continue to hear the commandment to approach our neighbor with full hands not empty, we hear it therefore under the New Covenant not only as a commandment that makes us sinners but also as a commandment whose promulgator has redeemed us and secured our forgiveness. We hear it not just as those called—chosen, Lévinas says—for obedience, but as those fallen away and yet restored. We hear the commandment to love our neighbor—Lévinas does sometimes use this phrase to express our responsibility—but we hear it as those called, lost, and bought back. We hear the call of the "ought" not as simple, and with the innocence of the Old Covenant, but as complex, modulated now by the sorrow of loss and the joy of restoration, and as the voice of experience, the experience of a particular moment when a death changed the ethical history of the world and the New Covenant was inaugurated.

I cannot here explore further the ways in which the commandment to "love one another as I have loved you" might be held to modify the import of Lévinas's ethical arguments when he conducts them in a nonbiblical context. Instead let me now point to a second way in which that new commandment modifies the unfulfillable obligation. The Old Covenant, I said, was made with Israel, but the New Covenant was made with "us." By "us," I am referring to those addressed as "you" in the new commandment, who are called on to love one another. For Hegel this was one of the essential features of Christianity, the absolute, revealed religion. The commandment of love imposed on Christians is not a commandment to universal benevolence or beneficence but specifically a commandment to love the brethren. It is the love Christians have for one another that is distinctive because it is, according to Hegel, the expression of the awareness that "God is love" (W xvii, 288). My Lévinas-inspired reading of the New Testament may help to clarify why Hegel gives such priority to the love of the *Gemeinde* one for another. I am called, Lévinas believes, not simply to responsibility for my neighbor, but to responsibility for my neighbor's responsibility. If we accept a New Testament modification of Lévinas's Old Testament analysis, I, as called, lost, and bought, must therefore be responsible for my neighbor as called to responsibility too, and as lost and bought as well. But only if my neighbor is one of the brethren, only if he or she knows himself or herself as called, lost, and bought, will that responsibility for my neighbor's responsibility be entirely free of any hint of domination, imposition, or usurpation of the other's status as other. A Christian, as one for whom Christ died, will of course love any other man or woman in his or her otherness as one for whom Christ also died. But that love cannot be reciprocal, as the new commandment requires, unless both relate themselves, in absolute equality, to the third party whom both know to have died for both. Only fellow subjects of the kingdom, only Christ's adopted coheirs, can love one another as he has commanded them. And therefore it is one of the first duties of Christians, as it was one of Christ's last commissions to his disciples, to seek out what was lost, to proclaim the good news to all nations, to extend the kingdom of the Lord to the ends of the earth and so to bring all within the scope of the commandment to "love one another as I have loved you." The commandment to love one another is indeed addressed only to members of the community, the church, but, proleptically and in principle, the church includes the whole of humanity; the Old Covenant was made with Israel, but the New Covenant is made with all, and all are bought back by God from outside the Law into his love. Some of the difficulties in Lévinas's hermeneutical position take on a new aspect when seen in relation to this New Covenant, and in the light that falls from the sacred Scriptures on the world-historical role, past and present, of both branches of Judaism.

CHAPTER 7

Lévinas (2): Two Branches of Judaism

PLAINLY, IF THE GOOD NEWS OF THE NEW TESTAMENT IS SIMPLY THE continuation and extension of the ethical kerygma of the Old its truth can no more be demonstrated than the truth of the original proclamation. These things do not come with observation. But there are certain points at which the difficulties in Lévinas's account of the Old Testament Revelation are eased if his ethics are given the New Testament gloss I have been suggesting. First, you may remember, he had some difficulty explaining why the Bible was necessary—what the relation was between the ethical imperative and this particular proclamation of it. In Hegel's account of the Incarnation this familiar eighteenth-century historicist difficulty evaporates in respect of Christ: Christianity is the absolute, revealed religion; that is, it is the religion which reveals the absolute, the divine, significance of historical human particularity. God is revealed as a particular historical human being who has died. (And from the recognition of this dead human being as God derives the overwhelming certainty of his resurrection.) Once we recognize Christ as the particular human being of whom the whole of the Old Testament seeks to speak, whom it signifies, then we can extend Hegel's point and see the whole of the Old Testament as sharing in the process of Incarnation, as preparing the entrance of the divine into the human. Thanks to Christ the Bible is Revelation, and part of what it reveals is the necessity of Revelation's taking on this particular form. As part of the humanity of Christ, the Bible shares in the revealing of his divinity and like any other aspect of his humanity is instrumental to it. Because the Word has become flesh—and *only* because it has become flesh—we can recognize that all along it was the Word of God and can recognize in the particular imperatives of the Old Testament the original and ultimate imperative that, in Lévinas's anthropology, founds and grounds our human existence.

Second, the Bible seeks to speak of Christ, that is, it shares in his human particularity, in more than one way. Ricoeur's appreciation of its variety seems intuitively more plausible than Lévinas's severely unifying approach. The Old Testament, read as the New Testament requires it to be read, does not, for example, simply provide the ethical, cultural, and cultic prescriptions which form Christ, and which he transforms by embodying their inner essence as proclamation of the one imperative. The Old Testament also prophesies him, that is, relates him to the social and political world as the inaugurator of the messianic kingdom which fulfills and terminates all collective human endeavor. It provides, above all in the Psalms and the Song of Songs, a lyrical vocabulary, a repertoire of poetic forms, in which human life irradiated by God—preeminently Christ's life but, thanks to him, the life of any one of us—can be articulated as love and trust, supplication and despair, desire and affirmation and celebration. The Old Testament also provides in its wisdom literature a more prosaic repertoire of questions and reflections about the course and purpose of human life, and God's intentions for Israel, which all find their answer and terminus in Christ. It provides too a developing historical narrative with an internal logic which culminates in him. That narrative also, however, gives a framework to the whole of the Old Testament: it relates the history of Israel to that of neighboring peoples and, possibly most important of all, it introduces in the Old Testament that awareness of historicity which makes the understanding of Israel's religious development towards Christ into a part of Israel's religion. This awareness of the developmental quality, of the Christ-oriented dynamic, of the Old Testament has itself taken on different forms over time: the manifestations of a historical self-consciousness in the Old Testament which I have already mentioned; the New Testament concern with the fulfillment in Christ of the Isaian prophecies; the patristic and medieval interpretations, for example, of God's words to the serpent as a prophecy of the redemption, or of the priesthood of Melchizedek as a foreshadowing of that of Christ; the understanding made available to us by scholarship since the eighteenth century of the historical development of the religion of the Old Testament and its continuation into the New—all of these seemingly different interpretative devices, of differing degrees of antiquity, have in common that they enable us to read the Old Testament as consciously confluent on Christ. Not on the New Testament, for if we read the text of the Old Testament as confluent on another text—as I think Ricoeur is tempted to do—then the textual complex that results would still be open to Lévinas's objection that it should be read as if only one form of discourse prevailed in it, whatever its apparent superficial variety, namely, the discourse of timeless ethical prescription. Only if the Old Testament is read as converging not on a text but on a man, not on yet more signifiers but on a signified, are we free to accept its generic variety and its historical development. But it also follows that no apologetic argument for the truth of this way of reading the Old Testament—no argument that the good news is not false—can be derived from these different forms of confluence, for the texts converge on this man and not on themselves, only on the assumption that the Word has indeed become flesh, on the assumption, that is, of the good news itself.

A third question which Lévinas, rather surprisingly, seemed to avoid answering was, who are the Jews? To that question the Old Testament, when read in accordance with the New Testament principle of Incarnation, that the Word has become flesh in a particular man, has no difficulty returning an unambiguous answer, if one that is quickly hedged around with qualifications that portend the later dark history of anti-Semitism. The New Testament principle is, of course, that the Jews are those of whom salvation is (Jn 4:22), and none of the qualifications controverts or could possibly controvert it. This principle in turn selects, or highlights, one particular Old Testament understanding of Jewishness as decisive: the Jews are the people who, according to the interpretation of Genesis 12:3 by the Septuagint and Ecclesiasticus, will bring on all the peoples of the world a blessing which will fulfill the promise made to Abraham (Sir 44:21); they are a servant of the Lord who, according to the final version of Isaiah 49, will be "a light to the Gentiles" and the Lord's "salvation unto the end of the earth." They are called to hear the kerygma, the annunciation of the Word, to conceive it through the ear, to give it human flesh, and to bring it to birth for the world. That at any rate is the definition of Jewishness offered by the Judaism that developed from the fourth century B.C. onwards under the pressure of the need to relate itself to larger and alien civilizations and that eventually bore the name of Christianity; it may well be that talmudic Judaism has other definitions to offer, though Lévinas seems not to wish to give them prominence and to prefer the definition "the people of the Book."

With this Christian, incarnational, definition of what we may call the world-historical role of the Jewish people we have reached the domain of the fifth Hegelian principle I outlined: the history of the church is the point of intersection in the Scriptures between the philosophy of history and the philosophy of religion. This is plainly a vast theme, and in the context of my dialogue with Lévinas I will say only two things about it. The first is that, as with the principle of Incarnation, it has, given the biases of Hegel's presentation, to be extended backwards to incorporate the Old Testament as well as the New Testament history of the church. The church, the community of Jesus' friends called to witness throughout the world to the good news of the kingdom, must be understood as the rebirth in a new era, the Roman era, of the chosen community of Israel. The event-sign, as Ricoeur would say, of Jesus' life, death, and resurrection, which stands in a direct if mysterious relation to the event-sign that is the destruction of the Temple, has joined the event-signs of the Exodus, the Davidic kingdom, the Exile, and the Return to define a life story for the Word of God in the world, the story of how the process of call, loss, and redemption has actually and particularly happened in the collective life of nations. The dialectical relation between sacred and secular, church and state, that for Hegel constitutes the conceptual backbone of human history since the rise of Christianity—through the Roman and medieval periods, the Reformation, the Enlightenment, and the Revolution—needs to be seen as the reiteration, the translation into the terms of the New Covenant, of a process that is already recorded in the Old Testament, even if there too it is only retrospectively apparent how ancient it is. From no later than the period of the Exile it was clear to some at least in Israel that the religion of the Exodus was a religion of redemption and that the redeemed people had thereby a special role in relation to other nations—whether in the theocratic exclusivism of Ezra, with its striving to make Israel unique in its purity, or in its dialectical opposite, the growth of proselytism and of the practice of translating the Hebrew Scriptures, with its implied invitation to all nations to come to worship in Zion.

My second point, however, has to be that at one point Lévinas is not unwilling to see an interrelation between the philosophy of history—that is, the philosophy of the interaction of states—and the philosophy of religion—that is, the philosophy of the manifestation of the Word of God in the human world. In general, it is true that for Lévinas the events recounted in the Bible exist, that is, contribute to life now, exclusively through the reading and the interpretation of biblical texts. Lévinas's God, in short, does not act. (One could draw a similar conclusion from his remarks on prayer.)

There is, however, one radical and terrible, though only apparent, exception. "For many Jews," he writes, "the only meaning of sacred history and the Revelation it brings us is to be found in their memories of the stake, the gas chambers. . . . Their experience of the Revelation is transmitted through persecution!" (R 56; *LR* 191–92). To two thousand years of Revelation not through God's actions but through the suffering of the people who keep His Law Lévinas gives, surely rightly, the name of the Passion of Israel, and there can be no doubt, alas, that the beginnings of that Passion are inseparable from the great schism in Judaism in the first and second centuries A.D. That schism was provoked by a radical and irresolvable conflict: between Rome, demanding emperor worship and armed with inexhaustible military resources and the state power of capital punishment, specifically of crucifixion, and Israel, the people of the Temple and the Book, armed in the end only with faith in the one invisible God. But the schism was not perhaps inevitable. For a while Christian Jews, Christian Pharisees even, still worshiped alongside other tendencies in the same synagogues. By about A.D. 130, however, the people of the Book had chosen to divide themselves so bitterly that they were unable to recognize themselves in each other, or each other in themselves, despite their common origins in Book and Temple. The worst possible reaction to so old a quarrel, with such terrible results, is to ask who was to blame. Much better is to engage in the conversation that is Revelation, to try to understand both past events and our present situation by seeking to read the Book aright.

Two distinct possible reactions to the Roman challenge were defining themselves in the time of the schism. On the one hand, there was the path of confrontation and denial—outright denial of the claims of Rome and confrontation with the military and civil power of the state. The military confrontation was eventually shown to be unviable, but in the civil sphere the ideological confrontation became all the more acute. The people of the Book could redefine themselves more narrowly as the people of the Law, and could redefine the Book itself through the codification of an Oral Law. The Law, thus understood, detached from any civil authority, could take the place both of the state which God's people had lost to the foreign conquerors and of the state of the foreign conquerors themselves with which they refused any compromise. At the cost of a certain isolation from that body politic they could seek exemption from the obligation to worship the imperial god-man and so could remain faithful to the one invisible God, the unknown and incomprehensible object of all hope and trust. By this withdrawal from the state they had confronted but failed to defeat, they would effectively withdraw from world history—the history of states—to become a people defined only by physical descent and their obedience to a transcendent Law. Having thus ceased to be actors in history they would be confined to being its victims. It was a terrible distinction—how terrible, those who accepted it can hardly have known—but it conferred in exchange the gift of purity, of never as a people being responsible for the oppression and persecution of others. Having lost Jerusalem, they would witness to the one pure and Holy God in all the lands to which they were scattered and not primarily, if at all, in Judaea. Having lost the Temple, the place of physical sacrificial worship, as they lost the state of which it was the focus and expression, they would devote themselves to the study and interpretation of the disembodied Word while trustingly awaiting the reestablishment of state and Temple, even if only at the end of time. In this way Israel would maintain, in a new form appropriate to the Roman era, a major part of what had been revealed to it in the days of its statehood: universalism, messianism, and the assurance that the Word of God is addressed to particular human lives. All of these beliefs, however, were to be maintained in a mode of externality, of confrontation with a secular world and distinction from it.

On the other hand, there was the path of mediation—the avoidance of military confrontation and the acceptance of the need for the sacred universality of Israel to enter into a relationship of mutual transformation with the secular universality of Rome. The people of the Book, true to its self-description as developing Revelation or Revelation of development, as not just Law but the history of Law, could accept that a moment of decision and, in a certain sense, of fulfillment had come. It would follow that continuity, even continuity of the kind that others sought through confrontation and denial, could be achieved only by conscious discontinuity and change. Other books were taking shape in the same process that was also leading to the writing down of the Oral Law. Interpreted as fulfilled in the events surrounding the life and death of the prophet Jesus of Nazareth the Scriptures held good news for all subjects of the empire. They were liberated for a life in the Spirit as a reconstituted chosen people, a renewed Israel under a new covenant, soon to be called the church. Without seeking to exclude or detach them from the empire the good news engaged with their condition in such a way as to subvert completely the instruments of imperial domination. The emperor, the embodiment of the state, could not be worshipped, alive or dead, as a human manifestation of divinity, for Jesus the Christ was already the only human image of the unseen God, manifested in accordance with a divine plan which ran through the Scriptures as the principle of their structure. The state power over life and death, symbolized in the terrible image of crucifixion, had been appropriated and transformed by the God of Israel. The cross had been made into the vehicle of the good news that, though called and lost, the new Israel—that is, in principle, the whole world—had been bought again by God. For the definitive new revelation, which marked off the new order from the old, was that God's action was passion. God had suffered, suffered in his Son, who had been coming into the world since the first utterance of the Word. No suffering that history could impose through the Roman state or any other was beyond redemption by him, and indeed since the Resurrection of Jesus that redemption was now always and everywhere already begun. Humanity was now living in the messianic age. Even the loss of land and Temple was already being made good in the Spirit through the construction of this new Israel. As the church, as the living Temple, the new people of God could live the life of the Roman state, and live it more abundantly for being liberated from domination by it—engaging in the empire's civil and legal, and eventually in its institutional and political structures, in order to consecrate them but at the same time preparing to outlive and transcend them. Israel reborn would thus join the actors in history. It would have the role of living in and through secularity in any time and place or political dispensation, in order to mediate to it God's redemption, so that eventually all nations would, in accordance with the promise, be blessed in Abraham.

The fearful temptation for the mediator, however, is assimilation: taking on unchanged the unholy characteristics of that which the mediator set out to sanctify. That is the temptation Satan puts to Christ in the Gospels, and it is the temptation to which, in his tale of the Grand Inquisitor, Dostoyevsky represents the Roman church as succumbing. Time and again over the centuries the Israel that sought to mediate the ethical kerygma to the state has sanctioned the state's violence against the Israel that has maintained the kerygma by confrontation with the state and exclusion from it. At such moments those who preach the Passion and Resurrection of Christ have recrucified their Master in the Passion of Israel.

The original point of intersection of the philosophy of history and the philosophy of religion is then the challenge to interpret the destructive collision of the Roman Empire and the ancient Jewish state. That point of intersection leaves an ineradicable trace in all biblical hermeneutics, for out of the collision there emerged in the first century A.D. a new Israel reading the old Revelation with new eyes. By the second century, with the disappearance

of the military and political option, this new Israel had crystallized into
two forms increasingly and tragically alienated from each other: the church
reading the Scriptures through the New Testament; and the diaspora, the
home of Lévinas's faith, reading them through the Mishnah. There is, however, a further fundamental division in the new Israel only fleetingly alluded
to by Lévinas: between the new development of the house of study as the
central expression of observance of the Law and the sacrificial worship of the
old Temple. Lévinas notes that the turn to the Judaism of study and away
from worship in the Temple begins shortly before the Christian era (and
therefore before the Temple's destruction) but pays no particular attention to
the decline in Temple worship itself. But we clearly cannot understand the
significance of the rise of the Judaism of study unless we understand its
dialectical opposite and complement. For the Temple worship did not end
with the destructions of A.D 70 and 135, though it could have no place in
the Judaism of Mishnah and Talmud. The Temple worship continued transformed in the theology and practice of New Testament Judaism, and it continues down to the present day with altar and sacrifice, priest and victim,
incense and perpetual fire, in the liturgy of the people of God, the universal
church. I am not suggesting that there is uninterrupted continuity of liturgical practice from the Second Temple to the Basilica of the Sacred Heart at
Notre Dame du Lac—though there may be more real continuity than we
imagine and there has always been much secondary influence of Old Testament sources on the design of churches, church furnishings, prayers, music,
and so on—but rather that there is an even more important conceptual continuity. The Temple was the place where before the Exile the physical vehicle
of the Covenant had been venerated and where various sacrifices by physical
means maintained or reestablished communion between God and his people,
most notably on the annual Day of Atonement. It was therefore the place of
material and bodily interaction between God and humanity, the sign and
instrument of his presence in a particular place, Jerusalem, among a particular people. It was thus in itself a means for the Revelation and Incarnation of God.

The Temple has recently been called the forgotten element in New
Testament Christology.[1] It is as a perfecting of the Temple ritual, a fulfillment of what the Temple was and did and promised, in short as the Temple
of the new Israel, that the New Testament writers understand Jesus and his
work, even before the destruction of A.D 70. Jesus completes the physical
Revelation and Incarnation of God in Israel above all when he comes to be
sacrificed in Jerusalem. He perfects and supersedes the Temple and so in a

sense himself destroys it (the story is told by all the Evangelists, including St. John),[2] but he raises it up in the Spirit and carries it on in a new, spiritualized, but still bodily form into the new, Roman, and universal era. He is the Temple (Rv 21:22) not just of Jerusalem but of all the nations, and for the New Testament writers the church throughout the world is building up both his mystical body and a new Temple.[3] The vocabulary provided by the Temple is central to the beliefs about Jesus of New Testament Judaism and not just for the author of the letter to the Hebrews: when Paul or the author of 1 John describe Jesus as the "propitiation" for our sins they have in mind the ceremonies of the Day of Atonement, in which the essential role was played by the "propitiatory," the one part of the furnishings for the Ark of the Covenant which was retained in the Second Temple. When Paul says that the cup of blessing is a "communion" with the blood of Christ he is assimilating the Eucharist to one of the most frequent and popular Temple rituals, the communion sacrifice. I would suggest that one reason this theme has been forgotten is that it requires a Catholic—rather than a Reformed or Talmudic—approach to reading the Bible to notice it, for it is the element that points us beyond the Book to that which the Book signifies, the material and particular presence of God in the world, first in rituals and in a building and then in a man and subsequently in other rituals and other buildings and other people insofar as they are related to this man. The Temple is the key to my seventh and eighth principles of a Catholic hermeneutic. The Temple is with and in Jesus himself, the material link between the Old and New Testaments. But it is more than that. The Temple is also, and necessarily, a link between the Spirit of Jesus and the Spirit of the church, between New Testament Christology and the self-consciousness of Jesus. It is inconceivable that Jesus could have reflected on his mission without considering its relation to the central public institution of Israel's worship, and there is no reason to suppose that he could not have done so in the terms which seemed natural to his earliest disciples.[4] If we know anything about Jesus' teaching it is that he taught that the kingdom of God was at hand and that Israel should repent and believe the good news. In Jesus' own time that message was capable of meaning that God was present, or imminently present, in Jesus' proclamation of the true Spirit of the Law, by word and deed, by life and death, and that Israel was in danger of losing that sense of the immediate presence of God which was the true Spirit of the Law and which had in the past been safeguarded in the Temple worship. Such a meaning would be truthfully represented by the New Testament witnesses we have considered. If Jesus thought of himself and his mission as comparable to the Temple and its ritual in its effect of making God present to Israel, then there is no reason to assume a radical discontinuity between his understanding of his life and that of the early Christian *Gemeinde*—rather the opposite, in fact. When, therefore, we, as the inheritors of that early Christian, Pentecostal understanding of Jesus' life attend Mass in the Basilica of the Sacred Heart we are indeed the continuators of the old rites of the Temple in Jerusalem, not directly, in some act of liturgical archaeology, but insofar as those rites have been reconsecrated and reinterpreted by Jesus, not just in his words, for we are beyond bibliolatry now, but by his actions.

In a world in which the Temple has been destroyed the Mass realizes, for the Israel of the spirit, the Temple-inspired eschatology taught by Jesus. The signifiers of the Scriptures find their signified in the flesh and blood of a man, raised, glorified, and rendered present without deferral. (There is of course also a Christian *future* eschatology, but that is a secondary matter which I cannot deal with here.) But what of the other Israel, the Israel of the flesh, confirmed by the destruction of the Temple in its turn to the synagogue, the house of study, and the Book, read not through the New Testament but through the Mishnah and the Talmud? For them too, and in the lifetime of many of us, eschatology has been realized; they too have moved beyond bibliolatry, and the words of the Book have found their signified in the land promised to Abraham and Moses. Lévinas's contrast between the unyieldingly transcendent biblical kerygma and the compromises of the notion of the Word made flesh has been growing ever more unclear since the foundation of the state of Israel in 1948. So too, therefore, has the contrast in postdestruction Judaism between the path of mediation and the path of confrontation with the worldly power of the state. In order to characterize a Catholic reading of the Bible that is truly contemporary we need to return to consider my sixth principle, which concerned the religious revolt of the first century not against Judaism but against Caesarism.

In 1948, after the millennial Passion of Israel had terminated in a descent into Hell, the Jewish people, in Emil Fackenheim's phrase,[5] returned into history—from which for more than eighteen hundred years they had remained excluded. With that a religious revolution began: the earth has quaked and the bedrock has shifted, probably forever, beneath what used to be called Judaism and Christianity. The consequences are of course more obvious for the Talmudic Judaism of the Diaspora. The self-definition of the Jewish people as the people of the Book and nothing else, as those who honor the Law of God in every corner of the earth because they have nothing else to rely on and nowhere in particular to call their own, as those who are pure because they are victims and nothing else, cannot possibly survive the establishment of a state which understands itself as Jewish, which has laws, institutions, customs, and culture that have to relate to their equivalents in other states, which has a particular territory on the shared earth to belong to and call its own, which as a nation among nations must henceforth be an actor in history and so must ineluctably have its own victims too. Through being, as Lévinas puts it, "engaged in events" (*LR* 283), Jewish Law has to change fundamentally from the form it took on eighteen hundred years ago as a result of its disengagement from events. It now has a state to run, but Mishnah and Talmud came into existence as the Jewish response to statelessness. To be exact, they came into existence as one Jewish response to statelessness, the response of confrontation, of the decision to remain external to the Roman Empire. There was another Jewish response, as we have seen, a response of mediation, and the foundation of the state of Israel has set what Lévinas calls Judaism on a path convergent with the future fate of what he calls Christianity.

But for Christianity too—for what I have called New Testament Judaism—the consequences of the foundation of the Israeli state are fundamental and very long term. The undoing of two millennia of "Jewish" exclusion from statehood also undoes elements of the "Christian" self-understanding so old that they already figure in the New Testament. "Christians," as they called themselves, had been defining themselves as "not-Jews" since perhaps the revolt of A.D 66–70. To the survivors of the Nazi genocide the advancement to statehood in 1948 gave, almost one suspects without its being intended, the priceless but ambiguous gift of recognition and equality. Gradually the term "Jews" faded out of the English vocabulary, especially in the language of the communications media, and became a historical term, almost like "Vikings," and gradually another term came to prominence: "Israelis," a term, which like "Pakistanis" or "Iraqis," simply referred to the citizens of another state—another, but not The Other, not the opposite by which identity was defined. The foundation of the state of Israel has gradually withdrawn from Christians the possibility of defining themselves by rejection of the Other outside them, and so it has freed them to recognize the Other within them—to recognize, that is, the extent to which their religion makes them Jewish too. Since 1948 Christianity has been set on the road to recovering its Jewish past.

And the existence of the state of Israel profoundly affects Christianity's future too. It points us onwards, as Lévinas recognized (*LR* 261), to a stage beyond the secular state envisaged by Hegel as the supreme culmination of Protestant Christianity. Not, however, as Lévinas also seems to have thought, simply because Israel sets the extraordinary example of trying to incorporate religious particularity into the foundations of a modern secular state. Rather, Israel is especially, perhaps uniquely, important because of its role as international irritant, because it gives the particular Divine Revelation a role in the world order that lies beyond the state. The long experience of statelessness embodied in the Talmudic tradition is after all peculiarly relevant to the future of us all. Christianity, which for most of its existence has been associated with the growth of state power, has to swallow its pride, learn from Israel, and proclaim the kingdom at that supranational level of human interaction at which the process of globalization is intensifying, states are losing their identity as they struggle to achieve or maintain it, and world religions are clashing, blindly or willfully, as the interests of local particularity are subverted by the worldwide power of consumerism. Catholic Christianity—Catholic New Testament Judaism[6]—is called more visibly in this conjuncture than at any time since its first spectacular failure in the first century of its existence to find a new mediation between two, perhaps the only two, possible readings of the Bible: that which sees its signified as Christ and that which sees its signified as the Land. That is not, in the end, a matter of declarations and diplomatic démarches by curial congregations and Vatican secretaries, nor even necessarily of authoritative teaching, though it may involve all of these. It is a matter in the end of making it possible to imagine a Mass, a proclamation of the word and an act of commemoration and thanksgiving, in the reconciling and redeeming presence of the Lord, and in lawful continuation of the rites of the ancient Temple, which would make God's peace for God's land visible and tangible and part of our daily bread.

In such a Mass, any Mass, which celebrates and effects the continuity of Church and Temple, we will, however, become aware, especially if it is said in Latin, of another force, another presence which, in addition to the Old and New Covenants, is determining the rite in which we are participating. That rite is not simply a re-presentation of the ancient rite of Israel made new and universal by our Jewish Lord's sacrifice of his life; it has also, at least to some extent, been made universal, catholic, as we say, by being made Roman. If we are liturgists what we see, hear, or smell will remind us as much of Rome or Constantinople as of Jerusalem. And if our Mass is not only High but pontifically so, it will bear the name of Rome's supreme

pagan priest and emperor, the Pontifex Maximus. The presence of what is
alien, pagan, unholy, unclean at the heart of the church is essential to its
nature. The church has always seen itself as sent, like its founder, to call not
the righteous but sinners to repentance; it is of its nature missionary, and the
nations it brings to Mount Zion will come bearing gifts from their own
lands, not from the land of Israel. The gifts may take strange forms. One of
them, we have seen, is the cross, a pagan instrument of death, an object as
repugnant to God's law as it is possible to imagine. It has been brought in
and given a place of unparalleled honor: captivity has been led captive and
made into a gift to men. From its very beginnings the church has been a
movement from the sacred to the secular and through the secular back to
the sacred again, and it is time to give some closer attention to these terms,
which I have so far used freely without further discussion.

There is a twofold movement here which is intrinsic to the church's experience of secularity. First, the Law defines a boundary, as it does repeatedly, say, in the Book of Leviticus: this is sacred, this is secular; on this side
of the boundary is the clean, beyond it lies the unclean. Second, Christ
transgresses the boundary, not in order to abolish it, but in order to save
what was lost, to recover what was unclean by bringing it back into the
sheep fold. When the church on its mission to the world encounters something alien and different from it, something secular, it knows that the difference is never absolute, for it can always, must always say of it: "For this too
Christ died." And indeed in the acceptance of the new unclean, in the forgiving of its difference from the Law, Christ dies a little more. He—God in
him—bears the pain of the recovery. In such moments the Church too must
die, must swallow its pride, give up the boundary which it thought defined
its existence, and discover a new and larger vocation. And that new vocation
will itself be defined by a new boundary which in time the church will also
have to transcend.

The church, the new and universal Israel, has always been intended for
this task; the task belongs to its origin and founding call, by which it became
the instrument of the plan of God revealed to Paul in the eleventh chapter
of the letter to the Romans, that by its turning to the Gentiles God would
secure the salvation of all, even of all Israel. The gospel gives us the para-
digm of the process in a saying of Jesus' which is often misunderstood, at
any rate by those outside the church. Lévinas, certainly, misunderstands it
(*LR* 268). "Render therefore unto Caesar the things which are Caesar's;
and unto God the things that are God's" (Mt 22:21). It sounds like a simple
division of life into two realms, a secular and a sacred, each with its own

authority, to whom appropriate obedience is to be paid. But to read it that way is to overlook both the dramatic context of the remark and the meaning of the words it uses. Jesus' remark is not a platitudinous "on the one hand . . . and on the other" but is experienced by his audience as a surprise—as so surprising that they do not dare to ask him any more questions. In fact it contains a double surprise, for the answer to the question, "Is it lawful to give tribute unto Caesar or not?" is concluded with the first half of the remark, and the second half is a completely unexpected appendix. The first half is surprising enough, a debater's reply to a debater's question, as clever as the trap it avoids, and evasive only because the question was not asked with any serious interest in the issue: "since Caesar has labeled the coin as his property, give it back to him; it is pagan and unclean, and you presumably wish to be clean or you would not have asked what is lawful." But the second half is utterly serious, calling on the audience to recognize the power and majesty and inexhaustible claim of the author of the Law, a Law which they have degraded into the material of debating points. They should not be thinking up trick questions about duties to Caesar, they should be earnestly meditating on their life-filling duty to God. For the word *God* does not refer to some more or less equal adversary to Caesar, with whom Caesar might divide the world. What is God's? What property has his name on it? "The earth is the Lord's, and the fullness thereof: the world, and they that dwell therein" (Ps 24:1). There is, then, a secular realm of pagans, outside the Law, who have to be dealt with on their own terms. But there is a greater realm too, the kingdom of God, the author of the Law, and that kingdom embraces everything, the fullness of the world and them that dwell therein, including the pagans to whom Israel, if only it will be renewed in the spirit and the Law, has its mission. The sacred, at first defined as excluding the secular, is discovered, in the surprise that is Revelation, to include it too. And in that moment of surprise we can hear an urgent appeal: "Come with me! Fulfill the Law! Include what is outside it, so that the full holiness of God may be praised by all!" Rome itself, the great outside, with its coin-minting Caesar, its pagan pontiff, may one day be included.

That day comes soon, the New Testament tells us. All the Evangelists present the origins of Jesus' life and ministry as deeply rooted in the traditions and history of Israel, through genealogies in Matthew and Luke, through the role of the Temple in Luke, of Herod the Great in Matthew, of John the Baptist and of citations of Isaiah in all four. The climax of all four Gospels is of course the narrative of Jesus' passion, death, and resurrection.

And in all four narratives an exceptionally prominent feature of this conclusion to a story of travels and meals and miracles, of preaching and argument with numerous different Jewish factions, of deep and urgent—and sometimes angry—conversations, in the Galilean countryside and in Jerusalem, is the sudden collision with Rome. Present hitherto only in the background, as a date or a centurion here, a coin of the tribute there, the Roman power becomes one of the three principal actors—alongside the Jewish authorities and Jesus himself—in a drama on which the fate of the world hangs. The centrality of Roman involvement should not be underestimated: after all, only three human beings are named in the creeds and one of them, alongside Jesus and his mother, Mary, is Pontius Pilate, an unsuccessful career official who, legends aside, was probably never a Christian. Rome is not present simply as the necessary historical framework to an essentially Jewish quarrel, implicated only because, as the occupying power, it decides in matters of life and death. Nor is it present—despite the arguments of those who find here the roots of Christian anti-Semitism—simply as a foil to the Jewish figures, in order to retort on them the blame for Jesus' death. No, Rome is presented as drawn, reluctantly maybe but willy-nilly, into the role no longer of supercilious imperial observer of minor colonial excitements but of an actor in a drama whose outcome it cannot foresee or control. "Have thou nothing to do with that just man," says Pilate's wife, according to St. Matthew (Mt 27:19), troubled by a dream which unsettles the imperialist's illusion of invulnerability. Pilate himself feels that fear, St. John tells us, not merely of a riot, but of an unknown power, of incalculable energy, when he hears that if Jesus' accusers are lying, as he suspects they are, he may be "the Son of God." Whatever that may mean to him, he recognizes an authority before which the command structure of the empire, perhaps even the emperor himself, is of no consequence, when he is quietly told that "Thou couldest have no power at all against me, except it were given thee from above" (Jn 19:11). All the Gospels show, in different ways, a man attempting to hold aloof—convinced of Jesus' innocence (Matthew, Luke), baffled by his mystery (John), or simply aware of the malice of his accusers (Mark)—but slipping inexorably under the pressure of circumstances into knowing involvement in a crime; his guilt is directly mentioned by Jesus in John and is implicit in the handwashing recorded by Matthew; even Luke, who wherever possible understates the Roman responsibility, equates him with the odious and frivolous Herod Antipas. With Pilate's involvement comes that of his underlings, the Roman military machine: every Evangelist but Luke narrates the flogging and mocking of Jesus by the Roman soldiery, and even Luke adds the mockery later. It might be thought inevitable that the Roman army should appear as the agents of the crucifixion itself (though Luke again does his best to obscure the point). But what was not inevitable was that in the mocking and buffeting, the dicing over Jesus' clothes, and the opening of his side with a spear, Matthew, Mark, and John should represent prophecies in Isaiah, Zechariah, and the Psalms as being fulfilled by *Gentile* powers. That the actions of the Roman Empire have given their full and culminating meaning to the Hebrew Scriptures is asserted by all four Evangelists in their giving to the Roman authority—identified by John as the pusillanimous Pilate—the responsibility for proclaiming Jesus to the world as "the King of the Jews," in the *titulus,* the inscription affixed to his cross. And the synoptic gospels all show the moment of Jesus' death as accompanied by the acknowledgment of an unnamed centurion, the voice of ordinary, middle-ranking, thoroughly pagan Rome, that insofar as he can understand the term, in some sense similar to Pilate's, this man was a "son of God." The proclamation and glorification of the King of the Jews has given a decisive role in the realization of the Law revealed in the Bible to a people outside the Law and with no knowledge of the Revelation. Indeed, they have appeared up to now as the enemies of the Law and oppressors of those who observe it. But the true spirit of the Law embraces even them and makes them, like Cyrus nearly six hundred years earlier, into the instrument of God's purpose that all nations shall in the end be blessed in Abraham. God's Law imposes on his people an unfulfillable obligation to be holy, but God's reconciling power gathers into his people even those whom the Law marks out as profane. Rome itself becomes a holy city, and the seat of God's vicar on earth. This reconciling interchange of sacred and secular, of what is inside the Law and outside it, continues throughout the history of Christianity, of New Testament Judaism. That interchange need not be presented in Hegel's systematic terms, not least because Hegel's final synthesis of the process in the secular constitutional nation-state of the immediately post-Napoleonic era has broken down in the new age, in which such states are dissolving into global order or disorder. But Hegel's fundamental insight was that the power of reconciliation which was at work in the advancement of the religion of Pentecost to the religion of Rome and so of the world has remained at work ever since. And that insight, with one or two Catholic qualifications, can I think still guide us in our attempt to find words which will express the good news of reconciliation in our time and context. "God

was in Christ, reconciling the world unto himself, not imputing their trespasses unto them; and hath committed unto us the word of reconciliation"
(2 Cor 5:19). Finding the word of reconciliation, finding the word which
tells how human works begun in the shadow of an unfulfillable obligation
can by God's free gift be completed as vessels of life, and life more abundantly, that is the task of a Catholic hermeneutics, whether of sacred or
secular scriptures.

Sacred and Secular

The Spectrum of Writtenness

PART 3 OF THIS STUDY IS CONCERNED WITH THE EXTENT TO WHICH secular, that is, nonbiblical and nonsacred, writing can be read, at times, with the advantage with which, at times, the Bible can also be read. The result, I hope, is the discovery of some new ways in which some of the greatest modern literature—and also some of the less great—can speak to us about the relation of the modern world to God, about God's hiddennness and the revelation of the hiddenness, and about his reconciliation of our world to himself through his Son and through his Son's mystical body, the church. In order to reach this goal, however, we need to develop a set of concepts that will enable us to relate what we have learned about the nature and genres of biblical writing to nonbiblical works. I do not suggest that these two kinds of writing are identical—that the Bible is really just poetry, as Herder proposed, or that poetry is really all a Bible, as Novalis suggested after him.[1] I do not distinguish two opposites in order to reequate them with one another, as a certain kind of deconstructive analysis is prone to do. I am concerned here with an area in which two distinct circles of writing overlap. Determining the distinctness of the two circles is as important as determining the area of overlap. I believe that a Catholic approach to this dual task is particularly suitable and particularly promising, for the Catholic tradition of the church has long been a tradition both of distinguishing differences and of reconciling what is distinct. In Johnson's phrase it is, at least in exegetical matters, the tradition of "both and" rather than of "either/or."[2]

Of the modern accounts of the Bible that have been discussed so far, and perhaps not only of them, the fullest and most dispassionate is that given by Ricoeur. In order to determine where the circles of sacred and secular literature overlap and where they are distinct, I shall concentrate mainly on some ideas of Ricoeur's—specifically, his ideas of revelation, authorship, and writtenness. Ricoeur's approach has its limitations, however. His modern, linguistically based hermeneutic has more in common than one might expect with the historicist hermeneutic of Schleiermacher, to which he seems superficially to be opposed. A Catholic approach to secular literature, like the Catholic approach to biblical exegesis that I have already tried to develop, will need to incorporate and go beyond both Schleiermacher and Ricoeur, for example, by turning to Lévinas. It should also treat with some caution Ricoeur's concept of poetry.

There is already a problem with Ricoeur's account of what makes the Bible different, what makes it sacred rather than secular writing. Ricoeur provides a comprehensive taxonomy of the forms of biblical discourse and at the same time identifies the unity and uniqueness of the Bible as lying in its content: its pursuit from many different starting points and in many different perspectival constructions of the single vanishing point that is the unnameable name of God. Yet if we are trying to explain what we mean by saying that the Bible is sacred, is *Holy* Scripture, it will not be enough to assert that the Bible is properly called sacred because in various ways, all of which betray awareness of the impossibility of the task, it says or tries to say something about God. That could be said, for example, of any work of theology, and even a work of theology is not Holy Scripture. An explanation of why the Bible is Holy Scripture must explain, among other things, why in its physical, written or printed form it is properly a holy object—to be incensed, sworn on, or preserved in an ark, to be treated with reverence even before or without being read—why it is to be copied or decorated with the utmost care, why it is a duty to expound, comment on, interpret or simply recite it, why it can itself provide a rule of life. Being Holy Scripture involves being read, and being assumed to have been written, in a way that is different from the way other books are treated, and that difference has to be explained. It is not just a matter of content. Even if being about God, the Unnameable and Unknowable, is not like being about Napoleon, you will not explain why Holy Scripture is Holy simply by saying that it is about God unless you are talking to a very sophisticated theological mind, or to an Absolute Idealist. To the ordinary mind Scripture is Holy not (just) because it is *about* God but because it is *from* God. Scripture is Holy because its author is the Holy Spirit, whether by direct dictation or by the more indirect process of inspiration. Holy Scripture is divine revelation and does not have human authors in any but a secondary sense. So exceptional, indeed unique, a book must of course be treated with the reverence due to the One who uttered it.

Ricoeur, however, is compelled to say that what makes the Bible special is that it is about God, because he has subverted and inverted that common-sense understanding—if, by way of paradox, we may so call it—of what differentiates sacred from secular writing. For he attributes to all poetic texts the features that might have been thought of as marking out the distinctively holy writings. All poetic texts, in his view, not just the Bible, communicate and constitute a revelation, manifest a world, the world, to us, and what they reveal could not be constructed by any process of reasoning however subtle or prolonged. All poetic texts, not just the Bible, are to be understood as themselves intending the world that they reveal, not as being the product of an author's intention or desire for self-expression: all poetic texts are effectively authorless.[3] And all poetic texts, not just the Bible, exist pre-eminently, perhaps exclusively, as written, not as some secondary fixing of spoken words which are imagined as possessing, if they could be recovered, some higher degree of authority or authenticity than what is written. What Hölderlin calls "the solid letter," "der feste Buchstab,"[4] is the keystone not just of biblical literalism but also of a secular literary criticism which stays close to the text and avoids psychological speculation about either expression—by a speaker—or impression—on an audience. Indeed, for this secular criticism, as for the older and oldest forms of biblical criticism, the object of interpretation is the word and even the letter of the text rather than its sense, even its literal sense. For Ricoeur it is not the sense but the word and the letter that make up the text—that, in the case of the Bible, are given by the Holy Spirit—and there may be no literal sense to the text at all, only various levels of metaphoricity.[5] Since, then, formally, at least in respect of being revelation, being authorless, and being text, there is no distinction between biblical and secular literature it is not surprising that Ricoeur has to seek the distinction in the content. But surely so important a distinction should reside at least partly in the kind of writing involved and not simply in what it is about? In order to understand how Ricoeur comes to his counterintuitive conclusion we need to look at his intellectual roots.

From the point of view of the intellectual historian, two features of Ricoeur's postmodernist hermeneutic of revelation particularly stand out: his indebtedness to German Romanticism and Idealism and his opposition to Schleiermacher. As to the first point: Ricoeur's transfer to nonbiblical writing of key characteristics of the premodern understanding of biblical writing picks up and renews a tendency which was part of the invention, around 1800, of a sacred realm of human Art as a kind of compensation for the simultaneous secularization and humanization of religion. It is in Art, and in poetry as the supreme form of Art, that the sacred flame of divine creation is relit by the early Romantic generation in Germany, from Karl Philipp Moritz to Schelling, Friedrich Schlegel, and the young Schopenhauer, and the French, English, and American writers who learned from them.[6] For Moritz every work of Art is a revelation and re-creation of the whole world, and for Schlegel and Novalis and other Romantic aphorists that principle applies even to the smallest fragment of utterance. (Think of Lichtenberg's two-word aphorism "Die Wörter-Welt" ["The world of words"].)[7] The concept of genius, of which Herder made a powerful instrument for the interpretation of the Bible, might lead in practice to an excessively personal understanding of literary production. The aesthetic theory of post-Kantian Idealism, however, transformed the concept of genius into the concept of the impersonal artist, who is a mere vessel of the creative powers of the world-spirit that interprets itself in the vast array of human culture. The understanding of culture as essentially linguistic was another of Herder's profound but half-conscious innovations, which bore fruit not only in the foundation by Romanticism of the science of comparative philology but also in a Romantic literary practice determined by the concept of poetry as pure "appearance" and ultimately as cipher, hieroglyph, or arabesque.[8] Sociologically, these remarkable anticipations of twentieth-century literary and linguistic theory are to be associated with the rapid growth of a mass literary culture which in Germany was for the first time entirely print-borne and print-created and unsustained by any metropolitan culture of conversation.[9] If Ricoeur sees all poetic texts as autonomous, impersonal, and revelatory, that is ultimately because he is the inheritor of Romantic and Idealist aesthetics which first took up the terms descriptive of sacred literature in order to apply them to secular literature.

The second prominent feature of Ricoeur's hermeneutic theory helps to explain the line of inheritance, the route by which the legacy of secularization descended from late-eighteenth-century Germany to late-twentieth-century France. I mean Ricoeur's evident and systematic opposition to Schleiermacher's hermeneutics. The young Schleiermacher shrank back from a final identification of poetic and religious genius, an identification which would have signaled his total acceptance of the post-Kantian religion of Art, at that time most systematically expounded by Schelling. His theological position was thereafter characterized by this refusal of the Idealist temptation, a refusal of which his final and possibly most influential expression was his posthumous hermeneutics. Schleiermacher's hermeneutics are based on principles diametrically opposed to those of Romantic Idealism and so to those of Ricoeur. Schleiermacher seeks not to extend a sacred hermeneutic to secular literature but to define a hermeneutic for secular texts that can be applied with minimal accommodations to the sacred. He starts from the presumption that hermeneutics is the art of understanding texts as if they were the speech of another; he does not regard the writtenness of texts as fundamental to their definition. He then assumes that texts emanate from an author and are therefore to be understood by analyzing the interaction of the author's intention with the language of his or her time. And the conclusion, in practice if not in theory, is that understanding a text is so much a matter of envisaging its relation to its historical and personal context that novelty is difficult to find in it and revelation virtually impossible. In rejecting these positions of Schleiermacher, Ricoeur returns, wittingly or not, to the positions of Schleiermacher's original adversaries, reviving premodern and prehistoricist approaches to sacred texts but treating them, as Romantic and Idealist aestheticians did, as applicable to all texts (or at any rate all poetic texts) and so not as reflecting any fundamental difference between the sacred and the secular.

If we see modern hermeneutics, whether biblical or nonbiblical, as poised between a revival of the antihistoricist aesthetics of early Romanticism and Idealism, on the one hand, and the historicist and academic tradition inaugurated by Schleiermacher, on the other, then it is obvious that a Catholic approach to literature cannot fully endorse either, whether in respect of revelation, or authorship, or writtenness. We would certainly want to assert with Ricoeur, and against the Deists whom Schleiermacher was trying to placate, that there is nothing absurd or self-contradictory or historically unwarranted about the idea that the biblical writings are the vehicle of revelation now (and not simply, as Schleiermacher would have it, the record of revelations made to certain individuals in the past). We would probably even welcome the idea that nonbiblical poetic writings can show us something at least of what revelation is and how it works. But we are unlikely to want to follow Ricoeur so far as to accept that all literary texts, biblical and nonbiblical, offer revelation—even in his rather special sense of the term—in equal measure. There is something reliable and constant about the presence of revelation in the Bible, whereas elsewhere it may be present, but then again it may not. After all, and to take the example of writers of real quality, the first time we open a book by P. G. Wodehouse or Georges Simenon may indeed be a moment of revelation, the manifestation of a whole way of the world's being that we could not have guessed at before. But if we ever get so far as to open our hundredth new Wodehouse or Simenon it is more likely that our predominating sensation will be of grateful familiarity than that we shall experience a lost Atlantis of being rising up before us out of the ocean of instrumental rationality.[10] And there are other factors besides familiarity which may severely restrict the possibility of revelations emerging from a nonbiblical literary text. The text may, in a more general sense, be too predictable: the settings, characters, or situations in a drama, novel, or film, the attitudes and expressions in a poem or song, may too obviously derive from conventions, whether literary or social, for them to reflect the mystery of life rather than the necessities of a genre. They may give a faded form of pleasure, the relief from care that comes with the reassuring repetition of verbal or other formulas with which we keep the truth at a distance. But they are too obviously the creatures of the powers that rule this world for them to be much of a revelation of its nature. In some formal sense every poetic text may be a revelation, but the revelations offered by most texts may be so similar as to make that sense not just formal, but trivial. A Catholic approach to literature, sacred and secular, requires a discrimination of revelations.

When we come to the central point of difference between Ricoeur and Schleiermacher, the question of authorship, we again find that distinctions have to be made. As part 1 has shown, there are compelling reasons for Christians to assert that the biblical writings are the work of the Spirit. We may prefer to speak of the Holy Spirit, or the Spirit of the church, rather than of the world-spirit, but we will join the Romantics and Idealists in asserting against Schleiermacher that the meaning of certain texts does not reside solely or even principally in what can be formulated as the original intention of an original author. There are sound empirical reasons for taking such a view. Multiple authorship, the collective handing on of a collective tradition, the processes of translation and commentary and redaction, may often make it impossible, or at least problematic, to speak of a single original author or of an original context which might help to define the author's intention for a particular text. But the main reason for the church to reject Schleiermacher's approach to the Bible has to be theological: his misrepresentation of the relation between Scripture and tradition and the need to preserve the priority of the dogmatic interest. Ricoeur's objection is equally fundamental: the intention that matters to him is not the author's intention

but the intention of the text, the world that it intends and reveals. Moreover, this revelatory intentionality is for Ricoeur a feature of all poetic
writing, not only of the Bible, just as the Idealist believes that the same
suprapersonal Spirit manifests itself in the products both of religion and of
Art. But is it necessary or even desirable to exclude the historicist concept of
authorship completely—either from literature as a whole or from sacred
literature in particular? Ricoeur's stress on the revelatory power of the text,
regardless of the author's intentions, may be of great value to biblical studies,
but does the point have to be universalized? When there are fewer empirical
obstacles to determining the author of a text—as is the case with much
secular literature—when there is ample evidence of the context in which
it was written—as is the case with most European literature since the
Renaissance—and when there is extensive documentation, contemporary
and even personal, of what the author believed his or her intention to be—
as is the case with most literary figures of the past two hundred or three
hundred years—then the denial of the significance of authorship seems more
unnatural and Schleiermacher's approach seems more plausible. Indeed,
Schleiermacher's hermeneutics seems to apply better to the secular literature
of two hundred or three hundred years ago than to the Bible for which he
designed it. Equally, a Catholic approach even to the biblical Scriptures
cannot entirely dispense with the historicism of Herder and Schleiermacher. Catholic Christianity reads the Bible as a self-conscious confluence of
traditions, a story told by the Spirit of the stories told by individual authors.
It requires, therefore, a sense of development in time, of changing contexts,
and of the placing in context of individual speakers and utterances, whether
David or Isaiah, John or Paul. That sense of historical difference, and so of
the context and individuality of authorship, is fixed for Catholic Christianity by the distinction between the Old Testament and the New. In expli-
cating and commenting on the record in the Old Testament of what the
New Testament calls God's "plan" (Eph 1:9), Catholic Christianity cannot
do without the historicism that follows the changing and developing articu-
lations of the plan.

A Catholic approach to literature in general can perhaps reconcile these
conflicting elements. For we need to be able to use Schleiermacher's historicist and essentially secular hermeneutic of authorship in order to explicate
certain aspects of the biblical writings, without allowing that hermeneutic
to dictate the meaning of the whole. Similarly, we need to be able to use Ricoeur's liberatingly reasonable concept of the revelatory text to establish that
the controlling interest in the interpretation of sacred scripture is dogmatic,

without allowing that concept of revelation to be so uniformly applied to secular texts that its use in reference to sacred writings is trivialized or aestheticized. We need, that is, to distinguish two areas of interpretative activity which overlap but which are not identical (as Ricoeur and Romantic aesthetics, on the one hand, and Schleiermacher and academic historicism, on the other, both imply that they are). A catholic or Catholic—a fully open and a fully orthodox approach to literature—will distinguish, first, the area of sacred writings, controlled by a hermeneutic of revelation, and, second, the area of secular writings, controlled by a hermeneutic of authorship. The area of overlap will itself then be twofold: there will be a subsection of the sacred area, under the sway of the concept of revelation, where the hermeneutic of authorship must also be applied; and there will be a subsection of the secular area, under the sway of the concept of authorship, to which the hermeneutic of revelation will also be plainly relevant. To some extent and under some aspects the Bible has to be open to historicist literary criticism. Equally, however, as we shall see, secular literature, to which Schleiermacher's hermeneutic is far better suited than it is to the Bible, is also capable, to some extent and under some aspects, of rising to a meaning that can only be elucidated by theological exegesis. The reason why this should be is closely connected to the reason for the Bible's openness, in certain respects, to the secular mode of interpretation: it is nothing less than Hegel's principle that Revelation and Incarnation are continuous, that the Word has become flesh.

But before I try to fill out this initial sketch of a Catholic approach to literature I must consider the third point of difference between Ricoeur and Schleiermacher: the question of writtenness. Here too we shall find that beneath the appearance of difference there is common ground of a questionable kind: neither thinker makes with sufficient force the distinction between sacred and secular writing, and as a result the significance of the area of overlap between sacred and secular writing cannot stand out. They appear to differ insofar as Ricoeur asserts the autonomy of the written text, its independence of the rules that govern speech and the task of recording it, while for Schleiermacher the written text and the spoken word are subject to the same rules of interpretation, and writing is simply a more durable form of speaking. They agree, however, in making no distinction in this respect between sacred and secular scripture. Schleiermacher sees both sets of writings as historically specific utterances of past, that is, dead, authors. Ricoeur sees both as written texts which, in virtue simply of their writtenness, are the vehicle of a nontheistic, nonreligious revelation, and in that respect he does not differ from his Romantic-aesthetic predecessors, for whom the monuments of Art and the documents of religion were equally self-expressions of the Spirit.

The different approaches have, therefore, two major assumptions in common both of which seem to me wrong—that there is no fundamental distinction between sacred and secular writing and that there *is* a fundamental distinction between what is written and what is spoken. I have to leave until later my reasons for seeing a radical distinction between sacred and secular writing. The second assumption, however, can be discussed now. For Schleiermacher the written text stands in opposition to the spoken word in two ways. First, as the instrument of tradition, as the medium in which an oral utterance is handed on by being given a permanency unnatural to it, the written text is the beginning of the betrayal of the act of speech. The task of hermeneutics, in Schleiermacher's understanding, is precisely to uncover what the written text conceals, to get back to an original meaning which, *ex hypothesi,* because it is original, is not what the text seems to offer us. Second, the text, seen either by the Calvinist as the revealed word or by the historian as the unchanging record of some original utterance, is opposed to the words with which subsequent interpreters, teachers and preachers, surround it—Scripture, that is, is opposed to tradition. For Ricoeur the written word is from the moment of its inception, from the "incipit" at the start of a book, distinct from the language of speech, and for him too the revelation that the written work provides derives from its writtenness, not from any communal tradition of exegesis. Both Ricoeur and Schleiermacher fail to take account of a crucial feature of written texts to which Lévinas draws attention and which we have already considered in relation to sacred scripture: the letter is kept alive by the Spirit; the written text is kept alive, is read, applied, and interpreted, through its breathing the atmosphere of an oral tradition; the revelation of Sinai continues in the latest question asked by the novice of the schoolmaster. The written Law and its oral interpretation cannot be separated. Lévinas made a similar point about secular literature in 1948 in an essay which drew down on him the hostility of the existentialist establishment. Expressing opposition to the aestheticist view, with its roots in the Romantic and Idealist period, that works of "art" are self-contained zones of a perfection uncontaminated by other human values, he wrote, "[C]riticism integrates the inhuman work of the artist into the human world. . . . [T]he immobile statue has to be put into movement and made to speak" (*LR* 142). The work of literature, which initially and by its nature as a written artifact, resists being reduced to concepts is forced to enter into a conceptual discourse—the language of critical discussion, whether in speech or in a form of writing which is obviously continuous with speech. Obvious or unobvious, there is a fundamental continuity between the written and the spoken word: Schleiermacher is wrong to cut the text off from subsequent traditions of interpreting it; Ricoeur is wrong to cut it off from the spoken language from which it emerges. The distinction between speech and writing is not absolute, and that it is not absolute is perhaps a good deal more obvious now than it was in the heady days of the mid-twentieth century when structuralism and Paul Ricoeur were young (as indeed was Nicholas Boyle). Since then an enormous expansion in the technology giving permanence to speech and an equally enormous increase in its sophistication has meant that, for example, telephone conversations or video-conferences or the most ephemeral utterances of public figures are nowadays also written documents, written in the digitalized electromagnetic codes which are not just a true language built up out of discrete signs or letters, unlike their analogue predecessors, but are actually today's universal metalanguage, thanks to which all documents are more or less readily translatable into and out of the older-fashioned forms of writing, such as print. (Newspapers no longer correct and tidy up the statements of politicians but print them with all the repetitions, incoherence, and errors with which they were spoken. The old practice maintained a distinction between the spoken word and the literary artifact that was the word in print. The new practice reflects that the printed word is only a transcription of another document that is already written—the digitalized recording, to deviate from which is simply a falsification, actionable in the courts.) Speaking and writing are a continuum. They always were, but technology has made the point particularly evident. All credit to Lévinas for noticing it at a time when electromagnetic tape recorders were available only to a few, and important radio broadcasts were still regularly preserved on shellac discs.

If, then, speech and writing are continuous and if, as I wish to assume, a distinction between sacred and secular must be made, then we can refine a bit more our image of the relation between sacred and secular scriptures and in such a way that the positive value of Ricoeur's emphasis on writtenness does not get lost. Our image of two different but overlapping areas of literature, namely the area of sacred writing approachable through Ricoeur's hermeneutic of revelation and the area of secular writing approachable through Schleiermacher's hermeneutic of authorship, can be developed into the image of a spectrum of numerous possibilities lying at different points along a scale between two extremes. The possibilities will be ideal literary types: genres of which individual texts or parts of texts might be instances; or aspects under which individual texts might be seen. We can now associate writtenness with the sacred end of this phenomenological spectrum of literature, and what we might call orality—the quality of being approachable through a hermeneutic which assumes that the rules of written and spoken discourse are the same—can be associated with the secular end. At the sacred end of the spectrum we will have more or less pure writtenness, the extreme case of the autonomy of the written word: the book that is venerated as it is carried in procession or that is shut away in an ark without being read. At the secular end we can find plenty of plausible candidates for the equivalent extreme case of more or less pure orality, of near-identity of the textual record and the spoken word—a semiarticulate quarrel in a reality TV show or a fly-on-the-wall documentary, for example. The two ends of the spectrum are as clearly distinct still as the red and blue ends of the optical spectrum. But between them, roughly in the middle, will lie the intriguing areas of overlap, or interpenetration, to which this study is dedicated. On the one hand, we have the sacred revelation gradually taking on orality, emerging, we might say, from the condition of the written icon into being read, then into being read as the spoken word of God to which human speech, in exposition and interpretation, is a response, then into being, in part at least, the work of authors whose intentions can be subjected to varying degrees of historicist interpretation, and then into having, again in part, not only authors but also subject matter and literary forms in common with secular literature. On the other hand, we have secular recorded orality gradually taking on the quality of written revelation. At first, at the secular pole, we have literature in a state of virtually pure interpretability—if that is an appropriate way to describe a spat on *Big Brother*—that is, a state in which the words used have their meaning almost exclusively from the personality and context in which they are uttered and the written (electromagnetically written) form of the work is all but irrelevant to the meaning. Then there is a stage at which the intention of the author of the words interacts, and has to be understood as interacting, not only with the linguistic and cultural context but also with the written medium itself: we say that a journalist has a good style, and we mean not just that he or she has an attractive personality or says intelligent things about their world but that he or she is making something with words that has a touch of permanency about it, the writing itself is a meaningful, an interpretable, achievement and belongs in the field of literature. Once the written medium has become independent in this way, as style, and is interacting meaningfully with authorial intention and historical context, it is possible for subject matter and genre of secular literature to develop in such a direction that the area of sacred Scripture comes into sight: the subject matter can become morally, even theologically, reflective—Pope's *Essay on Man,* Iris Murdoch's novels—the genre can begin to overlap with one of the biblical forms of discourse, historical or prophetic, lyrical or philosophical—Scott, Hölderlin, Emerson. This subset of secular literature constitutes what in the most comprehensive sense of the word can be called poetry, and its proximity to the area of sacred writing was already apparent to Aristotle. Aristotle, it will be remembered, remarked that poetry was more philosophical than history.[11] Whatever that remark may have meant in its time (i.e., if interpreted in accordance with Schleiermacher's principles) we may gloss it as meaning for our present purposes that the area of secular literature characterized in particular by the use of fictions and metaphor, whether in narrative or lyrical forms, is the area closest to some at least of the sacred writings in their attempt to name the name of God. It is the range of the spectrum where our two extreme possibilities most fully interpenetrate. This much we may, I think, take over from Ricoeur without misgiving. There is, however, an important respect in which his account of the relation between sacred and secular writtenness needs to be modified.

Ricoeur applies the term "poetry" and "poetic discourse"—in the sense of a written discourse characterized by fiction and metaphor, by what he calls "split reference"[12]—to too broad a range of phenomena. He applies it, not simply to the area of overlap between the larger areas of sacred and secular writing, but also to the two larger areas themselves. But it seems to me evident that there is more to sacred literature than the use of fictions and metaphors, and more to secular literature too. By extending the use of the term "poetry" to cover both, Ricoeur obscures not only what distinguishes them one from the other but also what both really have in common. (I shall from now on use the term "literature" to refer to those larger areas and "poetry" to refer to the smaller area characterized by the use of fictions.) The reason Ricoeur wants both sacred and secular literature to count as poetry—in the sense of written discourse characterized by the use of fiction and metaphor—is, I think, twofold. He wants to be able to describe the language of literature as (a) nonpurposive but nonetheless (b) having reference. I shall try to fill out my sketch of a Catholic approach to literature by investigating these two claims in more detail.

A Catholic Approach to Literature

LITERATURE IS LANGUAGE FREE OF INSTRUMENTAL PURPOSE, AND IT seeks to tell the truth. These are the twin premises of a Catholic approach to literature, whether sacred or secular. They are not however reflected without distortion in Ricoeur's otherwise productive hermeneutic of literature and particularly not in his conception of poetry, and it is worth asking why. I shall concentrate, to start with, mainly on the secular case.

First, then, nonpurposive use of language. We have seen that Ricoeur believes—rightly, I think—that both sacred and secular texts can, for their readers, be the vehicle of "revelation," though he adds of course that revelation in this sense is nontheistic and nonreligious. He further believes—also rightly, I think—that this revelation is a revelation of that which other forms of discourse—he specifies the "ordinary" language of everyday communication and "scientific" discourse—are too instrumental and purposive to let us experience: those other forms of discourse are too concerned with describing things in the world for manipulative and utilitarian purposes to let us see the world simply as it is, as something that is simply there. Now it is a most fruitful insight, I think, that both sacred and secular literature are said to be characterized by a nonpurposive, noninstrumental use of language, that they are said to have in common that they do not talk about the things of this world as, directly or indirectly, capable of fulfilling the desires of the speaker or writer but talk about them in a way that Kant, who had something like this insight before Ricoeur, called "disinterested."[1] It is helpful too that sacred and secular literature are in this way jointly marked off from what Ricoeur calls ordinary and scientific discourse, which are seen as un-selfconscious applications of a language that is for its users simply a medium of purposeful communication. But Ricoeur seems to me to go wrong when he equates this joint capacity of sacred and (certain) secular writings for a revelation that transcends what other, more utilitarian forms of discourse are capable of doing, with their being, in his sense of the term, poetic forms of discourse, that is, forms of discourse that make use of fiction and meta-phor. The common feature of sacred and secular literature that marks them off from other forms of discourse and makes them capable of becoming a vehicle of revelation is indeed, I believe, their nonpurposive and nonutili-tarian use of language, specifically, of written language. However—and this is the crucial point—these two areas of literature are nonpurposive in dif-ferent ways. The nonpurposive, or disinterested, use of the written medium by sacred literature will concern us later. For the moment I wish to concen-trate on the nonpurposive, the disinterested, use of the written medium by secular literature. It is the distinguishing mark of secular literature that it exploits writing in order to give pleasure, to entertain. Unlike Ricoeur's or-dinary or scientific discourse, secular literary discourse sets out not to com-municate or record information but simply to give pleasure in the written medium—to play with it, a whole influential branch of aesthetics would say,[2] even though this sort of play has a serious or at least, in Aristotle's sense, a "philosophical" meaning. As writtenness increases, as literature moves fur-ther away from communicative and purposive orality, so the element of play in it becomes more explicit and more "philosophical."

Let us consider for a moment how this works out in practice, following the stages I have already identified in the development of literature away from pure, or nearly pure, orality. First stage: Reality TV entertains by using spon-taneous utterance as if it were the material of such artificial and normally heavily scripted forms as TV drama, the news broadcast, or the scientific documentary, playing self-consciously—usually self-indulgently but some-times ironically—with the status both of the material and of the format. Second stage: The intention to give pleasure by having a good style, by writing well, perhaps even wittily, may already be apparent as a subsidiary feature of much journalism and accounts for the high estimation accorded in the past to the oratorical achievements of Cicero, Bossuet, or Burke. And then there is history, poor unphilosophic history—a third stage. It is less often appreciated than it should be that the writing of history is prob-ably, of all the genres of secular literature, the one in which nowadays most is written. It is also to a large and, despite massive studies by Ricoeur and

Hayden White, equally unappreciated extent a literary game.[3] Yes, historical works communicate information but rarely for any utilitarian purpose and never as directly as most of their readers—and perhaps many of their writers—imagine. The construction of a narrative, of an argument, even of the sentence which is thought of as recording a fact—these are all literary procedures. And, compared with a report in a biochemical journal on the pharmaceutical properties of a newly synthesized compound, there can be no doubt that what results from them is entertainment. Good history is made not just—and perhaps not even mainly—by what is called good research, but by good thinking and good writing. We enter fully into the realm of play, however, when we arrive at poetry in the broad, Aristotelian sense— the fourth stage of nonpurposive writing for the sake of pleasure. Here we find whole works that have as their primary intention simply to give pleasure in writtenness, by narrative and dramatic representations of fictitious events, for example, or by the measured expression of thought and feeling in verse. However noble the conceptions of poetry, however passionate or distressing the incidents it relates, they are all put into words as the fulfillment of an in- tention to entertain. That is the glory of poetry, and of secular literature generally, that out of such slight material as the pleasure to be had from the weaving together of words it can make analogues of revelation that can illu- minate and affect the whole of our life. And that brings me to the second reason why—I think—Ricoeur is wrong to regard literary discourse, whether sacred or secular, as, in his sense, poetic, that is, fictional and metaphoric. It is a very big issue—nothing less than the question whether literature tells the truth.

If poetry, as Ricoeur understands it (what I am calling literature), is to be capable of furnishing a nontheistic revelation, he ought surely to believe that in some sense poetry/literature tells us the truth about things. He is re- luctant, however, to say that literature makes true statements—though that proposition seems reasonable enough, provided it is understood that a state- ment can be as long and as unstraightforward as *Anna Karenina* or *Peer Gynt*. I suspect there are at least two reasons for this reluctance. One is that if lit- erature is involved in anything as obviously communicative as telling the truth it might become open again to a hermeneutic interested in the inten- tions and context of the author, in what he or she could have meant by as- serting that this or that was true. The written status of literature as text free from authorial intention—a status Ricoeur believes to be absolute—would then seem to be compromised (as of course I believe it is anyway, but on other grounds). Another reason could be that if literature tells the truth,

then there is a danger that what it says might prove to be useful, either practically or morally; it might help us to understand how things work or what
our duties are, and this would seem to be incompatible with its nonpurposive
status. Presumably for these reasons at least—there may be others—Ricoeur
prefers to say that all literature, all "poetic discourse" as he calls it, refers to
things—for otherwise it could not reveal anything about them—but does so
only indirectly; metaphorically, by saying one thing and meaning another. I
do not propose to go into this matter further, because while the approach
seems right within certain limits it also seems to me unnecessarily and mis-
leadingly circuitous as an account of all literary discourse.[4] The approach
does not even do the job it seems to have set itself to do. Even if literature
were all metaphors, the reasons why people utter metaphors are as open to
investigation by a historicist hermeneutic as the reasons why they utter what
purport to be statements of truth, and indeed much literary criticism is based
on that assumption. And there is no necessary association between the fic-
tive and the nonpurposive. TV advertisements demonstrate that fictions—in
every sense of the word—can be fully purposive. And if I tell a true story
for comic effect, or indeed write a history of the Roman Empire in many
volumes, I am engaged in nonpurposive entertainment in which fiction is at
most a matter of a little embroidery. Above all, though, Ricoeur's approach
is inconsistent, I believe, with our experience of by far the greater part of
that area of literature which does deal in fictions. For Dickens's characters,
let us say, may be fictions, but they are certainly not metaphors. Mrs. Jellyby
is not a metaphor for people who are so obsessed with the charity that operates at a distance that they forget the charity that begins at home; she is an
example of them. Larger, more horrible, more unforgettable than life, perhaps, but an example, not a metaphor—and perhaps even the concession is
not right, for G. K. Chesterton wonders whether those who accuse Dickens
of being unrealistic have ever opened their eyes to the extraordinariness of
the life around them. Literature, I think, shows us in words the truth about
life. That is not its defining feature, for the defining feature of literature is
its noninstrumental use of words, and the defining feature of secular literature is its noninstrumental use of words in order to give enjoyment. But if
we deny that the words literature uses tell us truths about things, about individual beings, natural, personal, or cultural, we shall have great difficulty
explaining how they tell us the truth about Being in general, how they
amount, or are capable of amounting, to a Revelation.

Even literature which is defined by its playing with writing, by its intention to use writing only to entertain, has to be understood, in the first

instance, as communicative utterance. It may have no nonliterary or non-linguistic purpose other than pleasure in itself, but still it makes use of the purposive capacities of language. They may not tell us how to operate a machine, or how a company managed to defraud its investors, or how a case is to be decided between two quarrelsome litigants, or why we should vote for one hypocritical politician rather than another—but nonetheless novels and plays and poems describe and narrate, instruct and judge, arouse, flatter, and persuade. They do so, of course, as we have already seen, in subordination to an overriding intention to give pleasure by what they do and how they do it, and in that way they differ from technical manuals, the reports of officials, and the speeches of lawyers and politicians. But only in that way. In principle those other documents could all be included verbatim in a literary work, just as dead animals and unmade beds can be included in works of sculpture, as long as the author can find a way to make us enjoy them. When Robinson Crusoe recounts how he built his boat, when Portia addresses the court of justice in Venice or Coriolanus the Roman tribunes, when Emma Woodhouse with a shock revises her opinion of Miss Bates, it is not only the characters involved or their hypothetical represented audiences that are informed, persuaded, affronted, or admonished, but we the readers of the book or the audience at the play: not in quite the same way, no doubt, but for us as for them the issues are technical and legal, political and conscientious. The difference is that for us they are also matters of what I have called enjoyment: we are not involved in legal or political confrontations, in crises of moral development or physical survival, but we are taking pleasure in being told about them. (We are not being told about nothing, or about something completely different.)

To be more specific, we are sharing a pleasure in being told about them. I cannot agree with Kant that our pleasure in beauty is morally disinterested, for I prefer to follow other accounts than his of the origin of moral obligation, but Kant was surely right to remark that our pleasure in beauty is conceived as universal. Whether or not the concept of beauty applies to the pleasure we take in literature, Kant's remark certainly does apply. My pleasure in the shape of the tulip, for example, is disinterested—that is, it is independent of any desire to possess it—not, as Nietzsche would have it, because of some effete lack of will on my part, but because I envisage everyone else as sharing it, and that universality is not compatible with any one-sided exploitation of the tulip for my own benefit. How much more must this argument apply to the pleasure I take in literary composition, which is a human, not a natural, work and which is constructed in the very medium of communication, in language? One of the oldest conundrums in poetics is why we enjoy tragedy and take pleasure in the representation of things not pleasurable in themselves. Aristotle explains that we take pleasure in the representation itself.[5] We enjoy, not the thing imitated, but the imitation. It is a terrible sight, but it is so beautifully painted, a terrible story, but so truthfully, so beautifully truthfully, told. When we read this answer to the puzzle we perhaps forget what was so obvious in Aristotle's time and place that it required little explicit analysis: representation, mimesis, was the work of actors, or mimes, in a public performance. It is not just imitation but public imitation of sorrowful events that makes them pleasurable. Or rather: imitation is of its nature public, whether it occurs in a painting made only for a second pair of eyes, in a theater before an audience of hundreds, in printed books circulated to thousands, or is simply done in words, the nature of which is to be accessible to everyone. The pleasure we take in tragedy is pleasure in the consolation that is the *sharing* of grief and horror. And our pleasure in the consolation can be the principal and defining characteristic of our experience because, though the bereavement is a fiction and our grief correspondingly hypothetical, the sharing is immediate and actual. Moreover, what we share is not simply the emotional reaction to a fiction. It is the emotional reaction to a truth which the fiction has expressed. We share the pain of knowing a truth about our shared condition. "Thou'lt come no more—Never, never, never, never, never." *Our* truth is being told to us and we look each other in the eyes and know that our truth is everyone else's— which is one reason why after a performance of *King Lear* there is not usually very much to say. We may not often see a life wasted as it is spoilt and wasted by Macbeth, or Hamlet, or Cleopatra and Mark Antony, but their plays show us, that is, they enable us to share the knowledge, that there is such a thing as life and there is such a thing as wasting it—that life matters. In Lévinas's terms, these plays enable us to share with our neighbors the knowledge that life matters, and to that extent our experience of them is a fulfillment of the Law of responsibility and so properly a source of pleasure. Existence is not a meaningless accident to which the only appropriate reaction is silent stoicism. It is, as Heidegger says, a source of Care, but it is not, as Heidegger implies, a source of simply individual Care. We are in it together, and sharing is as intrinsic to our existence of Care as it is intrinsic to the representation of that existence through literature or in any other art. The great tragedies, by giving us pleasure in the immediate awareness of the absolute generality, the absolutely shared quality, of pain and Care, furnish us with a hint or foretaste of the one great Christian truth: God, the source of all existence, suffers too, and therefore we can trust that in and beyond the suffering there lies redemption. In such works we need little help from aesthetics to discern revelation.

But not even tragedy, not even *King Lear*, is the whole truth that secular literature can reveal to us through the pleasure of sharing. There is, after all, comedy too. Chesterton's merits as a thinker are grossly neglected but are probably irrecoverable by the mainstream of modern criticism. He is the nearest thing to an English Nietzsche, but neither modern Nietzscheans nor modern Chestertonians are likely to welcome the comparison. Chesterton, however, has said exactly what needs to be said in this connection about Dickens, far better than I could say it:

> The art of Dickens was the most exquisite of arts: it was the art of en-joying everybody. . . . I do not for a moment maintain that he enjoyed everybody in his daily life. But he enjoyed everybody in his books; and everybody has enjoyed everybody in those books even till today.[6]

Every word and every step in this little argument is precise and correct: the choice of the word *enjoying* as the correct but subversive complement to the word *art* (itself subverted by its application to Dickens); the distinction between enjoyment in the purposive and instrumental world of daily life and enjoyment in—not "art," not "poetry," but the real and practical medium for the communication and sharing of truth—Dickens's "books"; the recognition that the enjoyment that the supreme work of art offers is an enjoyment that extends to every aspect of it, an enjoyment that does not eliminate moral interest—Chesterton goes on to talk about the enjoyability of Dickens's villains—but embraces it; and the final, brilliant—because gratuitously superadded—insight that the sharing of the pleasure that marks out the work of secular literary art is intrinsic to the pleasure itself, that it is a part of our enjoyment of a Dickensian character that we experience it as an enjoyment which must be shared and which, through the writing in the book, is being shared, with "everybody." A little later in the same chapter of *The Victorian Age in Literature* Chesterton addresses "the only elementary ethical truth that is essential in the study of Dickens," and again he strikes exactly the right note. Again he recognizes the universality of the work of literature, and its call to all of us to share in it, as the route by which the secular leads to the sacred. Even an essentially comic mode of writing can give us the pleasure of that shared recognition of the truth about our need-fulness which we might think of as reserved to tragedy, for breadth of sympathy is natural to comedy and Dickens

> had broad or universal sympathies in a sense totally unknown to the social reformers. . . . Dickens . . . really did sympathise with every sort of victim of every sort of tyrant. He did truly pray for *all* who are desolate and oppressed. If you try to tie him to any cause narrower than that Prayer Book definition, you will find you have shut out half his best work. (*VA* 121–22)

Chesterton is absolutely right—and how right he is too, in characterizing this most English of novelists, to invoke the English Prayer Book. Dickens enjoyed the existence of everybody, even of the convicted criminal, and his sympathy included even the guilty man in the condemned cell. As a child I was so profoundly struck by his account of Fagin's last hours that I read and reread it compulsively and became even then a firm opponent of capital punishment—as Dickens no doubt intended. But that moral intention does not compromise what Chesterton rightly calls Dickens's art. On the contrary, it is the condition of it; the moral concern is the vehicle of the sympathy with every sort of victim, a sympathy which is so certain of the need and so unprescriptive as to the means of relieving it that it resembles prayer; and the sympathy in turn is the condition of the universal enjoyment of every sort of existence. You cannot enjoy everybody unless they matter to you as they matter to themselves and to each other—unless, in other words, you can say of them what the Word of God said of the creation of the human race: "Behold, it was very good." Enjoying everybody without the belief that they matter would be the act of a Don Juan, who in the end condemns himself to the same eternal meaninglessness that he assumes in his victims.

Mattering, it may be recalled from the discussion of Frei and Auerbach, comes from the Spirit. A book becomes literature by using language for the purposeless purpose of enjoyment. But language is the medium of the Law, of the Word which tells us that everything matters, even the sparrows on the rooftops. By showing life as mattering, and thus sharing in the work of the Spirit, literature enables us to take pleasure in a truth about human existence: the truth that its constitution is inescapably moral. Literature, however, shows us more than just the way people behave in response to a commandment, more even than the presence of the commandment itself.

The pleasure Aristotle rightly says we take in representation, in the mere imitation of things, is the secular analogue of Redemption. Representation is the moral reality of Redemption projected into the secular realm of pleasure. Representation affirms—more, it enacts—the worth to God of what is represented. However appalling or dispiriting, however low or laughable, the life that is represented, sinful life just as it is, serving no further purpose but just being there—life as it is for its Maker and Redeemer—is affirmed by the act of representation to be worth the labor and love and attention that go into the showing it (by the artist) and the recognizing it (by the audience). *Così fan tutte* points to the real possibility of the forgiveness that it celebrates, and so too does *Waiting for Godot*. Life does not have to be shown as having a discernible purpose in order to be shown as capable of being forgiven: it only has to be loved enough to be worth representing, and worth the labor of understanding that goes into enjoying the representation. Nietzsche's formula that "only as an aesthetic phenomenon is the world and existence eternally justified"[7] could not be more wrong; it needs to be reversed, so as to run: only as a revelation that the world and existence matter eternally—matter so much that the God who made them died to restore them—is the phenomenon of literature possible. An event of representation is an event of forgiveness, a participation—imperfect, of course—in the divine act, not of creation (as a romantic aesthetics once maintained), but of re-creation. Such an event of remaking—of redress, as Seamus Heaney calls it—is not to be understood as the solitary act of an artist: like any act of communication, it exists only insofar as it is received. Because works of literature are made out of language, out of the original symbolic exercise of my preoriginal responsibility for my neighbor, they have at their heart a principled universality which fits them to participate symbolically in that interaction of Law and loss and reconciliation which Christians call Atonement or Redemption. Of course, a secular author cannot get it right all the time and the greatest always err by giving too much rather than too little. Moralizing and sentimentality are as inseparable from the genius of Dickens as the flight into bombast is from that of Shakespeare or Yeats: they are not accidental blemishes but outgrowths from the core, from the demonstration of the human and eternal value of his characters, which is what makes it possible to enjoy them. Fagin is saved from being a stereotypical instrument of anti-Semitism and is raised into literature by our enjoyment of his monstrosity, and that is made possible as much by Oliver's final prayer for him— "Oh! God forgive this wretched man!"[8] (in which a direct vocative can be heard behind the gasp of sentiment)—as by the relish in the caricature when we first meet him, stirring the coffee in an iron pot and serving hot rolls and, of all things, ham, to his "dears," while he inspects their pickings.

The fictions of human individuality that we call characters, the fictions of human interaction that we call plots, the fictions of a meditating and soliloquizing human consciousness that we call (lyric) poetry—they all tell us or show us many truths: about what people are like, about how they feel and behave, about what the world looks like to us and others. To that extent they are continuous with other nonfictitious forms of secular literature such as history, oratory, and journalism, which themselves may make occasional use of fictional hypotheses to communicate truths (Imagine a typical Parisian shopkeeper of the early 1790s, What might those bereaved by this latest atrocity be thinking? etc.). But literature in which fiction has become the dominant mode, what Ricoeur calls poetry, differs from literature in which fiction makes only an occasional appearance in a crucial respect: it hypothetically but systematically postulates the nonexistence of its author. "These words are not being spun out of a mind, they tell truth" is the fiction, the lie, Plato would say, with which all fictions begin. History, or memoirs, or speeches on public occasions are usually content to have authors, to originate in particular people who may have their own perspectives on things, their own motives for telling and concealing, and telling in a particular way, and whose products are therefore explicable by a historicist hermeneutic. Authors of nonfictional, secular literature accept that they will be contextualized. They may not like the idea, but they accept it. But fiction— "poetry"—is always striving to escape the historicist hermeneutic, to achieve a state of pure writtenness, to be simply the words that show the world as it is, that tell the story as it was and not as something interpretable as the consequence of quirks in the author's motivation or accidents of his or her sociolinguistic context. That striving may express itself in very different ways: in the noisy or discreet authorial self-reference of Fielding, Wieland, or Jane Austen; as the hide-and-seek of author and narrator in Sterne or Nabokov; in the pretense to omniscience of Balzac or the pretense of ignorance in Dostoyevsky; in the formal elimination of an authorial role altogether in drama or in the first-person narrative of Goethe or Raymond Chandler. All these are devices to allow the text of the fiction to stand on its own as the representation to an audience, the mimesis, of a world that is a part of the world. In fiction the aspiration of secular literature to total independence of an authorial perspective, to being pure text, pure transcription of how it is, is as nearly fulfilled as it can be. Fiction comes as near as any form of secular literature can to creating a world of the text in Ricoeur's phrase. It is therefore peculiarly able to tell us not just many truths but the truth. That it tells us many truths, that it is, as we say, true to life, is the guarantee of its veracity, the guarantee that the world of this text is a part of the world we know and inhabit: it shares with us what we share with one another. We nod and agree that we have seen hardhearted hypocrisy like that of the Dashwoods at the start of *Sense and Sensibility,* or even, if we look firmly enough in the mirror, like that of Goneril and Regan, that we have seen infatuation like that of Antony and Cleopatra, or Anna and Vronsky, that the soliloquies of Hamlet and Macbeth or their depicted relations with women or with their own fantasies put into words or into mimic show things that before we heard and saw them we did not know we knew. But now we know them, we *all* know them, for secular literature does not merely imitate truly. It publishes truths. And now that we are all agreed in recognizing in the world of the text the world that we share with one another, the text springs the surprise of which only fiction is capable, within the realm of secular literature: in *this* set of truths, in *this* represented segment of the world we share, in *these* people and *these* their destinies, or, in the case of lyric poetry, in *these* now known and worded moments and moods and layerings of memory, there is revealed a truth, the truth, which only a text which is all but free of contamination by authorship can reveal: the truth that regardless of who, for example, Shakespeare or Dickens may have been or what they may have meant by, let us say, *Hamlet* or *Great Expectations,* there is life, and there is the wasting of it, and there is the fulfillment of it too—fulfillment gained or lost but always at least present in the redemptive assumption that it is all, however hurtful, or absurd, or even banal, worth putting into words for all of us to share. And finally, because we recognize the contingency and uniqueness of this particular revelation, the dependence on an author of this particular moment of near-emancipation of words from authorship, there looms behind it, if not pure Being, at least the possibility of pure Being's revelation and the certainty of its primal modification by the call to responsibility.

So, for example, there are many fine things said and shown in *The Tempest* about art and age and resentment and drink and, possibly, colonialism. We recognize their truth and so recognize in the text the world we all share. But what makes the play almost a revelation is—to borrow a term from painting as much as music—its tonality, the unique harmony of its many voices, audible for a moment perhaps (though it is, strictly speaking, impossible for any one moment to contain it) in the exchange between Miranda and Prospero, the moment (again, if there is one) in which the text springs its surprise:

> M. O brave new world
> That has such people in't!
> P. 'Tis new to thee. (Vi, 183–84)

In those few words, and in the spectacle of the stained and sorry crew that call forth Miranda's exclamation, innocence and appetite and love and generosity and promise are married up with experience and disillusion and comedy and maturity and forgiveness, and the whole "world"—as the characters call it—is seen in a light at once multiple and strangely clear, like a landscape after the storm that gives the play its title. The world which is seen in the light of this dialogue, a light which is universal but not uniform, calm but not cold, is the world of the text—the world of *this* text, the play named after the storm. It is the world of Shakespeare's last play, of his farewell to the stage, to art, to life; it is mature, majestic, ascetic, virtuosic, renunciatory—however the interpreter chooses to specify its character. The world of the text, then, though we might call it impersonal, is impersonal with Shakespeare's impersonality: we identify it historically and even biographically as his world, or at least as the world of this particular play. But there is another world still that the words of Miranda and Prospero let us glimpse, behind even the world of the text, another world about which the play is telling us—or allowing us to sense—the truth. It is not the world that has such people in it, whether the people that Miranda or Prospero knows, or that Shakespeare knows and has at the end of his career learnt to see through both Miranda's and Prospero's eyes. It is the world that has such texts in it, that has among other things *The Tempest* in it and us, *The Tempest*'s audience. The world in which the understanding and desire and growth in forgiveness that the world of *The Tempest* contains is a representation or imitation, a miming, of what we all acknowledge to be, not life as seen by Shakespeare, but just life. At such a moment the play is as near as it can be to revelation of a truth, and Shakespeare is simply the instrument who has provided the words without which we could not have uttered or named it. The play has become a secular scripture. We no longer feel that the truth we are being told is to be found in Miranda's view (though that is true), or in Prospero's view (though that is true too), or even in the uniquely toned and nuanced and harmonized conjunction of both which is the wisdom the play enables us collectively to share and which we might call Shakespeare's view. Rather, the truth the play presents to us is that there is truth, that is to say, that life can reveal itself in words; that there is life, and that there is knowledge, and that the rule of right living and right knowing is the same. The play has shown us Prospero's growth from an autocratic and even vengeful old magician to a man who can cast away his wisdom in the more abundant life of the new world of forgiveness: it has shown us his growth into right knowledge. And so we can say that that rule of right living and right knowing, the rule of truth, is both represented and obeyed in this incomparable though still human work. It speaks truly of truth and so is poised on the verge of pure writtenness, pure independence of its author. Coincidentally the unreliable and fragmentary form in which it has come down to us also leaves this play as, of all Shakespeare's works, the one that is nearest to being pure text.

The greatest secular literature, then, comes very close indeed to telling us the truth, to showing us that there is truth. There is a way of seeing life as a whole, or rather there is a light in which life as a whole presents itself to us, for which the name, the only name, is *The Tempest*—just as (or almost just as) there is for every human being, every new child, a light in which life as a whole presents itself, as it never has before and as it never will again, and for that the only name is his or her own. But beyond the recognition that life always presents itself to us as named, as in a particular mood or key, lies the thought of life as it is in itself, unnamed, in all moods and none. No secular literature can show us life as it is in itself, what it is that presents itself in an unrepeatable way to every new human child, but the greatest literature, that in which the most distinctive mood is united with the greatest degree of detachment from the author's historically contingent personality, can bring us to the point where we can understand the possibility that the lost Atlantis of Being may reveal itself in words. Pace Ricoeur, that is as close as secular literature can come to revelation.

Let me summarize. Secular literature, though written down, can never be completely separated from the spoken language in which it has its origins and which, by means of the continuing discourse of critical discussion, keeps it alive. It can, therefore, never be finally detached from its author and always remains open to analysis in terms of his or her intentions and sociolinguistic context. Its defining characteristic is its nonpurposive, that is, noninstrumental, nonexploitative, use of language in order to give disinterested pleasure. But the language it uses for its nonpurposive and pleasurable end is the ordinary purposive language of communication, description, and moral evaluation; it is not necessarily a metaphorical language. Secular literature shows us what the world is like and what our duties are within it—that is, it shows the world as mattering—but as the object of a shared enjoyment. A part of secular literature, which we may call poetry, does this preeminently by means of fiction. Fiction is the device by which, above all, a text is presented as being authorless, and authorlessness is the supreme literary fiction, the ultimate untruth. Secular literature, particularly secular poetry, takes a nonpurposive enjoyment in the being of things which, to the extent that it approaches the state of pure authorless writtenness—for it can never actually attain that state—is capable of foreshadowing a revelation of Being and of the fundamental—preoriginal—modification of Being by ethical obligation.

Since this band in the spectrum of orality and writtenness, the band of revelatory or partially revelatory secular literature, shares so much of its territory with sacred writing, it is vital to our quest for understanding to resolve two problems: how this sharing is possible and what its limits are.

As to the first problem, Ricoeur states emphatically that the revelation imparted by a written text in virtue of its writtenness is nontheistic. I doubt whether a Catholic approach to literature can allow this. Indeed, I doubt whether a Catholic approach to philosophical theology can allow it either. For the revelation is said to be a revelation of the ground of our existence, and the ground of our existence can hardly be a matter of indifference to theology. Certainly not if we accept the guidance of Lévinas, for whom ethics, not ontology, is primary, and for whom being, even at its purest, is always adverbially modified by an "autrement," an otherwise. There is no *is* without at least the touch of an *ought*—without, specifically, the command to responsibility for the neighbor which for Lévinas is the preoriginal certainty from which the certainty of God is derivative. It is the Christian assertion, I believe, that the unfulfillable obligation, which all of us have from the beginning failed to fulfill, has been fulfilled for us by God who is the source of the obligation as he is the source—whatever that may mean—of all being. Literature approached by the Catholic route cannot, then, reveal simply the pure ground of our existence, for a Catholic cannot believe that our existence is simply grounded in that—pure—way: being is always adverbially modified by an otherwiseness that consists not only in responsibility, as Lévinas believes, but in sin and redemption too. We humans exist as called and lost and bought again, and we have no access to the being from which our existence emerges except insofar as it makes that threefold condition possible. We cannot know God as our Creator without knowing him as our Redeemer too, for we can know him only through the Second Person of the Trinity through whom all things were made, who was incarnate for our salvation, and whose Spirit is identical with that of the Father. What supreme works of secular literature reveal is, therefore, not some ultimate and homogeneous eternal moment, as Ricoeur's terminology might seem to suggest, but the permanent interaction of Law, judgment, and reconciliation which is the source of our existence insofar as it is open to us to know it. The revelation at the heart of secular literature is in the deepest sense a moral revelation, and therefore it is a revelation of God. Perhaps in the end all I am saying is that if we believe the teachings of the Catholic church to be true statements about human life, then we must necessarily expect literature that is true to life to reflect and corroborate them, whether or not it is written by Catholics.

The second problem that now forces itself on our attention is, where does this secular revelation stop? At what point in its development away from mere recorded orality does the secular written word cease to overlap with the forms and contents of the sacred books? How far does the band of secular literature extend along the spectrum that leads eventually to pure writtenness? For it clearly does not go all the way. The Bible and Shakespeare may be the works most in demand among castaways on desert islands, but no one swears an oath on a copy of Shakespeare. The family Bible may sit unread on the family bookshelf, but its presence still suggests an inarticulate seriousness about truth, while the equally unread Victorian poets in the same gold-lettered leather binding—in Germany, the unread yard or two of Goethe—are the material only of comedy. We incense the Gospels but not the *Iliad*. There are limits to the sacralization of the secular. The clue to what they may be is given again by the dialogue between Ricoeur and Lévinas. Ricoeur shows most uncertainty about including as an independent form of biblical discourse the genre which Lévinas believes to be all-embracing: the genre of prescriptive writing, of Law. Lévinas is right to hint that this uncertainty betrays a cardinal weakness in Ricoeur's account of revelation. Ricoeur is hesitating over the precise feature of the sacred books which marks them off from the secular, the one genre that does not figure in the repertoire of possibilities available to a secular writing that has become independent, as style, and is interacting with its author's intentions and its historical context so as to create new meanings. There can be non-sacred but morally and theologically reflective narrative, lyric, and wisdom literature—even, if marginally, prophecy. But there cannot be a secular literary simulacrum of Law. There are of course written bodies of secular law. But such rules for the functioning of the earthly city lack the nonutilitarian writtenness that would free them to signify outside their cultural context. Though written, they do not fulfill the basic requirement for any literature—that their writtenness should not be made instrumental to a purpose extraneous to itself—for they are written down only as a matter of convenience, only in order to be remembered in an unchanging form, that is, to be available to perform their function at different times in the same unchanging way. They certainly do not fulfill the basic requirement specifically for secular literature—that their writtenness should be intended as a source of pleasure. They are recorded orality without a trace of the intention to entertain (see, e.g., sec. 101 of the Settled Land Act, 1925).[9] Secular law has this purely instrumental relation to its own writtenness because all its imperatives are, as Kant would say, hypothetical. It prescribes what you are to do only on the assumption that you wish to achieve a certain goal or wish to avoid certain penalties. It is written in order to define and maintain procedures, not in order to state what is, or what ought to be. As it is wholly about procedures it is necessarily excluded from noninstrumental literature.[10] Its own being, as a body of writing, is, therefore, and has to be, of no interest to it: since secular law never states what is but only how things are to be done, it cannot state what it is itself. As secular law, as a body of hypothetical imperatives, law can be no part of secular literature. But as sacred law, as the expression of a categorical imperative, law can be no part of secular literature either. The Law, as categorical obligation, is the exclusive preserve of sacred scripture.

Uttering the Law, putting into words the preoriginal—Lévinas calls it an-archic, beginningless—obligation to responsibility is the task of sacred literature which therefore is properly called, collectively and simply, the Law. The words of the Law do not tell us how to do things on the assumption that we have reasons extraneous to the Law for doing them: the words of the Law tell us to do many things only as ways of fulfilling the one obligation which alone they proclaim. The imperative is one and categorical, not multiple and hypothetical. In that lies both the common ground shared by sacred and secular literature, the justification for calling both of them literature, and the limit which keeps them apart. Both sacred and secular literature involve the noninstrumental, nonpurposive use of words and in different ways assert our freedom from the tyranny of functional, goal-directed thought and language: secular literature by using words to give pleasure and so enabling us to enjoy what is; sacred literature by using words to utter obligation, and so to give us our identity, not as beings who perform a function, but as creatures who know what ought to be. Kant thought the analogy between the beautiful and the morally good worth a section in the *Critique of Judgement*,[11] and the analogy is particularly close when it is exemplified in two sets of ways of using the same medium, the written word. At the same time Kant is careful to point out that analogy implies difference too. Sacred and secular literature may make use of the same, or some of the same genres, they may even at times share similar subject matter, but the limit defining—putting the end to—the area of overlap between them is provided by the imperative form: "Thou shalt." Secular literature can go so far as to show us life lived under the sway of the commandment, it can let us glimpse Being modified by primordial obligation, as perhaps we do in *The Tempest* or, in the converse image of radical disobedience, in *Othello,* but it cannot utter the commandment itself, for it does not have the authority. It cannot strip itself of authorship to the point where its imperative is uttered by God rather than by a human speaker with his or her own intentions, subject to determination by a historical and linguistic context and so to analysis by a historicist hermeneutic. Equally, the authority of the commandment that defines sacred literature is expressed in its withdrawal from human authorship, in its presenting itself as written, ultimately and in the extreme case as nothing but written, as not even dictated, but directly inscribed by the finger of God on stone—as not even read but deserving divine honor even as a closed book. The genres used in sacred literature may take it far inside the territory of secularity. Sacred literature may make use of history, as in the Old Testament and the Gospels, of fiction and metaphor, as in wisdom literature and the New Testament parables, of lyrical meditation, as in the books of the prophets and the Song of Songs; it may make subsidiary use of an intention to entertain just as secular literature may strive to reveal the ethical undertone to existence. But it always retains the formal relation to commandment which marks the frontier with secularity. The dependence of a sacred text on an author can never reach the point where the text becomes simply an interpretable utterance by a historically determined individual and loses the writtenness that permits the direct enunciation of the imperative. It always remains Law. Even the wisdom books of sacred literature are expressions, however refined and derived, of the original obligation. Even Ecclesiastes, in which first-person utterance and the appeal to the author's experience are so prominent, enjoins us "Remember now thy Creator in the days of thy youth" (12:1). Even the Song of Songs, that torrent of sensual delight, shows us unwavering desire for a lover who knocks on the door saying, "Open to me, my sister, my love" (5:2), and—because this is a sacred text—the imperative, even in this gentlest of forms, is directed to us too. Even the oddly immoral stories of Jacob and Joseph are presented as the prelude to the liberation and the covenant in the time of Moses, part of the mysterious, even arbitrary, way in which the Law enters life and transforms it. It is possible to meditate on the most prosaic advice of the Proverbs, the most godless cynicism of Ecclesiastes, the most bellicose nationalism of the Psalms and to remount the stream to their source in the first commandment and the second that is like unto it. The structural parallels between biblical and nonbiblical poetry and fictional narrative may become very close, but there will always be the difference that is made by the dependence of the biblical text on the direct utterance of the Law. The relation between secular and sacred scripture is therefore very similar to that which Kant allows between the beautiful and the moral: the beautiful may be a symbol of morality, but the relation of symbolization implies difference and noncommensurability too. The beautiful cannot simply be equated with the moral without compromising the absoluteness of the moral command. There is, however, a richness to this symbolic relation which Kant also points out: it is a relation recognized both by the philosopher and by "ordinary understanding." The philosopher can show that judgments of beauty employ the same concepts of immediacy, disinterestedness, freedom, and universality as moral judgments, but ordinary, unphilosophical language also uses moral terms such as "majestic," "innocent," or "cheerful" to apply to beautiful objects, whether of art or of nature. There is thus in everyday life an easy and gradual transition (*Übergang*) from the material of sensual pleasure to the object of moral esteem "without too violent a leap" (ohne einen zu gewaltsamen Sprung).

In the remainder of this study I attempt to apply this Kantian principle to the case of literature. I attempt to read secular literature—noninstrumental writing for the sake of pleasure—as a symbol of sacred literature—noninstrumental writing that enunciates the preoriginal command. Unlike Ricoeur, I assume that such a term as "revelation," or for that matter "sin," "redemption," or "spirit," when applied to secular literature, is not nontheistic or nonreligious. On the contrary, whatever theistic and religious, whatever sacred sense those terms may have, we will in practice learn it by means of a gradual transition, without too violent a leap, from their secular application. Secular scriptures in short are the way in, the prolegomena, to the sacred scriptures. They provide the commentary that makes the original text accessible, the atmosphere of application, elaboration, and response that the written law needs in order to breathe and live. They most obviously perform this function when they are explicitly conceived as commentary, and we do not do them justice if we overlook that explicit commitment—if, for example, we do not ask what Tolstoy meant by his epigraph "I will repay" we shall not fully understand the moral seriousness and moral achievement of *Anna Karenina*. As it happens, and as Steiner has pointed out, a remarkable amount of Western literature has been conceived as theological commentary or explication, so I have no qualms about starting with a text, Pascal's *Pensées,* whose theological function is fully explicit. We shall, I think, find that there is an easy transition to texts that are normally thought of as fully secular—to *Faust, Moby-Dick, Mansfield Park.*

Why these texts? Well, of course it does not just happen that so much of Western secular literature has a concealed theological substructure. The secularity of a text exposes it to the historicist hermeneutic, and secularity itself has a historical definition. To ask what is the relation between sacred and secular scriptures? is necessarily to ask a historical as well as a conceptual question, and I have chosen these particular texts not only for their intrinsic importance and their variety but also for the light they can shed on the historical origins of modern secularity. Secular is what Western literature became as a consequence of a development in European society and economic behavior around A.D. 1200 that brought about a new understanding of what it is to be human. As a result of what Peter Spufford has called the Commercial Revolution[12]—the necessary long-term predecessor of the industrial revolution—a new sense of human identity and human worth became available: as determined by what one possesses, specifically, by one's liquid, investable capital, rather than by one's preordained and inherited status, as was the case in the preceding "feudal" era. From the twelfth century onwards the growth of the Italian, and later the German, cities and the monetarization of economic relationships put the feudal sense of what it was to be human under threat. In the culture of the high Middle Ages, from the twelfth to the fifteenth century, above all in the work of Aquinas and Dante around 1300, a synthesis was achieved of the new individualism, based on the sense of what one has, and the old order, based on the sense of what one is ordained to. In the sixteenth century, however, the new economic system entered into an expansionist phase with the founding of the first European extraterritorial empires, the synthesis was tested to destruction, and in the process that we call the Reformation the feudal order, consecrated by the old church, lost its hold over the European mind. In the Reformation Christianity set itself the task both of liberating the new area of life constituted by individual economic activity from the old authorities that called themselves sacred and of reclaiming the whole new area for God—the task of redeeming the time. If Christianity failed in that task it was because the process of reform lapsed into schism and neither institutional nor, consequently, intellectual coherence could be maintained. Modern being is secularity, a being that is forgetful of its origins in God, just as it is capital, a having that is forgetful of its origins in work, and since the Reformation, and because of it, the church has failed in its task of reconciling modernity to God—that is, of leading it back to its origins. In the culture of modern, that is, post-Reformation, Christendom the boundary between secular and sacred remains largely untranscended: the secular art and literature that are so glorious a part of its capital depend for their existence on a deliberate repressing or forgetting of their Christian origins; the forgotten territory is marked by a limit which may be approached but not crossed and therefore may not even be fully recognized; and only rarely, if at all, can the human life that art and literature present and celebrate appear in them as what it was ordained by God to be—the element in which his Word, his revelation, is made flesh.

The Christian faith, I have argued, is, however, the faith that Christ's redeeming work continues, bringing within the ever newly redrawn boundaries of God's kingdom his ever newly adopted children. Where there is a boundary established between what is within the Law and what is beyond it, Christ oversteps the boundary and seeks the incorporation of what was lost. "God was in Christ, reconciling the world unto himself, not imputing their trespasses unto them; and hath committed unto us the word of reconciliation." What is the word of reconciliation that we, Paul's addressees, are commissioned to speak in conversation with the secular scriptures of our modern era? It must be a word that opens the way back to the origin of those writings in God—in the primal and unfulfillable commandment to responsibility and in the primal act of forgiveness by which God has taken on himself all the pain of our failure to fulfill it. It must uncover the limit that makes the writing secular and by bringing to it the knowledge of what lies beyond, it must enable it to be recognized at last as a limit. It must, of course, impute no trespass. Rather it must accept the limit, it must read the point of trespass, the point which makes the writing secular, the point at which God is forgotten, as the point of forgiveness, the point at which God is incarnate, both revealed and hidden in flesh. Read as showing Christ in the moment in which they mark themselves off from their origin in God, secular scriptures become the limit case of sacred scripture, the word of God no longer as an address to us—as God's reply to our prayer—but as the inarticulate groanings of the Spirit within us—as our prayer itself. These words (the word of reconciliation enables us to say) say what it is about us that needs to be redeemed. For, as St. Paul continues in his letter to the Romans, "we know that all things work together for good to them that love God" (8:28). Even in the works and words that seem to hide God's face, or to spit on it, we can see God revealed at the heart of our world and in our culture.

Literature as Bible

CHAPTER 10

Wagers (1): Pascal's *Pensées*

IT OUGHT TO BE AS EASY AND NATURAL TO SPEAK OF LITERATURE AS Bible as it is to speak of the Bible as literature. The two concepts are, after all, strictly parallel. But there is an awkwardness and unfamiliarity to "literature as Bible": the area of overlap, in which sacred and secular writing share similar genres and subject matter and poetic devices and are open, at least partially, to interpretation by each other's proper hermeneutic, is tilted so that normally traffic takes place only in one direction. A historical bias, which this investigation may perhaps help to explain, ensures that in that area of overlap the sacred is secularized more often than the secular is consecrated. There is an assumption that the secular, historically based hermeneutic of authorship normally has priority over the sacred, dogmatically based hermeneutic of revelation. In the third part of this study I try to restore the equilibrium. I will try to trace the boundary between sacred and secular in a number of nonbiblical works that belong in the area of overlap, and to show the boundary as the place not only of division but of forgiveness and reconciliation, the place where the sacred is not only marked off from the secular, but where the sacred reenters the secular and reclaims it.

I start therefore in the field of wisdom literature, the literature in which God, the origin of the preoriginal command, is present in his absence, is hidden, and has to be sought. Much of wisdom literature belongs under the general heading of poetry as, in modification of a usage of Ricoeur's, we have defined that term: the literary realm of fiction and metaphor, of lyric poetry, as in the Psalms, of fictional narrative, as in Tobit or Esther, of drama even, as in the Book of Job, which is surely as much a drama as Aeschylus's *The Persians*. But the realm of poetry, of fiction and metaphor, whether as song or story or drama, does not exhaust wisdom literature or its possibilities of overlap with secular writing. Somewhere between biblical poetry and biblical history there lies an area of wisdom literature of the greatest importance, in which fiction and metaphor play a role only episodically, and which is closely related to nonbiblical literature, both in its form and in its content. Indeed, we have seen that it contains some of the earliest and clearest examples of the intercourse between sacred and secular words in the Bible itself. It is the area of prose or verse teaching or preaching, either in extended form as a sermon or letter or meditation, or in the briefest form of all as a proverb, a wise saying of one or, perhaps more usually, two lines. This genre is characterized by its often explicit understanding of itself as the words of a teacher to a pupil or group of pupils. In the Old Testament it shares in the general characteristic of wisdom literature that it treats the world not as the place where God acts or speaks but as the place where he is absent or has to be sought. In the New Testament this characteristic is of course profoundly modified by the principle that Jesus Christ "is the image of the invisible God" (Col 1:15). Invisible, however, God remains even in the New Testament wisdom literature of sermons, letters, and apophthegmatic discourses, which are not only to be found in the books explicitly denominated letters. The longer and the shorter of these two forms of what might be called sapiential discourse originally had rather different statuses. The prose letter, genuine or fictitious, already had a clear literary standing in pagan antiquity, but the collection of aphorisms or sentences, *sententiae,* was little more than a teaching tool in medicine or philosophy, and remained so throughout the Christian Middle Ages. In the period of the Renaissance and Reformation, however, some typically modern changes to these ancient patterns occurred: the essay was invented and given a name by Montaigne in the sixteenth century as a consciously modern transformation of the models of Plutarch and Seneca, and as a perhaps unconsciously secular transformation of the sermon. Shortly afterwards, in what might be called the school of Montaigne in seventeenth-century France, the collection of short remarks became a fully literary genre. The maxims of La Rochefoucauld and, in eighteenth-century Germany, the fragments and aphorisms of Friedrich Schlegel and Lichtenberg belong to a genre which does not fulfill some pedagogical purpose as a teaching aid, whether in the sciences or in the art of courtly manners, but is a nonpurposive source of pleasure, just as the biblical collections of sayings are nonpurposive aids to reflection on the application of the Law to social and personal life.

This emergence of the essay and the aphorism as literary, that is, secular but noninformative, genres was accompanied by a shift away from a crucial structural feature of ancient wisdom writing, whether biblical or pagan, a shift which was caused, I believe, by the close relation between these new genres and the new medium of printing. The old genres present themselves as the words of a teacher passing on understanding and experience to disciples, an "I" speaks to a "you"—"All this have I seen," says the Prince Preacher of Ecclesiastes (8:9)—as the basis for his imperative. "Remember now thy Creator in the days of thy youth." The modern essay and the aphorism, however, present themselves as the words in which a solitary mind engages with its world but talks only to itself. At best its words make up a letter to the anonymous and unknown public created by the mass-produced book, but they do not need to emerge from monologue into addressing anyone at all, for the audience which hears or overhears them is silent and absent. The supremely purposeful practitioner of the new art of the monologue of a mind shut up in a room on its own, and simply overheard by the readership of a book, was Descartes: his *Philosophical Meditations* set out to ground a new system for understanding and changing the world, a new philosophy and a new applied science, on the solitary reflections of a man passing the winter in the snug behind a stove. Augustine and Anselm developed their understanding of God through a sustained address to him—even Luther, possibly the first of the modern solitaries, in his room in the Wartburg, conversed with the Devil, or at any rate threw his inkwell at him—but for Descartes God is not the inescapable partner in any conversation, even of the mind with itself: God is simply one possible thought among others that may help him towards his goal. Pascal, Descartes's younger rival in mathematics, and in much else, could not, he said, forgive Descartes for his instrumental attitude to the thought of God.[1] In his own writing Pascal sought to give expression to his sense of the overwhelming, and overwhelmingly paradoxical, fact of God. But utterly different though his sense of God may have been from Descartes's, Pascal did not abandon Descartes's presupposition about the context—perhaps we should call it the dramatic context—in which the modern search for God took place: a man in a room, alone with his thoughts.

Pascal's *Apology for the Christian Religion,* the uncompleted project of which the fragments have become known as his *Pensées,* was conceived from the beginning as a work of modern wisdom literature which would be a bridge between sacred and secular writing, sacred and secular worlds. It was to be the easy transition, without a violent leap (as Kant would say), from one to the other, which is why I have chosen it to begin the discussion of secular scripture. Even after his conversion Pascal moved in a circle of skeptics, who read Montaigne, admired at least some features of his idiosyncratic style, and found in his unapologetic self-cultivation a model for a life that thoughtfully confined itself to knowable pleasures, companionable but respectful of the autonomy of others. Pascal intended to undo this work of Montaigne's from within, to understand and express the appeal of Montaigne's model of life and, by calling only on its own resources and its own inner logic, to transform it into the similarly but far more powerfully appealing model of a life lived for Christ. He wanted to find a way of writing that would entice readers from Montaigne to Holy Scripture and would enable them then to read the Scriptures with understanding and with profit. Attracted by the pleasure of an account of the human condition that had the aptness, and perhaps even the vocabulary, of Montaigne they would read on with a growing sense of the seriousness of their own situation. From being disinterested readers of an account as eloquent and disillusioned as Ecclesiastes of the absence of God from the world, they would become readers as thirsty as the Psalmist for the knowledge of the hidden God, present in that absence. To transform Montaigne Pascal had first to imitate him, and the imitation was to begin as a literary imitation: Pascal recorded his intention of following the model of Montaigne's digressive manner, the only manner appropriate to the most difficult of subjects, a manner which he thought also exemplified in Holy Scripture (P 283) and completely opposed, of course, to the systematic exposition usual in contemporary philosophy and theology. Many of Pascal's longer notes read like concentrated essays, in the manner of the master, and were described as "essais" by the first readers of the *Pensées* on their posthumous publication in 1670.[2] After the Bible Montaigne's is the book most frequently cited in them. However, other genres from the wisdom tradition were also envisaged. One chapter at least of the completed work was to consist of apparently disordered aphorisms (P 373), so the form in which Pascal's notes finally became public was not perhaps wholly alien to his original intentions. Letters seem also to have been considered: there was to be a letter "to bring [the reader] to seek God" (P 184), and perhaps there was to be an exchange of letters between the author and an unbeliever. If that became unwieldy as argument grew more rapid, a dramatic form could be used: an "order in dialogues" is mentioned (P 227)—both letters and dialogues had recently been successfully used by Pascal in his satirical *Provinciales*—and there are clear traces of a dialogue structure in the most celebrated of all the *Pensées,* the fragment known as Pascal's "wager."

Pascal's wager (*P* 233) has acquired an almost lurid notoriety: as an ingenious but sophistical proof of the existence of God, a "dismal conceit"; as the culminating, even "terrifying" application of the powers of a mathematician of Newtonian rank to the problems of faith; as the inaugurating act of the modern mind, responding to the scientific revolution of the seventeenth century and the collapse of the medieval world picture with an existential leap in the dark.[3] In the period since 1945 the most influential reading of this obscure and—to be honest—ill-written text has probably been that of Lucien Goldmann in his great study, *The Hidden God.*[4] Not that Goldmann's appropriation of the wager in the interests of his own existentialist Marxism has worn particularly well. Goldmann saw Pascal as initiating a tradition of dialectical thought continued by Kant, Hegel, and Marx, and the wager on the existence of God as prefiguring what one might unkindly call a wager on the existence of the proletariat—a commitment of one's life to the future fulfillment of history, in accordance with Marx's program, of which, he seemed to be implying, there was no more empirical evidence than there was of Pascal's God. Such grand gestural thinking—Goldmann called it tragic, but perhaps it was really Byronic, Byron smoking a Gauloise—now seems more clearly trapped in its immediately postwar era than the contemporary thoughts of Lévinas or even Chenu. But in order to defend this catastrophist reading of the wager Goldmann had effectively to deny that this text had any part in the project for a Christian Apology that I have just outlined: the project of establishing a transition, a transition from secular reading to sacred reading, from a life in and for the world to a life in and for Christ. While I think we may be certain that it was no part of Pascal's conscious intention to exclude the wager from his project, I also think Goldmann may be right that the wager, by its own internal logic, excludes itself. That does not necessarily make Goldmann's interpretation of the place of this text in intellectual history any more appealing. But before we consider Goldmann's thesis any further we must look more closely at what the text is and says.

First, then, it is true that the two small pieces of paper, scribbled over horizontally and vertically and in every spare corner, that constitute what is called Pascal's wager do not seem to have been assigned a definite place in what remains of Pascal's scheme of argument. In that they are not unusual: more than half the surviving *Pensées,* including some of the best known, had not been finally classified at the time of his death. The fragments he did classify, however, make it certain that Pascal intended to give to the advances he had made in probability theory an important role in his exposition of the human condition in the first chapters of his Apology. In the fifteenth of twenty-seven chapters a hinge or turning point was to come, as is clear from its title: "Transition from the Knowledge of Man to the Knowledge of God."[5] There is, furthermore, a cluster of allusions or parallels to the wager text itself around the twelfth chapter, entitled "Commencement," as if it were to inaugurate a movement into a specifically Christian apologetic.[6] It is certainly possible that the wager was intended to have a place in a developing argument that was to lead its addressee away from a worldly and towards a Christian life, and it is possible, even likely, that chapters 12 to 15 of the *Apology* would have furnished that place.

The essential presupposition or starting point of the wager, however, is that no progress in such an argument has been made. God, if he exists, is infinitely incomprehensible, and it is absolutely impossible for reason to determine whether he exists or not—as impossible as it is for reason to determine whether the infinite number is odd or even. But though our reason cannot determine the matter, the matter may still very greatly concern our interest. There are many contexts in life—battles, commercial ventures, games of chance—in which reason cannot determine an outcome in advance but in which it is perfectly possible to make a rational calculation of the interest it is wise to take in the event, a calculation, that is, of the prudent extent of one's investment, or, as people were learning to say in the seventeenth century, of the risk. The question of the existence of God is like a game of chance, a coin being tossed at the other end of infinity: reason cannot determine whether the result will be (or, since it is infinitely distant, even whether it is) heads or tails, but reason can perfectly well determine what risks are involved in the game. At this point Pascal pounces on his interlocutor: "What will you wager?" he asks, knowing the popularity of gambling in the worldly circles from which the reader of Montaigne is likely to come. Men venture money, time, and life on much less significant matters than this, and the new mathematics of probability can define the extent to which they are right to do so. So how about a bet on the existence of God? The interlocutor shrinks from the challenge: oh no, in so important, or possibly so uncertain, a matter it would be better not to take sides, better to suspend judgment altogether, as Montaigne so often does. But Pascal cuts off this retreat: in this matter, in the choice for or against God, it is not possible to suspend judgment; to do nothing—so I interpret what he now says—is already to have decided against. "You have to bet," he says, "you are not at liberty"—"Il faut parier; cela n'est pas volontaire"—"you are already embarked"—"vous êtes embarqué." The image of embarkation is extremely powerful but not entirely clear. I think Pascal has in mind—as would be natural for a seventeenth-century Frenchman from inland Clermont-Ferrand—a riverboat, for, as he says in another detached remark, "Rivers are moving roads that take you where you want to go."[7] The image implies a current as well as a boat: life is already under way, and even if we do nothing to alter our course we shall still arrive at one destination or another. Once it is established that a wager is anyway unavoidable Pascal's duel with his opponent is soon over. Only two more assumptions are required: first, if God exists he offers an infinite reward to some at least of his followers, and, second, if he does not exist no more is lost than if he does, namely, the life of transient and insubstantial pleasures which has to be given up one way or another, either on death, for the unbeliever, or on conversion, for the Christian. The conclusion then is immediate: "If you win you win everything; if you lose you lose nothing. Then wager that [God] exists, without hesitation."

These two lines are Pascal's wager. There is much else in the fragment, but this is the kernel of the mathematical argument which the rest of the text elaborates but does not advance. The elaboration, however, reveals the sense in which Goldmann may not after all be wrong to question whether the argument can be part of the Apology that Pascal certainly envisaged and in which he may have wanted the wager to play a crucial role. It reveals, in other words—and this is why we need to pursue it now—that the continuity of secular and sacred scripture which Pascal hoped to show is interrupted and rendered ineffective by a crucial feature of modern secularity.

The elaboration is of course intended to do the opposite—to render the argument entirely compelling through being put in an even more rigorous mathematical form. It consists of the reply to two possible objections to Pascal's conclusion that we must wager—that is, act, at a certain cost, on the assumption—that God exists. These then lead, not entirely clearly, into two important provisos. The first possible objection is that the cost, the stake required, is too high. The second is that the improbability of God's existence is too great. In reply to both objections Pascal shows that even in the most unfavorable case the wager on God would still be reasonable, that in any case which is even minimally *more* favorable it would be imprudent not to wager for God and that in the real case, in our actual circumstances, it is infinitely more reasonable to back God than not to. Even if the stake required were the highest that a finite being can put down and even if there were only one chance in an infinity of chances that God exists, it would still at least be reasonable to wager for God. But that is not in fact our situation. Two crucial provisos have to be made. First, Pascal's interlocutor asks, is it possible to see "le dessous du jeu"—the cards that are in the dealer's hands—is it possible to get a hint of the future course of the game on whose likely outcome we are wagering now? Yes, says Pascal in reply, there is Holy Scripture "and the rest," meaning no doubt the evidence of sacred history, the miraculous preservation of the Jews and of the church and so on. Moreover, there is the example of those who have gone before you and whom you can see farther down the road ahead, those who have staked all their worldly goods on the rightness of this path and are training themselves in the discipline it imposes. So the second crucial proviso is that those who wager for God can expect their circumstances to change, and with that change the calculation of probabilities that we and they have called a wager will change too. As they discover that the way of life of the believer has benefits which were previously invisible to them, so "with each step that you take along this way you will see such certainty of winning and such nothingness in what you are risking that in the end you will recognize that you have wagered for something certain and infinite for which you have given nothing." The wager in fact will have ceased to exist: it will have been transformed into infinite grace abounding.

Now this conclusion, it seems to me, disproves Goldmann's view that the life of Pascal's believing Christian, like the life of the believing Stalinist, is a continuing wager on an unprovable assertion. To the one caught up in the business of decision the believers farther down the road ahead may still appear, in Pascal's phrase, to be "wagering all their goods" on the rightness of what they are doing, but to their own eyes their situation appears quite differently. For them, and indeed for anyone, staking nothing on a certain outcome is no wager. For them the wager has been a kind of Wittgenstein's ladder into faith, which they have drawn up after them and dispensed with and which has now lost its relevance. And for that reason something in Goldmann's view seems to be correct, after all. The wager has no part in the process of growth in faith: it neither belongs to nor includes a progressive conversion, a gradual transition, without violent leaps, from a secular to a sacred life. Yet that is how Pascal's Apology was to be constructed, along lines laid down six years or more before he started making notes for it, in his famous "Conversation with M. de Sacy on Reading Epictetus and Montaigne."[8] Reading human life in Montaigne's terms was to lead gradually into reading it in terms of Holy Scripture. But Holy Scripture is almost dismissively excluded from the text of the wager: as "l'Écriture et le reste" it is no more than the first term in a long etcetera. Scripture has no part in the game played strictly according to the rules: to read it is to sneak a glimpse at "le dessous du jeu"; it is to cheat. The wager, then, is an account of the fundamental relations between the soul and God in which Scripture has no legitimate part. As if this were not strange enough, Pascal also stresses the difficulty of the transition from the wager to leading the Christian life that will cause the need for the wager to disappear. To bet on God is not to believe in him, it is merely to want to believe in him. Belief will come only with an act of violence of the self against itself forcing itself to do as it wishes, training body and mind in ways of thinking and living that will eliminate that equivalence, that equal plausibility, of belief and disbelief, which made the wager possible and necessary in the first place.

But if only violence will release us from the wager into the gradual growth into certainty that is the Christian life guided by Scripture, it is only by violence that the wager was first imposed on us. "I am forced to wager," laments Pascal's interlocutor, and it is essential to the mathematical argument that nonparticipation is not an option, that we are not at liberty but are already embarked. We might well ask, what is the force that has pressed us aboard? but in Pascal's account it remains anonymous. Once embarked, however, we find we have been given a new and equally unexplained liberty: a complete freedom of choice between two absolutely equal alternatives. Our reason faces the dilemma, does God exist or not? uninformed by any prior knowledge. The Scriptures play no part even in formulating the terms of the question. This seems implausible—how can we ask whether God exists unless we have learned his name from somewhere?—but it is essential to the scenario that Pascal constructs for the wager that the Scriptures are excluded from it, just as they were not invoked to explain what forced us aboard or what was the source of the current that sweeps us along. The apparent liberty of the choice Pascal offers between betting on heads and betting on tails in the great game being played at the other end of infinity is an artificial and illusory liberty compared with the true and original compulsion to which we are all subject and about which he remains silent. The liberty—or rather the appearance of liberty—is achieved by the exclusion from the rules of the game of the compulsion that really matters: the original command to responsibility for the neighbor. If that command, which runs through the books of the Law from the beginning of the Old Testament to the end of the New, were included in Pascal's schematic representation of the decision about God, then it might not seem in the least plausible to say that life is like staking all your money on one of two equally possible alternatives.

There is no possible alternative to the Law, to the command without origin, to the source from which all currents flow. If that is the absolutely fundamental fact about life and Being to which the name of God refers, then the question, does God exist? is an evasive trivialization.

Neither the liberty of our choice nor the arbitrariness of our condition is as great as the wager pretends they are. The rest of Pascal's Apology, insofar as it can be reconstructed from his notes, appears throughout to have been intended to make full use of the Scriptures in its description and diagnosis of our state. Job and Ecclesiastes would have been the principal sacred sources, alongside Pascal's reinterpreted Montaigne, in the account of human misery; the Gospels, the prophecies, and a figurative interpretation of the Old Testament would have contributed the counterimage of the felicity Christianity has made accessible. But the wager is sealed off from this progressive argument: both at the entry to Pascal's gaming house and at the exit from it there stands the violent assertion that the moral and historical experience embodied in writings, whether sacred or secular, is irrelevant to what goes on inside. It is not perhaps surprising that Pascal could not finally decide where to locate this fragment. There is a profound tension, even incompatibility, between it and the gradual argument in the rest of the Apology for an eventually overwhelming consonance of the witnesses of experience and secular and sacred writers and for the appropriateness of the Christian scheme. The Apology and the wager emerge from and represent two different worlds. The Apology is continuous with the long tradition of Christian and indeed Jewish exegesis and apologetic—the later sections were to make extensive use of Talmudic material—and the satirical humanism of its theological interrogation of the secular life owes almost as much to Augustine as it does to Montaigne. The wager presents us with a tabula rasa, and in the ruthlessness with which it sweeps all historical encumbrances aside we can recognize the radicalism of Descartes. Out of this void modernity is born, and, for our purposes at least, the wager is a deeper and more revealing account of this birth than Descartes's *Discourse on Method*. Out of the void emerge three distinctive elements of the modern way of being: a modern form of the question about God; a modern form of the concept of reason; and the modern form of being as, par excellence, wagering. The first two points belong closely together. The question of God is simplified by the wager into a question put to a single mind, to be decided one way or the other, and it is made into a question of existence: does God exist or not? The single mind is itself simplified into two faculties: "vous avez . . . deux choses à engager," you have two things to stake—says Pascal—"votre raison et votre volonté," your reason and your will. This reason has the function, in the argument of the wager, of recognizing that it cannot determine the question of God's existence one way or the other, and it is thoroughly Cartesian. That is, it is a faculty for mathematical thought which takes no account of potentially unclear or unreliable empirical data; in particular, it is capable of doing without the Scriptures, without, that is, the benefit of previous human experience of God committed to writing. This rather implausible account of human thinking ignores, for example, that much human thinking is done by directly engaging with language and that language is a collective cultural and historical artifact which no mind can invent for itself. The revolution—the cultural revolution—which has given this implausible account of thinking currency cannot of course be attributed solely to Descartes; that would be too Cartesian an approach to cultural history. It is part of a general revolution in human self-understanding which separated Europeans of the sixteenth to the twentieth century from their ancient inheritance and, for example, both substituted the question, Does God exist? for the traditional questions, what is God? or, older still, who is God? and substituted for the notion of tradition the notion of "reason" (or for that matter, "scripture") "alone." "Reason" in Pascal's wager is a characteristically modern concept. What the character of modernity is, is revealed by the third feature of the vocabulary of the fragment.

As a result of the continuing process of simplification, and of a conceptual slide which I will not go into here, the final form in which Pascal forces his interlocutor to confront that peculiar modern dilemma, does God exist or not? is this: "God is, or he is not. . . . What will you wager? . . . [Y]ou have . . . two things to stake: your reason . . . and your felicity." The question of God, we note, is not an interrogation of the being of the questioner: it is not a question about him or her at all but a game played at an infinite distance; there is no hint here of Augustine's God who is closer to me than I am to myself. Being—or at any rate existing—is a matter for God; what concerns this questioning and wagering mind is having. "You have two things." At the bottom line, as accountants say, when our life is reduced to its simplest, purest, most original terms, when we try to envisage ourselves with the utmost clarity, earnestness, and honesty, we find—in this modern version of the question of God—not what we are, which remains unstated, presumably forever, but what we have. Living, in its purest, most fundamental sense, is said to be not being and doing but having and risking—wagering, putting at risk what we have. So pure, so fundamental is this sense, in fact, that the wagering is utterly unavoidable. As surely as we are alive we must wager, we are not at liberty, we are already embarked. As surely as we are alive we put at risk what we have—or, as the accountants say, we invest. The seemingly, even provocatively, frivolous vocabulary of gaming conceals that Pascal's fragment puts the issues of God, and so of being, of what is and who we are, in the terms which in the modern age—that is, since, probably, the twelfth and at the latest since the beginning of the sixteenth century—are the most serious at our disposal, the terms of capital, risk, and return. Nothing gives confidence like capital, like the certainty of having what the suppliant have-nots are intent on borrowing. The extraordinary confidence with which Descartes sweeps aside all the usual petitioners, clamoring for him to invest belief in them, is the confidence of a new age with a new relation to God, to the world, to being, to itself—the age of capital.

Capital is forgetting: it is the power of forgetting where it comes from, namely, the work of others. It becomes capital by becoming what "I" "have" and forgetting that it is the separation, the alienation, of others from what they have worked to produce. Descartes does not ask where he comes from, where the confidence comes from that enables *him* to doubt everything. Pascal's risk-taker—perhaps we should call him Pascal's venture capitalist—does not ask, and is not asked, where the two things he has, his knowledge and his felicity, come from: he forgets that the whole human race has labored to produce and make available to him—in language, for example—the ways of knowing and enjoying that he thinks are his possession. Indeed, he thinks they are him, that the possibilities of knowledge and enjoyment that others have made are aspects of his potential, are his faculties, his reason and his will. He is what he has—but capital does not exist unless it is invested, and so what he has he must risk. He has to wager on something. The "I" that wagers has no past; it will not look back and see itself as the product of others' labor, it even forgets the origin of its concept of God in the Scriptures. Instead this "I" has a future, indeed it has only a future, for what it has it must risk in order to possess it and only because it possesses things is it an "I." Pascal aims to take to the extreme this venture-capitalist logic of his interlocutor, the logic which leads from capital to risk to the return of yet more capital and so on. He aims to make this logic subvert itself in the interests of the older conception of the "I" and the world, the conception that the modern self has had to forget in order to come into being, the conception that takes its origin from God. Take the supreme risk, he says, give up all your capital—that is, give up all your power of risk-taking—for the sake of the supreme, the infinite return. In this way Pascal hopes to transform the Cartesian confidence back into the old faith that it has, more or less politely, to dismiss or subvert. Pascal hopes to turn having back into being, to leap over the infinite distance that separates the capitalist from God, and to set him on the road of gradual progress or regress, of gradual revelation of the sacred in the secular, the road on which the drama of having and risking can fade back into the nonentity from which it came, on which forgetting can be forgotten (negation can be negated) in the different confidence, the confidence in otherwiseness, that is faith in God's forgiving grace.

That, I believe, is Pascal's intention. But the logic of capital is stronger even than Pascal's dialectic. Even an infinite return is still a return, and even the possession of God is still possession—having, not being. To be precise, it is having God, not hearing him. Because in the wager fragment Pascal's Cartesian interlocutor merely presupposes his own being as one who *has*— even only as one who has thoughts—because he does not first of all interrogate his own *being,* he does not address the question of God from the one place from which it is obvious that it also puts the self in question: from the command to responsibility which is so primary that it precedes even the constitution of the self. The wager therefore cannot deliver the one who wagers into the hands of the living God, the God who issues that word of primal command, or into the company of those who hear the word of God and keep it. That is not so much a weakness of the wager as a measure of the honesty and rigor with which Pascal has represented the operation and the limits of his argument. Pascal envisages the condition from which the wager is intended to release his interlocutor as—probably—a dungeon, a *cachot,*[9] in which a condemned man is awaiting death in, perhaps, an hour. Yet even when the interlocutor's will has been turned towards God by the operation of the wager he remains imprisoned and unable to take even the first step along the road of salvation: "My hands are tied and my mouth is dumb," he says. "[W]hat do you expect me to do?" The answer that is given to that question—"Hear God" (*P* 434); that is, perform the least of his commandments: use holy water, have masses said for you—is an answer that could have been given at any earlier stage in the story, for it presupposes the interlocutor's recognition that I am not one who has, risks, receives, and reinvests, I am one who hears the original commandment. And how is *that* recognition to be achieved? As we have seen, the only exit from Pascal's dungeon-casino is by violence. And Pascal has represented that truth, deliberately or involuntarily, by the isolation of the wager fragment from the rest of his Apology. The *Pensées*—the collection of aphorisms that the intended

Apology deliberately or involuntarily became—reflect, truthfully and rigorously, the conflict between the new Cartesian venture-capitalist self and the traditions of those who have heard the original commandment, and they reflect also his failure to resolve that conflict.

The *Pensées*—a work of wisdom literature that cites the Bible, imitates and explicates it, that stands therefore on the margin between sacred and secular writing, and that makes the transition from secular to sacred reading its central project—draw the boundary line marking off the secular from the sacred that is characteristic of the modern Western sense of what it is to be human, and the wager shows that to be human, in the characteristically modern sense, is to have capital and to risk it for future gain. It is to what defines the secularity of a text that we must look if we are to see where it utters the need for the forgiveness of God and so functions as the limit case of written revelation—the frontier between the revelation of being and the revelation of what ought to be, of the Law. Pascal's *Pensées,* deliberately poised on the boundary between secular and sacred scripture, are therefore exemplary. The boundary runs right through the work as the line, transgressable only by violence, which separates the wager from the rest of the Apology. The modern secular self will not be integrated into the medieval sacred pattern, and the *Pensées* trace out the contours of that refusal.

The leap from the self that has its capital to the self that hears the command even before it is constituted as a self is too great. Perhaps because of his Jansenism, his Reformation-influenced theology of grace, Pascal cannot imagine that transition except as a complete self-surrender, the disappearance of the wagering self altogether and of the calculations on which its decisions were based. Alternatively (though this may be the same thing) the transition would have to happen as the operation of an irresistible prevenient grace coming from a source entirely external to the self. Secularity seems impermeable to redemption: even the wager, the self-subversion of the logic of capital, can only make the interlocutor will to believe, it cannot make him believe. Shut in the dungeon of selfhood, bound and gagged, he seems doomed to spend his little store of time meditating the game of being and nonbeing played by an unknowable player at an infinite distance, like a Descartes forever unable to emerge from his snug. Somewhere out there is human community, the fellowship of the road, companions who once were bound as he is and now jointly wager all their goods, treating them, apparently, as not worth a bean. How he longs for their freedom, and the sunlight! The Christian society, the church, is strikingly imagined by Pascal in the later section of the Apology as a body with "thinking limbs," "membres pensants" (*P* 473–75). It is, in other words, a society built up by the very power that isolates his Cartesian venture capitalist, that imprisons him in selfhood, the power of thought. But the transition from the thought that isolates to the thought that establishes community seems to the man in the dungeon as impossible as the transition from self to society, the step out of the dungeon into the open air of belief. This impasse, however, is not a terminus. The boundary which defines secularity has a far side, and the *Pensées* include a literary principle which oversteps it and stands on both sides, a principle which does not have to reduce one domain to nonentity in order that the other may exist. It is a principle which mediates between the wager and the Apology, between the one in the dungeon and the many on the road, between having and living, and which therefore enables the text to function as the literary symbol of the moral event of forgiveness, as a word of reconciliation. I mean the figure of the author, of Pascal himself.

Pascal becomes a distinct actor in the drama of his Apology in various ways—some scarcely visible at first glance, others more explicit—and most evidently when the different currents in his dialectic separate out into dialogue. Thanks to the incomplete and fragmentary state of the text some of his most powerful and deliberately sublime evocations of human solitude float in an indeterminate context, implying often at least the potential for dialogue and drifting towards that urgent discussion on the existence of God in which Pascal will attempt in his own person to bridge the gulf between the solitude of uncertainty and the community of faith. Before I consider that culminating case, let me give three examples from elsewhere in the *Pensées,* of increasing degrees of explicitness.

The first example is one of Pascal's most famous lines, an evocation of the modern scientific vision of things created by Galilean astronomy: "The eternal silence of these infinite spaces terrifies me" (*P* 206). The disproportion between the single person who speaks and the silence infinite in space and time that surrounds him or her is surely an echo[10] of the wager fragment, in which the disproportion between infinity and nothing has more than merely mathematical consequences. But in its arrested state, as a detached aphorism, the remark leaves it indeterminate who is speaking, Pascal or his interlocutor: it is both the remark of a solitary who has to face the necessity of the wager and the citation of such a remark by one who belongs already to a communion of believers and has that moment of decision behind him. The transition from one possibility to the other is the movement of grace, the work of redemption and reconciliation of which the indeterminacy of the text is here a symbol.

Second example. The isolation of human beings one from another is the hidden theme in one of Pascal's dungeon scenes (*P* 199), which at first sight seems to be describing a collective fate: humanity is like a group of men in a condemned cell, some of whom are every day selected for execution in full view of the others; they read their condition in each other's eyes, but they do not speak a word of it. The absence of words in this little tableau is perhaps its most terrifying feature, and what makes it an image not so much of a shared destiny as of individual isolation in the face of death. But we also sense that we are not alone. We sense the presence of the author, the man who is terrifying us, and for his own purpose, the man who springs on us such rhetorical traps as the final sentence of his fable: "This is the human condition." But Pascal is not present in this aphorism simply as the implied puppet master, the manipulator who, having lured us into a dilemma, will reveal his own, only possible, solution. He is also present as one who shares in the terror that he has created, who is one of the men whose condition is described. For the silence of the prisoners about the horror they are seeing is never put into words. The writer of the aphorism tells us only of the prisoners' glances. He passes in silence over their silence—and thereby he shares in it. He too is one of the grim figures in whose eyes, not words, we read the atrocity of life. So our situation as readers is both solitary and shared, and Pascal as writer is playing a double role: he is with us, inside the dungeon, and he is outside it, overstepping the boundaries of our desperately constricted condition, endeavoring to compel us to see ourselves in the broader context of his apologetic project, as potentially liberated by faith. That dual role for the figure of the author is the enduring trace of the need for the transition from a secular to a sacred perspective—a need which this secular text cannot satisfy but of which it can be a symbol.

Third example. Often in the *Pensées* Pascal's role as author is made explicit by his use of the first-person singular, and the presence of a partner, as reader or interlocutor, is thereby implied whose viewpoint both is and is not identical with Pascal's own. In this role Pascal, as an observer of the bizarreries of human conduct like Montaigne or even Augustine, can speak in the third person of those caught in the absurd logic of having and risking capital—a having that requires one to give up what one has and risk it in a chase after more of the same. At first sight, he says (*P* 139), it seems as if all their misery comes from not knowing how to sit alone in a room. If they could but do that, they would be spared the fears, uncertainties, and disappointments of the absurdly risky chase. But then, he says, he discovered that after all their behavior was perfectly reasonable. Had they stayed alone in a room—alone, that is, with what they have—their solitary state would have furnished them with quite as many fears and miseries as they experience by venturing into the busy world: fears of loss and the miseries of unfulfillment. So it is after all true in a second sense that all their miseries come from not knowing how to sit alone in a room. Not only do they flee solitude and try to lose themselves in distraction. If they recollect themselves and return to solitude it becomes apparent that their vaunted self is anyway of the wrong kind, in fact it is a nonentity. In the terms derived from Lévinas that I have been using, because it is not constituted in response to a preoriginal obligation, a call from God, it is a hollow fraud. In Pascal's terms they are not Christians. But how to make them Christians? They are so trapped in the secular cycle of distraction and illusory self-possession that they are impervious to persuasion. Only with those who are willing to listen, only with those whom Pascal can address in the second person, is it possible to begin the dialogue which will lead them right up to the frontier of the sacred realm where their self can be refounded on the response to the divine command. The others must remain in the third person as examples of God's plan in distributing light and darkness unequally across the world, as occasions of humility should they anyway be converted independently of any efforts in the Apology, and, if all else fails, as objects of vituperation. The other party, the second person, explicit or implied, for whose sake the third persons are identified as examples, or are made the object of some of Pascal's cruellest rhetoric, is by definition the one who, though not sharing Pascal's viewpoint at the moment, is invited to do so by the operation of the Apology. The task of refounding the self of modern secular human beings is thus symbolized in the text by the task of transforming third-person specimens of fallen humanity into second-person partners in a developing dialogue: the transformation can be performed only by a power external to the text, but the figure of Pascal the author, facing like Janus in both directions, is there in the text to vouch for its possibility. *His* words—the words identified in various ways as belonging to this figure—utter in the text the possibility of reconciliation. In this text Pascal himself embodies the offer of redemption.

The dialogue which is the central episode in the wager fragment is the supreme example both of the attempt to lever the secular self out of its Cartesian self-sufficiency by its own resources and—after the necessary failure of that attempt—of a mediating role for the figure of the author. It symbolizes precisely the mode in which, I believe, secular and sacred writing can be reconciled—the mode of prayer. I need hardly say that this is not the view of Lucien Goldmann. Goldmann thinks that Pascal makes his wager with himself. This is surely wrong, but Goldmann is not wrong to stress the degree of Pascal's self-identification with the wagerer. He overlooks, however, the double nature of Pascal's role. Pascal speaks, first, as one who can make the gambler's calculations better than the gambler himself. "Voyons," he says, "Let us see," as he settles down with his interlocutor to work out the odds. The first-person plural—what I like to call the preacher's "we"—is not uncommon in the *Pensées,* but here it is virtually a dual rather than a plural, and as that it is possibly unique. Even if it is only the "voyons" of the mathematician talking to himself, it shows that Pascal has made the gambler's concerns his own. At the same time, however, Pascal speaks, second, as one who already belongs to the cheerful company of those on the road for whom the wager has shrunk into insignificance. As we have seen, the transition from being a gambler to being a member of that company cannot be made by taking a gamble: the transition from a self that has capital to a self that is the response to an obligation is not a new kind of investment. Pascal acknowledges that he has met a limit, a boundary which the language and reason of Descartes cannot traverse, or at any rate a radical discontinuity within them, when he recommends to his bound and gagged inquirer after truth to abandon reason, pride, and even language and submit to the mechanical externals of religion. This will be, he says, the first step towards building a faith that is based in the body (*naturellement*) as much as in the mind. But if the inquirer is bound and gagged, how is he even going to take holy water of his own volition? And how was Pascal able to converse with him? Even if Pascal was only a voice whispering in the inquirer's head their conversation was as much a miracle as any conversion would be. And it is as a miracle that Pascal, on reflection, decides to present it—as a divine intervention in answer to prayer. In a later and separate note which the editors have, no doubt rightly, treated as a conclusion to the wager discourse, Pascal tells the inquirer that if he has seen any force in the argument—and, a fortiori, if he has seen its infinite force—that effect is not due to the discourse itself, nor to him its lowly originator. Before and after composing it— surrendering, therefore, both the intentions and the consequences of what he said into the hands of God—he went on his knees to pray to God for a conversion in the interlocutor similar to that which God had already effectuated in himself. We see that everything depends on an "if": that "if" expresses the limit on Pascal's apologetic purpose in writing the wager, the rift between modern selfhood and God that only God can heal. However much

Pascal has exerted himself and his intellect, however compelling the argument may seem to be, it is effective only if God's grace makes it so. Even the existence of a dialogue between him and his interlocutor, even the possibility that an argument might be brought to bear on the self which "has," even the possibility that it should hear a voice in its head whispering to it of infinite possibilities, is a miracle of God's mercy. The surrender by this text of any claim to its own moral efficacy—any claim to be able of itself to change its recipient's life—its recognition that it has reached its limit, is represented within it by the image of Pascal on his knees at prayer. Pascal praying is here the point of mediation, of transition between sacred and secular, of the impossible union between God and Man.

I am not concerned here with the specific ramifications in Pascal's text of this idiosyncratic and not entirely wholesome self-stylization of its author. The *Pensées* are a limit case of secular literature, and on the limits, as Lichtenberg remarks, we always find the oddest creatures.[11] The *Pensées* are the extreme case of a work of secular writing that attempts to have a moral effect, to relate its reader to the origin of ethical obligation and, by showing the world as mattering, to make the reader live life as something that matters infinitely. But achieving a moral effect, causing moral change, is beyond the capacity of *any* text that is not sacred, that is not ultimately, in however derived a way, an articulation of the original "Thou shalt." All that a nonsacred text can do is utter—directly or indirectly—the desire for a moral effect, the fulfillment of the desire being left to a power absolutely beyond the text. The utterance of such a desire is a prayer, and insofar as a prayer implies a pray-er, one who prays, the desire for moral effect uttered in a work implies an author of the work who has that desire for it and makes that prayer to the power absolutely beyond the text. Unlike sacred texts, which are written by the Spirit, secular texts are written by authors. The failure to make this distinction was the principal error of the Herder and Schleiermacher school, which set out to read the Bible as poetry when it should have been trying to read the Bible as Law and poetry as prayer. Equally, it was Ricoeur's weakness that he failed to recognize that the lost Atlantis of Being revealed beyond the text by its writtenness is always aboriginally modified by an ethical command and that the beautiful aspires to symbolize the good. In a Catholic reading of a secular work, the work's commitment to symbolizing the good and the author's humility in admitting the ultimate impossibility that the work should do good—in admitting that there is a limit marking off secular from sacred literature—are recognized as together constituting a prayer.

From a Catholic point of view a book that is not a sacred book is not simply a written text, but a gesture and vehicle of hope launched by a human being, its author, on to a boundless and unpredictable world of interpretation and response. The hope, the prayer, it contains is that the good it symbolizes may be effective, may be done—that the revelation it contains may make the world a better place. Literature is not just texts, but read texts, and the nature of the texts changes with the nature and the situation of the reader. The hope a book contains—its author's prayer—is most completely fulfilled if the book becomes part of lives already in-formed—given form and substance—by the sacred books, the books of the Law. Through being read by the company of those seeking the Kingdom, the forgiven forgivers, the book finds the wound of its own secularity being healed. The limits that mark it off as secular, that cut it off from the possibility of passing on the divine command as the sacred books do, are transcended as it is reclaimed for the Kingdom by those readers to whom the word of reconciliation has been entrusted—that is, as St. Paul says, by us. That reclamation is achieved, if it is achieved, not in our reading and interpretation, though it begins there, but in our lives, for it is only there, not in any book at all, that the Word can become flesh, that the sacred word of command and forgiveness can be enacted in secular, bodily doings and sayings, thinkings and feelings. If a book becomes part of our habitual reflection in attempting to discern the path of justice, if its images and enactments of need and fulfillment, of tact and competence and love, contribute to in-forming our understanding of what we are praying for, then its own intrinsic prayer to be effective has been answered. By forming us, who have heard the call of sacred scripture, and whose flesh has both historically and through the sacraments become the receptacle of the Divine Word, it has, after all, joined its action to that of the original "Thou shalt."

In our lives, that is, in a way which collectively and individually we decide for ourselves in the light of the Law[12] and of our own situation, secular literature ceases to be a mere symbol of the good, acquires and fulfills a moral purpose, and thereby surrenders its secularity. In the particular historical situation in which we find ourselves the secularity of the texts we read is largely determined by their making written for us the concept of a self that has, and has forgotten the origin of what it has, rather than of a self that is formed in response to a command that it hears. Pascal's *Pensées* illuminate with merciless explicitness the limits of that secularity when, in the wager fragment, they show us the self of the interlocutor as incapable, in the moment when it most clearly understands the logic of its own selfhood, of being in-formed by a previous, or indeed a subsequent, hearing of the Word spoken in sacred scripture—at the very best the Scriptures are an after-thought, a cheat. But by reading the text in such a way that we recognize the limits on this secular self and know what it has forgotten, we have al-ready begun to transcend those limits. For us the *Pensées* are a prayer that the self-understanding of the modern intellect, shown to us here by and in one of its supreme examples, may issue in a forgetting of the forgetting which is its basis, so that it may dissolve into a new self living on every word that comes from the mouth of God. To the extent that that is the life we lead and that the *Pensées* accompany us on our way, as they have already accom-panied believers for three and a half centuries, Pascal's prayer will have been heard. The self for whose dissolution Pascal prays came into existence, I have suggested, in the twelfth century or thereabouts, and I have argued elsewhere that we may now be at a turn of the times in which it is already beginning to pass away.[13] Whether it will be replaced by the alternative en-visaged by Pascal, and by the New Testament, is, to say the least, doubtful. But the loosening of its hold perhaps makes it easier for us than it was for an earlier generation to transcend the limits within which secular literature used to be firmly confined and to see its relation to its forgotten theological context. In what follows I take some more or less exemplary cases of secular literature from the period since Herder and Schleiermacher which can, I be-lieve, be read as prayer. These texts aim to show the world as mattering, while they acknowledge that their secularity limits the extent to which they can impose an explicit ethical obligation and do the good that they sym-bolize. Their implicit desire to transcend those limits is answered when they are brought into a relation with sacred Scripture through being taken up into lives which sacred Scripture has formed. But in themselves—imagined as unread—they remain, permanently, prayer: gestures of hope and suppli-cation for the reconciliation that alone they cannot effectuate. To that pos-ture of prayer—Pascal explicitly says he has gone down on his knees—it is essential that the work, in some way or other, identifies itself as made by an author, a historically limited and interpretable figure (who of course may coincide closely or only distantly with the figure that, on other evidence, we know, or think we know, to have written the book).

I now move on, though, to a case that might seem counterexemplary, a text that could seem programmatically determined to take back and undo the work of the *Pensées*. Goldmann calls Goethe's *Faust* the most important of all the works of literature that express the dialectical vision that he attributes to Pascal. By contrast, however, with the many pages he devotes to Kant—whom he most implausibly endeavors to characterize as a tragic thinker—he gives only half a page to *Faust*.[14] In one sense this is not surprising for his interpretation of *Faust* is based on that of Lukács, which is too coarsely ideological to withstand any close confrontation with the text. But it is certainly odd given that Kant makes only one rather parenthetical allusion to the role of wagers in matters of belief, while a wager is central to the structure of both parts of Goethe's great dramatic poem. We must look into this more closely.

CHAPTER 11

Wagers (2): Goethe's *Faust*

GOETHE'S VERSION OF THE GREAT MYTH, THE PERHAPS UNIQUELY modern myth of Faust—the man who sells his soul to the Devil in exchange for unnatural powers—differs profoundly from all its predecessors, from the printed chapbooks that circulated in Germany in the last two decades of the sixteenth century, from the work of dramatic genius that Christopher Marlowe made out of them around 1590, and from the many popular versions and adaptations of Marlowe's play that continued to entertain the European, especially the German, public long after their source had been forgotten. The story of Dr. Faustus is not just one of the very few genuinely modern myths (by which I mean universal symbols whose origins nevertheless lie clearly in the last half millennium), it is also—and this no doubt is why it originated when it did—a myth of modernity. It is the story of a man who deliberately cuts himself off from his past, from what he has been taught. Faust rejects the learning that gives him his title "Doctor," he rejects the tradition, in favor of the promise of something new. Well before Descartes, Marlowe diagnoses and dramatizes the starting point of self-conscious modernity: a man alone in his study, sifting his books. Faustus turns from the old book of the Scriptures that the Good Angell urges him to read to the "damned booke" that will enable him to "search all corners of the new-found-world For . . . Princely delicates" and make his "servile spirits" invent "stranger engines" than any yet seen.[1] And the supreme symbol of the power brought him by the magic books that one day he will wish he had burned is wealth. Wealth, in the great sixteenth-century inflation, seems to be expanding as rapidly as Europe's physical and mental reach, in a system of trade and exploitation that generates ever more capital:

> From *Venice* shall they [the spirits that will serve Faustus] drag huge
>   *Argosies,*
> And from *America* the Golden Fleece,
> That yearely stuffs old *Phillips* treasury (*MF* I, i, 130–32)

For that promise of emphatically material possession—weighing down the imagination by the shipload, bloating it to the point of constipation—Faustus exchanges what he has, his soul. His soul is not what he is but what he has, and why should he not buy with what he has?—"[I]s not thy soule thine owne?" (*MF* II, i, 67) he asks when an angelic sign seems to be warning him to stop. By an elaborate "deed of gift," as it is more than once called, which he signs, seals, and delivers and which lays down his expectations in "Covenants and articles," he makes his contract of sale with the Devil. For twenty-four years Mephostophilis will bring him what he wants, and thereafter he belongs to the Devil, body and soul, forever.

But the appealing ambiguity of Marlowe's play is that it remains poised on the threshold of modernity. The Bad Angell promises Faustus not only "wealth" but also "honor" (*MF* II, i, 21), and "honor" is not a modern but a feudal category. It is in the terms of a feudal code of what is high and what is low that Marlowe's hero expresses his disgust for the learning that he discards—Philosophy, Law, Physicke and Divinitie are "obscure[,] . . . petty[,] . . . base [,] . . . contemptible"—and we hear in his lines the aristocratic grandiloquence of Tamburlaine. Yet the deed which follows on these fine words could not be more pettifogging or less feudal. This deed is a document, not an achievement, a purely commercial transaction in pedantically precise legal form. In the pursuit of wealth Faustus shrugs off the consciousness of sin which St. Paul sees as a necessary consequence of the Law, but he still wants "honor," the nobility of an identity determined not by what it has but by what it is and does. Faustus has entered the modern world, but he still speaks the language of the world it has displaced. And that residual adherence to the feudal and Christian past leads to the paradoxes at the heart of the play: Faustus believes in the Christ that he rejects; God is acknowledged as all-powerful but rejected in favor of a subordinate creature, the Devil; the soul is acknowledged as eternal but is exchanged for a finite benefit. Two generations later Pascal saw more clearly that the modernity for which we are what we have could be accommodated to Christianity only if it immolated itself in an act of self-subversion. Marlowe allowed Christianity and modernity to subsist side by side in contradiction of each other, however absurd the dramatic consequences: "When Mephostophilis shall stand by me," Faustus boasts of the power his contract has bought him, "What God can hurt me" (*MF* II, i, 23–24).

Goethe began to consider writing a drama about Faust around 1770, just one hundred years after the first publication of Pascal's *Pensées* and perhaps two hundred years after stories about the historical Dr. Faust (for there was one) were first committed to manuscript.[2] He completed the second part of the play sixty years later, in 1831, at a time when the first passenger railways were already running (he was very pleased with a model train sent him by his English admirers), when not Venice but the London East India Company held the gorgeous East in fee, and when the British and Iberian colonies in America were independent states stuffing nobody's treasury but their own. The self that has had subdued the world. For Goethe the paradoxes of an age of transition written into the story he had inherited were wholly obsolete. Consequently nothing gave him so much trouble in his revival of the story of Faust as the contract scene which has to specify its relation to the Christian tradition. For nearly thirty years, during which much of his new story grew up round the lacuna that this scene had to occupy, the scene itself seems to have remained unwritten. Finally, in about 1800, at the high point of German Idealism, when all around him thinkers and writers, from Kant and Fichte to Novalis and the Romantics, were reinterpreting or restating Christianity for the modern age, Goethe found the form in which his modern Faust could bind himself to the Devil. The form, however, could not be that of a contract of sale between parties already agreed about the nature and value of what is being exchanged, the goods that are being bought, and the coin in which they are being paid for. Goethe's Faust disagrees with his Mephistopheles about virtually everything. While he retains, as it were, a cultural memory of the figure of Christ, and has behind him a period of enthusiastic personal faith which may have influenced his current attitudes more than he realizes,[3] and while he never explicitly denies the existence of God, Goethe's Faust finds no practical use for the concepts of God or Christ and certainly not for that notion of Sin which Marlowe's Faustus already found the most distasteful feature of "Divinitie." This Goethean Faust has no belief or interest in a future life of rewards and punishments beyond death. He does not think there is an immortal soul for him to sell. He does not think there is an external or higher authority that could enforce the terms of any contract he might choose to repudiate, however many covenants or articles it might be loaded with and whatever it is written in or on, ink or blood, parchment or marble. More immediately and more practically, he does not think the Devil has anything to offer him. The sensual pleasures offered to an earlier Faust cannot seriously attract him. The one thing of value in Faust's world Faust has already—himself. Nothing can equal or even resemble the power within himself, the power by which he denies value to anything else. That power he is prepared to call God, though it is shut up and immobilized within him as if bound and gagged in a dungeon (F 1566–69). For there is nothing outside himself in which he could recognize or find himself again, nothing which could compromise the solitude of omnipotence, the solitude of the only thing that *is,* namely, the power to have. And so an agreement is possible with the Devil after all, but by way not of a contract but of a wager. Faust bets that, however much the Devil exerts himself to provide the delights and satisfactions of this world that meant so much to earlier Fausts, indeed however much the Devil exerts himself to provide experiences of any kind, pleasurable or unpleasurable, he, Faust, will find nothing in them comparable to himself, to the power he *has* of *having* experiences. To each and every one, he wagers, he will say no—this cannot detain me—I do not recognize myself in this— on to the next. It will after all always be something to have, never something that is.

> Die Wette biet'ich. . . . Werd' ich zum Augenblicke sagen:
> Verweile doch! Du bist so schön!
> Dann magst du mich in Fesseln schlagen,
> Dann will ich gern zugrunde gehn (F 1698–1702)

> Here is my wager. . . . If I say to the moment: stay a while, you are so fair, then you can cast me in chains. I will happily go down to ruin.

To a certain extent, then, and at a certain level, Goldmann is right to see this wager as a continuation of Pascal's, even, we might say, an intensification of it. Everything the world can offer (in Goethe's play to be provided by the exertions of the Devil) is weighed up and found wanting in comparison with the promise held out by an idea: in Pascal's case, the idea of a rewarding (and, he also notes, a punishing) God; in Goethe's case, the idea of an endlessly active and responsive (and, we also have to note, negating and dismissive) self. In both cases the logic of venture capitalism, which requires one to risk what one has in order to have more, is carried to the extreme point at which it seems to detach one from possessions altogether. And it is understandable that, seen in this way, Faust's wager should appear to Goldmann to foreshadow his own Lukácsian wager that all the values of bourgeois society are as nothing compared with the future (possibly, always future) triumph of the proletariat. But this interpretation overlooks two features of Goethe's text which betray an understanding of modernity far too profound to be captured in the terms of Marxist millenarianism.

The first is the feature which makes it possible to see Goethe's *Faust* as a programmatic undoing of the *Pensées*. Goldmann, like Lukács, favors what might be called a religious interpretation of Faust's wager, an interpretation that maintains a continuity with the vocabulary of the *Pensées* and that leaves Goethe's play open to reinterpretation as an early document of the existentialist-Marxist religion in which the communist fulfillment of history takes the place of life after death and with God. Goldmann therefore makes an error in his reading of Goethe's text which, it has to be admitted, is very common. He thinks that Goethe's Faust wagers, as Marlowe's Faust sold, his eternal and immortal soul. But Goethe's Faust is more deeply detached than that from the Christian past, and Goethe has, in this respect at least, undone the ambiguity of Marlowe's play. Goethe's Faust, as I have remarked, regards the immortality of his soul as at best an irrelevance. In the dialogue with Mephistopheles which constitutes, or appears to constitute, the agreement between them, there is no explicit mention of Faust's soul and only vague and uncertain mention of an afterlife. It is nonetheless quite clear what will happen if Faust loses his wager. If he says to any moment "stay a while" he will have done what he has wagered he will never do, and he will die. No talk here of covenants for twenty-four years. Faust undertakes to live the venture-capitalist life at the maximum possible intensity, giving away every moment as he receives it in order to invest in the future; and if at any point he hesitates he will pay the ultimate and only price there is: the process will stop. Faust's wager is therefore not so much the intensification of Pascal's as the reverse of it—not the wager of the interlocutor whom Pascal seeks to direct towards Christian belief, but the wager of which Pascal's text says nothing, that of the freethinker who chooses not to believe. What specifically Pascal's text does not tell us (and by not telling us this, Pascal makes it impossible to assess with any clarity the mathematics of his argument) is what the freethinker expects to win if he turns out to be right, and, as Pascal puts it, God does not exist. Goethe's Faust provides us with the answer; the answer is: everything. Every moment of Faust's life is to be a wager in which he gains all that in that moment human life can offer him—provided that there is no God to make of the moment of human life a means or pathway to anything other than Faust's own possession and enjoyment of what lies beyond it. If life were to contain anything to make him deviate for a second from the headlong rush of gain, reinvestment, and further gain, if there were to be any hint that what he gains serves any purpose other than maintaining his own cycle of experience, if it were to be valuable in itself, beautiful, for example, or touched by a suggestion of some immortal longing, if it were to impose some constraint on Faust's freedom to go on from it to new possession and new enjoyment, then life would not be worth living—or so Faust has asserted by making his wager with the condition that if he loses he shall cease to live. The value of life is in the living of it, he wagers—and living it means having it, enjoying it as his possession and as the material in which he feels his power and freedom to go on living new life—and if life proves him wrong he is not interested in having it on any other conditions. In those circumstances, he says to Mephistopheles, that is, if he is unfree, it makes no odds whether he is the slave of God or of the Devil. "If I come to a stop, if I stagnate," he says, paraphrasing the more famous words of the wager I have just cited but not adding to them, "I'm a slave. Whether yours or another's, what does it matter?" (F 1710–11).

Goethe's Faust wagers, therefore, against God, against any power that might seek to give a meaning to his experience other than that *he has* it. His wager is a counterblast to Pascal and in Pascal's terms. Since it originates in the freethinker rather than in the seeker after faith it illuminates even more clearly than Pascal's wager the foundations of secular modernity. Indeed, Faust's wager, rather than Goldmann's, is the true secular and modern alternative to Pascal's. Goldmann's existentialist-Marxist gesture is simply a pale echo of Pascal's religious reinterpretation of the logic of capital and has little to do with the deeper analysis of that logic offered by Goethe's version of German Idealism. In Goldmann's conception of the wager there still lurks the idea of an immortal soul, of a reward in the afterlife that pays for all, even if it is only in the historical afterlife of the proletariat. Goethe's Faust is a good deal more hard-nosed than that.

I mean, of course, Goethe's Faust, the character. Goethe's *Faust,* the play, raises different and more complex questions. In particular, there is a second feature of Goethe's text to which Lukács gives the wrong kind of attention and Goldmann gives no attention at all, namely, that it is a tragedy. Lukács rightly sees that Goethe's play is concerned not simply with Faust's making a wager, but with the consequences of his making it, and he also rightly sees that those consequences are tragic.[4] However, he concentrates on the story of Faust's love for Gretchen in the first part of the play and so makes it easier for himself to conclude that the tragedy of *Faust* resides in the tragedy of Faust's victims, the used and discarded who lie in the ditch alongside modernity's high road to self-realization. That sort of thing. It is easy to write high-sounding twaddle about the victims of history. In the end, though, it comes down to the sanctimonious Leninist principle of which George Orwell was a scathing critic: that you can't make an omelette without breaking eggs. And whatever else is wrong with that repellent principle, sanctimoniousness is not the stuff of tragedy. Goethe's *Faust* is not the Communist Party at prayer, even though, as we shall see, prayer has an important part to play in it. Goethe's *Faust is* a tragedy, but it is the tragedy not simply of Faust's victims but of Faust himself. The self-destruction of great qualities is one of tragedy's principal themes—*Oedipus, Hamlet, Phèdre*—and, for all the creative energy that it releases, Faust's wager proves self-defeating. It opens up to Faust every kind of experience, except the kind that cannot be opened up by a wager, and that proves to be the only kind that matters. The logic of the wager is the logic of capital: forgetting the labor of others in order to have, having in order to risk, risking in order to have and forget again. Goethe's Faust, like Marlowe's Faustus before him, forgets where he comes from and all that he has learned in order to define himself simply as one who has, one who has the power of having experience, and in the wager he risks that power, he stakes his life, in order to have ever more experience, dismissing what he has into oblivion for the sake of what is to come. But this potentially endless and self-accelerating cycle is based on a great denial. Goethe shows it, immediately before his Faust makes his agreement with the Devil.

Faust, in the blackest of depressions, brought on by the frustrations of powerlessness, of pure having with nothing to have, curses all the analgesic illusions—as they seem to him—with which human beings conceal their condition from themselves. He curses the narcotics of drink, of love, of hope, of faith, and above all of the patience that sees things through and sees us out, the dogged determination to survive that is the most contemptible illusion of all. The wager is Faust's response to Mephistopheles' attempt to coax him out of this depression and into admitting that life holds some desirable satisfactions after all. Indeed, taken to the letter—as it must be taken—Faust's wager is simply the exasperated assertion that he is right and that the world contains nothing to satisfy him. The wager is not merely associated by Goethe's dramatic art with the curse that precedes it; it is a reformulation of it. The wager is a denial of value to the world, particularly of the value attributed to it by the religion of faith, hope, and love. True, it is also the device by which this denial is transformed into the instrument for endlessly multiplying and extending the experience of the world. However, the experience it brings can be of a certain kind only, the kind that can be possessed, and assessed, and dismissed, and all in a moment. What the wager cannot bring Faust is a share in the life of those who live by the virtues that he has denied, above all the virtue of patience. For patience is the virtue which gives value not to the moment but to time, to duration and to persistence—not to acts and fulfillments but to states and qualities and waiting. Of course, Faust can experience such a life, for the wager allows him to experience anything but only on the wager's own terms—as something possessed for a moment—and that destroys it in its essence, both in itself and for him.

Gretchen lives a small-town life strictly constrained economically and socially, mentally and morally: those limits determine both the real happiness she has in the hard work of looking after her little household and the transfiguring consolations of love and religion aroused in her by the stirrings of eros and its conflict with her circumstances. Thanks to the wager, Faust can glimpse her life of simple virtue—the "bliss" in her "prison" as he puts it (F 2694)—and also her yearning and loss and anguish in the real prison in which her life ends; but he can only glimpse it. He cannot share it, make it more than a moment, make it a condition of his own existence—for example, by marrying her as she imagines he will. To ask the moment of love to stay a while in marriage would be to lose his wager, to arrest the never-ending cycle of having and risking, and from the earliest chapbooks onwards it is an article of Faust's agreement with the Devil that he will not contract a lawful marriage. So Faust's life and Gretchen's intersect in one moment only. That moment causes Gretchen's destruction, and affords Faust a glimpse of a happiness and sorrow, a way of living and a way of dying, whose possibility he denied in making the wager and from which the wager has now cut him off—except, that is, for such a moment. And since it is only a moment, as soon as it is over it is forgotten. Part 2 of the play begins with a ceremonial forgetting of Part 1. So it is, in the consumer society that capitalist modernity has created for us: any form of life is available to us—whether Buddhism, or ocean racing, or love—provided it is treated as a consumable commodity, capable equally of being bought and of being discarded.

At the center of each of the two parts of *Faust* Goethe has constructed such a moment which reveals the true character of his hero's wager. The central scene in Part 1, the thirteenth out of twenty-five, is a scene in a summerhouse in which Faust and Gretchen declare their love for each other and exchange kisses. For a moment Faust stands in a relation of complete equality with another human being, for a moment he is not having an experience but recognizing, and being recognized by, another independent existence. The moment, however, is immediately interrupted by Mephistopheles, as if he were challenging Faust to utter the forbidden words "stay a while, you are so fair." Faust does not utter them and so commits himself either to leave Gretchen or to exploit her—in any event the moment of equality and mutual recognition is gone forever. In Part 2 there is a precise structural parallel: the central scene of the central act, act 3, is a scene in a crusader castle in which Faust gives his hand to Helena, the resurrected spirit of classical Greek beauty. It is a moment of inspired and moving complexity, a synthesis at once erotic and poetic, dramatic and cultural-historical, which I cannot analyze here, but it too is interrupted by Mephistopheles, bringing to Faust the challenge of the wager: to move on or die. This too is a moment in and out of time in which the alternative to the wager becomes visible both to us and, before he forgets it, to Faust. Faust briefly articulates the wisdom that the wager does not deny but simply leaves out of account—not that he was wrong to assert that nothing in this world would satisfy him, but that the deepest truths of life do not relate to possession and satisfaction at all. Immediately before the entry of Mephistopheles he utters the couplet which transcends the terms of the wager altogether and retracts the great denial on which it was based:

Durchgrüble nicht das einzigste Geschick!
Dasein ist Pflicht, und wär's ein Augenblick. (*F* 9417–18)

Destiny is utterly unique—not to be pondered over and weighed up [as the wager formula does]. To exist is duty, even if it lasts only a moment.

Faust's meeting with beauty, with the principle that he wagered he could resist and always leave behind, reveals to him that our unique existence, the life we only live once, is not properly the subject of a wager at all. It is not something to be weighed up and measured against something else, not something to be possessed or evaluated or even enjoyed. It is not even a thing. It is an obligation. To exist is to be subject to a moral command. It is to hear the call to responsibility. For a moment in Part 2, as in Part 1, Faust experiences life beyond the wager—beyond the limits of secular modernity. But because he is bound by the wager it is only an experience, and only for a moment. He cannot live life as subject to an "ought" and capable both of beauty and of love, for he remains bound to the logic of having and risking. His tragedy is that the magical and unnatural power of the wager brings him to the frontier from which he can see the land beyond but then necessarily drags him away, back into forgetting and eventually into literal blindness. For Faust's tragedy in Part 2 as in Part 1 is not just the tragedy of missed opportunity: it does not just arouse the sadness of seeing someone hear the call to the right life but fail to live it. Faust's entrapment by the wager, at the two crucial moments in his life when its terms put him to the test, is the tragedy of great achievement brought to nothing by the falsity of the moral principle that inspires it. In that sense it is, of course, also the tragedy of Faust's victims, disaster not just for himself but for those around him. In Part 1 his inability to respond to the moment of love turns his relationship with Gretchen into a heartrending story of seduction, infanticide, madness, and death. In Part 2 his inability to respond to the call that reaches him through an embodiment of human perfection leads him to embark on a quest for power and property ("Herrschaft . . . Eigentum," are his words) (F 10187). He destroys an empire, sets up a trade system that plunders the remote parts of the world, and at home establishes a modern, geometrical, and wholly artificial land and townscape, by means of magic and the labor, torment, and death of many and at the expense of the few remaining representatives of the old order, who are expropriated and burnt in their homes by Faust's hired henchmen. Forgetting the Arcadian image of a human society at peace with itself, the gods, and nature, which he enjoyed for a moment with Helena, Faust, now a blind centenarian, projects himself, as he dies, into a wholly groundless vision of a future materialistic mass society of millions like himself, strictly disciplined by the permanent threat of collective destruction. *Faust: Part Two* ends with an extraordinary symbolic prophecy of the political and economic horrors of the twentieth century. I see in it no comfort for the apologists either of Lukácsian socialism or of liberal capitalism. Faust's story is tragic—not just tears shed by the crocodile of historical progress—because his victims are the victims of a cause which may once have been good but which, by the time they suffer from it, has been thoroughly perverted. The two moments in which Faust's fate is sealed are also the moments in which we see the happiness and—within the limits of secular literature—hear the call that Faust has chosen to ignore. In those moments we feel the pang of true tragedy.

Within the limits of secular literature. Because Goethe's *Faust* is a tragedy it symbolizes, in a complex way, a complex human good—the good that is shown as lost, as surviving the loss, perhaps even as having the loss as its necessary condition. But because Goethe's *Faust* is secular literature it cannot effectuate that good, in the sense that it cannot make us recognize what is lost, or survives the loss, as good, as good for us: it can show us someone heeding or failing to heed the call, but it cannot utter it to us. We can hear the words "Dasein ist Pflicht," "To exist is duty," as obligating Faust, and forgotten by him, with the tragic consequences we see, but we cannot hear them as spoken to us and for our sake. These are words of extraordinary weight. They express a truth which has been ever more neglected, for which there has been ever less space, in our collective life for at least eight centuries. But they are written down as part of a structure of words which has the noninstrumental purpose of giving pleasure. They are not written down as part of the text which has the noninstrumental purpose of affirming the ethical command; they are not written down as part of the Law. Can they nevertheless function for us as a paraphrase or commentary on the Law? Can they be for us at least marginalia, marginal comments or glosses on the wisdom literature that is part of the Law (so that we could, for example, without violating Goethe's work, say that our society had made a "Faustian" pact with forces of negation; or, conversely, could claim that a critique of Lukács's interpretation of the Gretchen story would be a political critique, not just an intellectual critique of a certain political ideology, but a moral critique of a certain political practice)? I have argued that the words of secular poetry can function for us in this way precisely insofar as they aspire to and recognize their status as limit cases; insofar, that is, as they press forward to enact the words "Thou shalt" and then defer, as to something beyond them. At the last they pass to their readers the task of transcending the limit that marks them off as secular. At the last they recognize that they can never be more than indirect utterances, echoes, as it were, of the call, of the command that can be directly spoken only in the sacred books of the Law and whose fulfillment can be found only in the living temple that is the bodies of the faithful, vivified by the Spirit. The supreme indirect secular echoes of the Law—and I certainly believe the culminating moments of Goethe's *Faust* to be among them—are characterized by their supreme awareness of standing at that limit. On the one hand, they come as close as it is possible to come to the state of authorless, written revelations of being, adverbially modified by the preoriginal command; in other words, they come as close as possible to being literature as Bible. On the other hand, they recognize that nonetheless, and for all that effort to become impersonal revelation, they are in the end the words of authors trying to tell the truth, utterances in a medium that is of its nature spoken. They recognize that they are texts with an origin, somebody's fictions. Specifically, they are the fictions, the weavings of words, of somebody who is not fundamentally different from the audience for whose benefit the mimetic performance, the public fictional imitation of truth, has been put on. They recognize that their author is part of the public, is one of an inclusive "us." By incorporating that recognition, the works of secular literature that define its frontier with the sacred open themselves to a dialogue with the audience that they postulate. They make themselves part of a living discussion, a discussion among those on whose hearts the Law *is* written, a discussion for which they provide some but not all of the words. In this way they are after all joined to the words that utter the Law and they become part of the revelation. By showing the world as mattering to somebody, they show it as matter for prayer, the general prayer "for all sorts and conditions of men" which takes those who utter it across the frontier between the secular and the sacred and is the first word of reconciliation between God and the world.

In the case of Pascal's *Pensées* we have seen every stage of this process in operation. The wager endeavors to compel a revelation; it pushes the text to the boundary between secular and sacred utterance. But it is unable to release its readers from the characteristically modern, secular way of thinking in terms of having and risking. This inability is reflected in the text's inability to establish communication between the wager and an apology based on Scripture and, ultimately, in the fragmentary nature of the *Pensées* themselves. The figure of the author, however, performs an essential role in making the limits of the text apparent and moving the thought processes of the work from monologue towards dialogue. Eventually the author becomes a concretely, indeed physically, envisaged figure as the man on his knees in prayer who asks for God's grace to secure the transfer of the interlocutor—or is it the reader?—to the company of those who are already on their way and who need no wager, no *Pensées* at all.

In Goethe's *Faust* the same processes can also be seen. The limit of secularity, the inability of the self that has and risks to hear the primal command that establishes the ethical character of existence, is of course the work's tragic theme. To that extent the play seems to aspire to the status of an authoritative diagnosis, a revelation, of the human condition. But that tragic theme is accompanied throughout the play by a formal feature that keeps the limits of the text before our eyes, an irony that repeatedly identifies the work as a modern retelling of an old story, that places it historically as a Faust story that is post-Christian—in which the Devil is an anachronism and part of the time a figure of fun—as an eighteenth- or a nineteenth-century story replete with allusions to historical and literary figures from Shakespeare to Byron, and as a commentary on Goethe's own life and times. Just as Faust cannot escape from his venture-capitalist modernity, so the text cannot escape from its historical identity: just as Faust can only glimpse a transcendent perspective before he forgets it, so the work can only hint at an impersonally authoritative vision of being before it reverts to an ironic awareness of its own limitations.

Towards the end of Part 2 the self-conscious duality in the play becomes acute. As it comes closer to revealing a moral truth about secular modernity, so it comes closer to revealing its own artificiality. This internal division is manifest in two remarkable features of the play's conclusion. First, taking up a device of Romantic drama, Goethe introduces himself into the action. The old couple, Philemon and Baucis, the last survivors of the ancien régime swept away by Faust, are visited at their cottage by a "Wanderer" whom long ago, as a young man, they tended after he had been cast ashore in a shipwreck. He has returned to thank them and to look again at the sea from which he narrowly escaped. But the coastal region has been enclosed by Faust in a polder, what was once the seabed is now densely populated, and the sea itself is scarcely visible on the horizon. The Wanderer is struck dumb with astonishment, and we later hear that he dies that night as he vainly attempts to defend the old people from the assault by Mephistopheles and Faust's thugs. The scene of his reunion with Philemon and Baucis is picturesque, idyllic, and richly suggestive of the art of the sunset years of the eighteenth century—of Philipp Hackert, for example, whom Goethe knew well—but it has undertones of nightmare—of Fuseli, perhaps, whom Goethe also admired. But its full daring becomes apparent only when we realize that "the Wanderer" was a sobriquet of Goethe's from his earliest adulthood, that he cast himself in the role of the Wanderer in some of his greatest early poems—among them a dialogue piece which shows a troubled victim of the modern Sentimentalist movement finding a brief refuge with a simple family—that he continued to use the term in allusion to himself throughout his life, and that rescue from shipwreck was one of the most important metaphors by which he explained to himself his role in the culture of

Germany, and of Europe generally, with particular reference to what he achieved in Weimar. In the figure of the Wanderer Goethe therefore shows himself, the author of the play, reduced to silence by the activities of Faust, his central character, and eventually murdered by him. The moral truth about the secular modernity represented by Faust's wager seems to be strictly un-utterable. Perhaps it is too appalling for anyone, perhaps it is just beyond the powers of this particular writer. At any rate the task of uttering it causes the work to display its own limitations, the extent to which it is not just a truth-telling fiction but the artificial construct of a historically specific personality.

The scene with the Wanderer, Philemon, and Baucis opens act 5 of the play and is a prelude to the closely linked series of scenes that brings Faust's life to an end. The second remarkable feature of these scenes, however, is that they offer not one end to Faust's life and to the play but two. The device of two alternative endings is no more peculiar to Goethe than the introduc-tion of the author into his own work, of course. Here as elsewhere it has the function of drawing a limit to what the work is able to say—pointing to something that lies beyond it that is for the audience to say, act on, work out for themselves, or indeed make the object of prayer.

I have spoken so far of Faust's career as a tragedy, the tragedy of a life that is a wager on what it can have rather than a response to a call to what it must be. That life is shown to run its destructive and self-destructive course, and as the play nears its end it becomes more nearly and clearly a showing of Goethe's own time and place: the modern world in the early stages of indus-trialization and imperialism. The question what the end of Faust the char-acter will be thus becomes ever more clearly an interrogation of the moral character of that world—a question of hope. Is there any? Does the world matter? Is the play a tragedy, final and unredeemed? To these questions we are given two answers. The first is spoken by Mephistopheles, contem-plating the decrepit body of the Faust who has chosen to die reaching out for the realization of his megalomaniac dream of a mass society of millions of Fausts, like himself "not secure, but active and free" (F 11564). The dream, Mephistopheles says, is as worthless as anything that has gone before it. Dreams and achievements and sufferings—they are all over, and, being over, might as well never have been. The pretension of all this activity to being anything is intolerable. Mephistopheles would prefer eternal emptiness: "das Ewig-Leere" is the last word of his long dialogue with Faust, begun more than ten thousand lines earlier, and it is the last word uttered in a scene set unambiguously on this earth and in our time (F 11603). It is the last word on Faust's career spoken in the frame of reference within which Faust made his wager. Eternal emptiness, it says, is the end to which the wager, and all that is built by it, must come. It is difficult to imagine a grimmer or more tragic conclusion to Faust's life of desire, struggle, and, to be honest, crime.

Yet Goethe notoriously follows it with a second conclusion, set in an unearthly world, or at any rate a world between earth and heaven (hell too puts in a marginal appearance, its jaws at one point being wheeled in on the side of the stage). The frame of reference of the wager is gone, and the wager itself is forgotten, though Faust's death continues to have its effect: the world in which he chose to speak and act is no more, and, as he promised, he does not adapt himself to a new one. He utters no further word and is wholly passive. In the half-reality of the last two scenes Faust is simply an object: the object of reflection, as sense is made of his life at last; the object of love; and the object of prayer. If Faust is saved by love, it is not by any love that he has for anyone else—and if he has loved anyone it can only have been momentarily—but by another's love for him. Gretchen is found waiting for him on the threshold of heaven, and her continuing love for him, a love to which she sacrificed her life, expresses itself in intercessory prayer. Her prayer, joined to that of other fallen women, for the intercession of the Blessed Virgin is enough to gain the promise that Faust will now follow where she leads. Goethe thus makes use of an adapted Catholic theology, and of allusions to the end of Dante's *Paradiso,* to express a hope that the world still matters, dominated though it is by the wager, and that it will remain open to the saving influence of the powers that the wager denies or at best forgets.

We must remember, however, that this hope is balanced by Mephistopheles' preceding assessment, from which all hope is absent. There are two ends to this play, not one,[5] and as the task of mediating between them is passed to us, so also is the task of formulating and living out a hope for the world the play depicts, which is ours. The play acknowledges that it is beyond its competence to express the moral truth of things—to pass judgment. The play acknowledges that it is in the end somebody's piece of writing, and it does not so much reveal being as defer to it. This transmission of moral responsibility, from the text to its readers, is itself part of the play's last ecstatic episode. The scene is not a scene in heaven, as is sometimes asserted. It is a scene of permanent transition, moving always upwards towards a heaven that is never reached. And in its course that movement is imparted to its readers too. The movement of prayer, which begins even before the pleadings of Gretchen and her companions, broadens out to include all the inhabitants of the intermediate realms in which the scene is set.

All the penitent turn their eyes upwards and are drawn on by their gaze (fixed on a female Godhead, the counter to Mephistopheles' principle of eternal emptiness) into the empyrean. But the famous words that enact that final movement, the last words of the entire play, incorporate not only all those whom the play represents but all those it addresses as well:

> Das Ewig-Weibliche
> Zieht uns hinan. (*F* 12110–11)

The eternally feminine principle draws us on.

The "we" of that final line refers not only to those who are represented in the play as praying for Faust but also to those of us who, having read the play and having heard the moral call that the play cannot utter, still have hope for the world devastated by the principle of having and risking, and so can include it in our prayer for all sorts and conditions of men and women.

CHAPTER 12

Faces (1): *Moby-Dick*

SO FAR WE HAVE SEEN HOW ONLY A WORK OF SACRED LITERATURE can represent the preoriginal ethical command to responsibility, the "Thou shalt" of the biblical Law. Works of secular literature may strive to represent it as the source of our fallen state, the reason why we can recognize the world's sinfulness, but must at the last defer to reality and recognize that it is unrepresentable. This act of deference is, I have argued, synonymous with a recognition that the work originates in a particular historically and culturally limited author and is part of a spoken conversation that is also subject to historical and cultural constraints. However, by representing the world as worth representing, as mattering enough for it to be worth putting into historically and culturally conditioned words, works of secular literature show the world as forgiven, as reconciled with God thanks to God's own action through the incarnation of his Law in Christ. Whatever its sinfulness it has been redeemed, and the writer's loving exertion in putting it into words is an attempt to express that redeemed status. We can therefore incorporate secular literature into our lives as commentary on the sacred Scriptures that give us the Law, for such secular scriptures show us the world to which those sacred Scriptures apply, show it as under the Law, as fallen and forgiven. Secular literature therefore articulates the world for us, puts it into words, as the material of our prayer—as the place in need of redemption, as the place that has received redemption, and as the place that our own lives are called to cooperate in redeeming.

Lévinas tells us that the immediate expression to us of the preoriginal command to responsibility is the face of another human being.[1] Not anything the face says or implies about some person distinct from—or, as we often say, behind—it, not any particular expression that the face may bear as the vehicle of some particular message, but its mere capacity for expression, the mere fact that faces speak to us, whatever they say, exposes us to our responsibility for the other. We live in a world of faces and therefore we live in a world that is from before its beginning ethically meaningful. That quality of ethical meaningfulness, of expressing an aboriginal command to responsibility, is connected by Lévinas to the name of God, in a way that it is beyond the scope of this work to investigate. But the connection is very close. "The dimension of the divine opens out from the human face," Lévinas writes, ". . . the proximity of the neighbour is . . . an ineluctable moment of revelation."[2] A commentator, ignoring Lévinas's principled objection to the idea that the Word of God could become flesh, has even paraphrased him as saying "The Logos does not just become flesh, it becomes face."[3] Though that is not a step Lévinas could take, I believe it is a legitimate step. For Christians Jesus the Messiah is the face of the invisible God and the opening forth of the divine dimension in every human face. For Catholic Christians there is a further consequence: for them the divine dimension opening out towards us in the face of the other is divine not only as the primal command to responsibility, and not only as the word of forgiveness spoken by Jesus, but also as comembership of the body of the forgiven. For Catholic Christians the face of the other, through being a face at all, speaks with the voice of God; through being *this* face it is the face of Christ; and through being a face among others it is the face of a fellow Christian, another for whom Christ died, and lovable accordingly, a member, potential or actual, of Christ's spiritual body, the church. If, then, a secular literary work is to represent the world as ethically meaningful, as mattering, it will represent the world not only as a visible face which speaks a command that can be heard but cannot be seen, not only as a face that suffers and forgives infinitely, but also as many forgiven faces—for the ethically meaningful world is a place of forgivenness in which the faces of those for whom God has suffered crowd together, whether in heavenly choirs or in earthly institutions and traditions, to speak of what God has done for them. A Catholic approach to literature will therefore be alert not only to a written work's attempt to reach the boundary beyond which lies the unutterable "Thou shalt," the original divine command; nor will it only be alert to the extent to which the work embodies the reconciling and forgiving belief that what it represents is worth representing. A Catholic approach to a literary work will also involve asking: how far and how well does this work represent worth-whileness as shared, as a feature of many faces gathered by the Spirit into social institutions, specifically, into the church?

Even without the assistance of Lévinas this approach to literature and to life has been spelt out for us by a great Catholic thinker and poet, Gerard Manley Hopkins. In 1881 Hopkins wrote in the sonnet "As kingfishers catch fire" that the fundamental principle of natural existence applies in the moral world too: we are what we do, our identity lies, not dormant and hidden within us, but in our interface with all other things. In moral terms, he says, "the just man justices": the just person is the presence of justice in the world and so the presence of God, for God called him or her for that purpose precisely, to be those just actions, those enactments of the primal command. And thereby, Hopkins continues, as only perhaps the Catholic Christian can continue, to be just is to be Christ in the eyes of God, for it is to be one of the myriad facets of the presence of the Just One in material and moral creation. It is, without prejudice to one's unique identity and vocation, to be one of many, a countless number, whose unique faces bear each of them the Grace of Christ:

> for Christ [he writes] plays in ten thousand places,
> Lovely in limbs, and lovely in eyes not his
> To the Father through the features of men's faces.[4]

This is a vision, I believe, not only of the Church, but also, within the limits that I have already discussed, of the art of the poet, considered from a Catholic Christian point of view, and particularly perhaps of the art of the novelist. For the novelist the enjoyment of all the ten thousand forms and conditions of men is also a prayer for them, because they matter—that is, because, having been called and forgiven by God, they are worth representing as they are. The novelist seeks to discern, in the features of men's faces, the lineaments of a world that matters, and looks in ten thousand places for the justice that, though the novelist cannot say it, comes from God: as with sacred wisdom literature, the search may end in the questioning of Job or the agnosticism of Ecclesiastes, but it may also approach the confidence in the Law of Ecclesiasticus or the author of Tobit. For the Christian, who reads the Old Testament through the New, the secular wisdom of the novel, like the sacred wisdom of the Bible, is taken up into the ten thousand faces of the Christ, risen in the Spirit, who is the supreme Wisdom of the Father.

The two exemplary nineteenth-century novels I now wish to discuss so mingle realistic fiction and moral reflection that they clearly belong in the category of secular wisdom literature. They are poems as Esther or Jonah, Tobit or Ruth are poems; like their biblical analogues their horizon is provided by the name of the Unnameable God; but they mark themselves off as secular by incorporating, in different ways, an acknowledgment that they cannot speak with the authority of the Law. They also betray their historical position—that is, they date themselves—by their concern with the issues I elicited from Pascal's *Pensées* and Goethe's *Faust:* the moral consequences of the change in economic and social structures which, gathering pace from about 1200 onwards, defined itself publicly as the birth of modernity in the explosion that was the Reformation. We can find in them too the confrontation between the lure of having and risking, the act and attitude of the wager, and the call of the Law, the primal command to responsibility which says that existence is duty.

On completing *Moby-Dick* in 1851, Herman Melville wrote to Nathaniel Hawthorne: "I have written a wicked book, and feel as spotless as the lamb."[5] *Moby-Dick* is undoubtedly a wicked book. The challenge for a Catholic reader of the book is to find out whether, or how far, Melville was right to feel as untouched by that wickedness as Christ, the lamb, by the sin he came to forgive—whether, or how far, the book itself embodies that redemptive purity.

Moby-Dick is in one sense the story of Faust carried to its logical or illogical extreme—a rejection of Christ and a pact with the Devil which takes the Devil fully seriously. Charles Olson has proved how deliberately Melville omitted any mention of Christ from the motto formula Ahab uses at the forging of the harpoon he intends to plunge into the White Whale: as the barb is tempered in the blood of non-Christians he "deliriously howled," "Ego non baptizo te in nomine patris, sed in nomine diaboli."[6] During the electrical storm described in the chapter "The Candles," when the whole ship glows with St. Elmo's fire, Ahab defies the image of the Trinity, "the lofty tri-pointed trinity of flames," formed by the three flaring masts of the ship. "I own thy speechless, placeless power," he cries, "but to the last gasp of my earthquake life will dispute its unconditional, unintegral mastery in me" (*MD* 507). As a sign of his defiance he waves over the terrified crew the harpoon he has consecrated to the Devil, while a flame comes from it "like a serpent's tongue," and he recalls, and thereby renews, the vows which have committed them all to their single-minded, hate-filled quest:

> All your oaths to hunt the White Whale are as binding as mine; and
> heart, soul, and body, lungs and life, old Ahab is bound. (*MD* 508)

But as if to demonstrate that he will not waver as Marlowe's Faustus wavered, that, whatever diabolical power he has bound himself to, he will persevere in his pact to the end, Ahab blows out the fire on the harpoon with the words, "thus I blow out the last fear!"

However, the similarity with the Faust stories lies deeper in *Moby-Dick* even than the fabric of imagery and allusion. The similarity is structural. Whaling, after all, the central and sustaining image of the entire work, is, and is presented as, a particularly cogent example of the process of having and risking in order to have more. The purchase and fitting out, supplying and manning of a whaler such as the *Pequod* is a significant investment of capital which will be risked on the high seas for perhaps four years before there is a chance of its returning filled with neatly stacked barrels of spermaceti oil, the predecessor in the American economy to petroleum.[7] "People in Nantucket," Ishmael tells us, "invest their money in whaling vessels, the same way that you do yours in approved state stocks bringing in good interest" (*MD* 73). Before the appearance of Ahab the *Pequod* is presented as the property of its shareholders, a "crowd of old annuitants; widows, fatherless children, and chancery wards; each owning about the value of a timber head, or a foot of plank, or a nail or two," but above all of the principal investors, Captains Bildad and Peleg. Though Quakers, committed to nonviolence, Bildad and Peleg have spent a lifetime in whaling, the most violent and bloodiest of trades. Bildad has concluded, we are told, that "a man's religion is one thing, and this practical world quite another. This world pays dividends" (*MD* 74). Bildad and Peleg engage Ishmael, after some readjustment of his expectations, for a 300th share of the net profits. So our narrator too is a speculator, though we are then given some statistics about whaling from which we can work out that Ishmael's return on his three years' investment of labor, apart from his "beef and board," is not likely to amount to much more than $90. Melville's figures, incidentally—more than 700 ships, worth a total of $20 million, employing 18,000 men and bringing in annually some $7 million—seem to be fairly accurate for the 1840s,[8] though they considerably understate the overall importance of the industry since they refer to the ships alone and omit the associated activities. Whaling, then, in *Moby-Dick* is not just a metaphor, but a metonymy, or example, of the process of venture capitalism. The famous chapter, "The Try-Works," depicts the business of rendering down the whale blubber into oil, the culmination and end purpose of a whale hunt, as a scene from the furnaces of the mid-nineteenth-century industrial revolution: the ship is transformed for a brief period of intense and laborious production by day and by night into a place of fire and metal, stone, and heavy stinking smoke. At the same time, however, the description relates the scene to the Faustian motif of the pact with the Devil. The *Pequod,* garishly lit up by the fires beneath the pots of boiling oil, is a "red hell," and the "pagan harpooneers" feeding the pots or the flames with the aid of "huge pronged forks" seem "fiend shapes" to Ishmael, "capering half in smoke and half in fire":

> Then the rushing Pequod, freighted with savages, and laden with fire, and burning a corpse, and plunging into that blackness of darkness, seemed the material counterpart of her monomaniac commander's soul. (*MD* 423)

At this point, however, the analogy between *Faust* and *Moby-Dick* might seem to meet with a check. For the soothing, regular, three- or four-year cycle of the whaling tour, from capital to risk to return, is interrupted by Ahab's single demonic purpose. All the savings and investments of Bildad and Peleg, all the fractions of the ship owned by the other shareholders, all the products of earlier voyages with which the *Pequod* is fitted out and adorned, the whale teeth cleats, the whalebone tackle blocks, the whale jaw tiller, all the "beef, bread, water, fuel, and iron hoops and staves," all the "spare boats, spare spars, and spare lines and harpoons, and spare everythings" that have been loaded aboard, even the jar of pickles, the bunch of quill pens, the nightcap brought along in various last thoughtful moments by Bildad's sister, Aunt Charity, even the last of the spares, a spare Bible (*MD* 96, 102)—all that capital disappears into the whirlpool of nothingness into which Ahab directs the ship, its boats, and everything that belongs to it:

> And now, concentric circles seized the lone boat itself and all its crew, and each floating oar, and every lance-pole, and spinning, animate and inanimate, all round and round in one vortex, carried the smallest chip of the Pequod out of sight. (*MD* 572)

Ahab brings to nothing, literally, every last solid fragment of capital invested in the *Pequod,* every last chip of having is risked and lost, and there remains, we are told, only the watery chaos that reigned before the creation, the eternal emptiness that Goethe's Mephistopheles would prefer to the pretense of being that is the memory of what is no more.

But this negation of all the capital represented by the *Pequod* and the lives of its crew is no mere tragic mischance, as if it could have been avoided had Ahab been more fortunate or more skillful in his final battle with the whale. Ahab has from the start of the voyage and throughout it denied the significance of the economic and speculative purpose for which the owners and the crew—at first, at any rate—think it has been undertaken. That "natural, nominal purpose," the slaughter of whales and the garnering of their oil, he pursues, we are told in the chapter "Surmises," only as a means to keep his "tools," the men of his crew, in order. "I will not strip these men, thought Ahab, of all hopes of cash," even though "the prime but private purpose" of the *Pequod*'s voyage, the killing of Moby Dick, has in him wholly usurped that pecuniary motive (*MD* 212–13). Other whales are dutifully hunted down, but when one is killed

> some vague dissatisfaction, or impatience, or despair, seemed working in him; as if the sight of that dead body reminded him that Moby Dick was yet to be slain; and though a thousand other whales were brought to his ship, all that would not one jot advance his grand, monomaniac object. (*MD* 291–92)

Ahab's monomaniac object, or project, has the form of whaling, the risking of capital, if necessary of everything, of the entire ship, for the sake of the gain represented by killing a whale. But it has only the form, not the substance, for his purpose is not the gain but the killing. Ahab, like Faust, commits himself to the process of risking everything in an endless pursuit, regardless of the destruction he causes and the appeals of humanity and duty. But unlike Faust he does so not for the sake of the pursuit and the affirmation of his own existence that the pursuit involves but for the sake of the destruction it generates. It is true, though, that Ahab does not value the destruction simply in itself. The story describes his motive for the pursuit as the desire for vengeance, vengeance on the white whale that has taken off his leg. That is to say, he seeks vengeance on the process of whaling that has wounded him. This huntsman is a victim, the victim of the hunt in which he engages himself heart, soul, and body, lungs and life. There is after all no malice in Moby Dick, devilish though he is often said to be, that is not there beforehand in his Satanic pursuer. Moby Dick turns no violence against the ship and Ahab that has not first been directed at him by those that seek to take his life and boil him down in iron cauldrons to make lamp oil. Ahab is the image of all those maimed and dehumanized by the process of having and risking for the sake of having more, and his pursuit of the White Whale, in supremely arrogant disregard of the imperative to profit, is the image of the revolt of the victims against the Leviathan to which they are enslaved. Unlike the tragedy of Goethe's Faust, however, Ahab's tragedy is not the tragedy of the man condemned to graze the orbit of an alternative existence, to hear the call of duty and love, and promptly, and by his own choice in the wager, to forget it. Ahab's tragedy is that of a man who pursues the devilish wager with total—monomaniac—single-mindedness to the point of ultimate absurdity, the point where everything is risked and nothing is gained and where he destroys himself by the sheer consistency of his self-assertion. Revenge has no place in the account books of Captain Bildad, for all that he has devoted a lifetime to killing whales, but in seeking revenge, in seeking killing regardless of profit, Ahab succeeds in making the process of whaling destroy itself: the attempt to kill the whale kills all who attempt the killing. And in that act of self-immolation Ahab does not merely forget or ignore the call of love and duty, he explicitly rejects it. Besought by the captain of the *Rachel* to join in the search for his missing son, asked most urgently to show solidarity with and responsibility for other victims of the business of whaling, the purpose of which his own quest denies, Ahab turns away and commits himself consciously and exclusively to his pursuit of vengeance on the business and to the one and ultimate whaling voyage, the search for Moby Dick.

The—literally—central image of the paradox that is the voyage of the *Pequod* is the ounce of Spanish gold, the doubloon, the reward for the first man to sight Moby Dick that Ahab nails to the mainmast when he prevails on the crew to join him in his quest. There it stays through all the leagues of sailing, throughout the storms, encounters, and meaningless butcherings of anonymous whales—an image of profit that will be realized only when the voyage is on the point of achieving a purpose that has nothing to do with profit and will in fact prove the negation not only of profit but of all invest-ment too. The doubloon is the image of the *Pequod*'s purposeless purpose, and the reward is never awarded. Ahab claims it for his own, for who else could be the first to sight his uniquely personal adversary? And he and the crew engage in the final battle uncontaminated by any calculation of profit and loss.

The voyage of the *Pequod,* originally simply an example of the venture-capitalist existence of having and risking in order to have more, is reinterpreted by Ahab, through his imposition on it of the purpose of profitless killing, into a quest for what lies beyond having and risking, what lies beyond the existence that has wounded him. By reducing the logic of wagering to absurdity, he seeks to penetrate to the being which wagering, over the centuries, has concealed from the once-Christian world. To say that harpooning is an image of penetration would be an understatement. It is explicitly in terms of breaking through into a beyond that Ahab interprets his purpose of killing Moby Dick when Starbuck, his Christian mate, objects, "[To seek] [v]engeance on a dumb brute . . . To be enraged with a dumb thing, Captain Ahab, seems blasphemous." Ahab replies that visible objects, events and deeds, "are but as pasteboard masks," the contours of which both reveal and conceal the feature of the "unknown . . . thing" that lies behind them.

> If a man will strike, strike through the mask! How can the prisoner reach outside except by thrusting through the wall? To me, the white whale is that wall, shoved near to me. Sometimes I think there's naught beyond. But 'tis enough. (*MD* 163–64)

It is enough that the wall is there to be breached and that the means of breaching it has been put in his hands, in the form of the destructive power generated by the business of whaling. What lies beyond whaling, beyond the wall, behind the mask? Freedom from the prison, certainly, freedom from the wounding and maiming cycle of having and risking, but what is that negation of the existence in which Ahab and the crew and the entire whaling industry and all it stands for are trapped? Is it being—or is it, as Ahab sometimes thinks, nothing? Is there a face behind the mask? Or is the mask one with the face, a persona of impersonality?

The mystery of the face, however, as Lévinas has shown us, is that it is not a mask. What it reveals or conceals is not something that lies behind it: its mystery lies in its surface where it utters without mediation the command to responsibility. The face may be distorted by suffering, by the wounds the world inflicts, it may be the face of the man of sorrows, an Ecce Homo, but we can come no closer than that to pure being, we cannot break through to a pure being beyond and before the primal otherwiseness of responsibility. Ahab, however, is intent on just that—on seeing the Father without seeing the face, the ten thousand faces, of the Son. He explicitly rejects the Christian mediation, by his commitment to the Devil, and as a consequence when he confronts the Father, or rather when he confronts the place where the Father should be, the wall shoved near to him, he finds no face but only inscrutability.

> I see in him outrageous strength [Ahab says of Moby Dick], with an inscrutable malice sinewing it. That inscrutable thing is chiefly what I hate; and be the white whale agent, or be the white whale principal, I will wreak that hate upon him. (*MD* 164)

Ahab seeks vengeance not just on the existence, the whaling, industrial existence, that has wounded him but on the being that has made that existence possible, the principal of which that existence is only the agent. Ahab hates and seeks revenge on God, on being itself. But we have no access to God except through his Son, and so Ahab's rage remains futile and in the end objectless. The whale on which he focuses all his hate has no face. Its inscrutability is chiefly what he hates, and through that no harpoon can find a way.

Moby Dick inspires horror not just by his size or his power, but by his facelessness. The sperm whale, Ishmael tells us, has a forehead or brow of superhuman dimensions, such that nothing else in the world can be a better image of God, but he has no face:

> [I]n the great Sperm Whale, this high and mighty god-like dignity inherent in the brow is so immensely amplified, that gazing on it, in that full front view, you feel the Deity and the dread powers more forcibly than in beholding any other object in living nature. For you see no one point precisely; not one distinct feature is revealed; no nose, eyes, ears, or mouth; no face; he has none, proper; nothing but that one broad firmament of a forehead, pleated with riddles; dumbly lowering with the doom of boats, and ships, and men. (*MD* 346)

The sperm whale, according to Ishmael, makes visible not merely the facelessness of God and the inscrutability of pure being; he makes visible specifically the facelessness of the God revealed in the Old Testament. In Exodus 33 God tells Moses that no one can see his face and live, and when he passes before Moses, sheltered in the protecting cavity of a rock, Moses is allowed to see only his back. When Ishmael, a few chapters after describing the whale's forehead, comes to speak of his tail and the "inexplicable" gestures it seems to make, he alludes directly to the God of Exodus:

[I]f I know not even the tail of this whale, how understand his head? much more, how comprehend his face, when face he has none? Thou shalt see my back parts, my tail, he seems to say, but my face shall not be seen. But I cannot completely make out his back parts; and hint what he will about his face, I say again he has no face. (*MD* 379)

By referring to the previous occasion when he said the whale has no face, Ishmael links the biblical allusion with that first passage also. At the same time he makes clear that his remarks are as much a commentary on the Bible as on the natural history of the whale, for the words "hint what he will about his face" have no possible reference to the whale. They can refer only to the hints about God's face contained in Exodus, and perhaps also in the New Testament, the good news about the shining forth of God's face. The appalling facelessness of the whale as his forehead bears down directly on you with annihilating intent, a wall shoved ever nearer, makes visible a God who in no way condescends to the human condition, who communicates nothing to and shares nothing with those who futilely confront him, inscrutable, "unappeasable," "all-destroying" (*MD* 570–71). This is a God whose face has been doubly denied: the New Testament face of Christ, the image of the unseen God, has been stripped away; and so too has even the Old Testament face that is no face, the hidden face of the God who shows only his back parts, who is only heard, the God who utters the law. No command to responsibility, no command of any kind, is uttered by that lowering forehead which is all Ahab can find beyond the process of having and risking that is imaged by the industry of whaling. That is all he can find, for he has sought what lies beyond the business of whaling and wagering, what is on the other side of the wall, only by carrying the business of whaling and wagering to its last extreme. It is a God who, as he admits, is scarcely distinguishable from Nothing. The true alternative to that business lies altogether elsewhere, lies in hearing the command voiced in the Scriptures which in Melville's novel are everywhere parodied, misapplied, upbraided for their inaccuracies, or ridiculed. The beyond is to be found not by a having and risking of which the culminating expression is risking one's life in order to kill but by an attentiveness to being which hears the voice that is always otherwise than being and imposes responsibility. To hear and respond to that voice is impossible for Ahab, Ishmael, and probably Melville too. The only possible response from Ahab to the Sonless and voiceless God he alone can encounter is to oppose to him the same faceless and destructive intent that he finds in the whale. "Forehead to forehead I meet thee, this third time, Moby Dick!" (*MD* 565) Ahab cries out on the third day of the chase, when he at last meets the destruction that, as the whaler par excellence, he embodies.

The theology of *Moby-Dick* has in it, therefore, no place for Christ, the Son, the Second Person of the Trinity. Jesus is mentioned by name only once, in the main narration, by Starbuck, Ahab's weak-willed, Christian mate, when after two days' chase, with boats lost, and Ahab's whalebone leg taken off a second time, he begs the captain to desist (*MD* 561). Ahab interrupts the funeral service of one of Moby Dick's victims before the sentence naming Christ as the resurrection and the life can be completed (*MD* 541). When the carpenter caulking the seams of the coffin that is to be the ship's lifebuoy—and so the means of resurrecting Ishmael—interjects in passing, "Faith, sir," Ahab sharply interrupts. "Faith? What's that?" He allows the carpenter to continue only when he has received the halting explanation, "Why, faith, sir, it's only a sort of exclamation-like—that's all, sir" (*MD* 528). "Christian" is in the vocabulary of the novel a synonym for weak of mind and courage and is associated with superstition. When the *Pequod* passes some rocky islets where bereaved seals are howling, "[t]he Christian or civilized part of the crew said it was mermaids, and shuddered; but the pagan harpooneers remained unappalled" (*MD* 523); and at the end the same "pagan harpooneers" (*MD* 572) stay unmoved at their lookout posts on the masts as the ship sinks beneath them, while to one of them, Tashtego, is given the final emblematic act of defiance with which the story ends—nailing the sinking *Pequod*'s flag to the mast and catching a seagull with his hammer as he does so. If, then, the novel acknowledges no mediator, no Second Person to be the Face of God, has it any place for the Third Person, that Spirit who speaks with ten thousand tongues through ten thousand faces? Is there any representation in it of the Church of the Redeemed? Strange to say, there is. There is a representation in the novel of the solidarity of the human race as lovable, and as redeemed by love, but it is a representation marked by defiant rejection of the Christian church of the novel's time and place.

The crew of the *Pequod,* "a crew . . . chiefly made up of mongrel renegades, and castaways, and cannibals" (*MD* 186), is the chorus surrounding the protagonist Ahab. His monomaniac obsession is refracted into their collective willingness to follow him, and their bond with each other is the counterweight to his monumental egotism. At the last Ahab will cut himself off from any responsibility to another that threatens to obstruct him on his one predestined path. Not only does he reject the appeal from the captain of the *Rachel,* he rejects even Starbuck, on whom he has to rely for the control of the crew, when he opposes him: "be the front of thy face to me . . . a lipless, unfeatured blank" (*MD* 561). But the relations of the crew members to each other sound an altogether different note. Theirs is a rela tion not so much of sight as of touch, not so much face-to-face as hand to hand, and it has a wholly distinctive affective quality. The sensibility of *Moby-Dick* is emphatically homosexual, and one has to admire the courage—or is it the effrontery?—of the emphasis. What other great Victorian novel in its first few pages shows two men embracing naked in bed together, "a cosy, loving pair" "in our hearts' honeymoon" (*MD* 52, 53)?[9] It is no doubt in the nature of the book's theme that apart from one or two shadowy figures in the early chapters in Nantucket—the significantly named Aunt Charity and Mrs. Hussey—there are no women in the story at all. But out of this con straint, whether or not we regard it as self-imposed, Melville has fashioned one of the main elements in the structure of his book's meaning.

Like their archetype, Dr. Faustus, the captain and crew of a whaler have to renounce wife and family for the duration of their contract. As in the Faustian model too, this renunciation is made a part of a conscious rejection of a Christian pattern of life. The construction in *Moby-Dick* of a homo-sexual alternative to heterosexual love and reproduction is at the same time the construction of an alternative religious model, an alternative model of existence and redemption. The chapter "Cistern and Buckets," for example, tells how Tashtego, the "Indian" harpooneer, is accidentally buried alive in a sperm whale's head while the spermaceti is being removed from it. The head breaks loose from the tackle securing it to the ship and falls into the sea. As it sinks, another of the pagans, Queequeg—"my brave Queequeg," says the affectionate Ishmael (*MD* 343)—dives into the water and by slashing open the side of the head delivers Tashtego from what promised to be his tomb. The operation is more than once described as obstetric; it even includes the midwife's device of turning the baby in the womb to prevent a breech de-livery. It has, no doubt rightly, been called a "second birth"[10]—but if that phrase refers to the new birth through the waters of baptism which sym-bolize death, then the episode is an image, not of Christian baptism, but of an alternative to it. This is, as Ishmael says, a "queer adventure" (*MD* 344), an adventure in inversion. If it is a triumph of obstetrics, it is performed by a male midwife on an adult encased in a thoroughly male, a sperm-secreting, womb. Similarly, if it is a baptism, it is a baptism performed by a pagan on one who remains a pagan. The elimination of femininity from the world of the whaler is synonymous with the elimination of Christianity. We are here in the presence of the extreme case of what Charles Gordon has called "the controverted feminine,"[11] a rejection on theological grounds of feminine language and imagery characteristic of the Reformation and early modern period and particularly of the legend of Faustus. Melville's case is extreme, for his Ishmael rejects the Son of God himself as too womanly. With withering irony he writes:

> [W]hatever they may reveal of the divine love in the Son, the soft, curled, hermaphroditical Italian pictures, in which his idea has been most successfully embodied; these pictures, so destitute as they are of all brawniness, hint nothing of any power, but the mere negative, feminine one of submission and endurance, which on all hands it is conceded, form the peculiar practical virtues of his teachings. (*MD* 376)

The substitution of homosexual and masculine values for heterosexual and feminine makes it possible for *Moby-Dick,* however, to contain a representation of solidarity and redemption despite its rejection of Christ. In the chapter "A Squeeze of the Hand," Melville fully exploits the ambiguous reference of the word *sperm,* along with other puns and incantatory repetitions, in order to create a mood of homoerotic ecstasy in which all human discord passes away forever, an eternal paradise, he says, in which angels in long rows have each of them their hands in a jar of spermaceti. The crew of the *Pequod* squeeze the congealed oil to restore it to its liquid state:

> Squeeze! Squeeze! Squeeze! . . . I squeezed that sperm [Ishmael writes] till a strange sort of insanity came over me; and I found myself unwittingly squeezing my co-laborers' hands in it, mistaking their hands for the gentle [perhaps also "genital"] globules . . . and looking up into their eyes sentimentally; as much as to say,— Oh! my dear fellow beings, why should we longer cherish any social acerbities, or know the slightest ill-humor or envy! Come; let us squeeze hands all round; nay, let us all squeeze ourselves into each other; let us squeeze ourselves universally into the very milk and sperm of kindness. (*MD* 416)[12]

This is the counter that the novel offers to Ahab's monomaniac destructiveness, a universal love embodied in the fellow feelings of the male crew. It was of course totally contrary to the moral teaching of any Christian church in Melville's time and was scarcely mentionable, even in the allusive terms he had chosen, in contemporary secular society. But Melville at the beginning of the novel, like Tashtego at the end, nails his colors to the mast, for the words of the sermon in the Nantucket chapel, which in a sense inaugurates Ishmael's voyage, tell us in what spirit the story that is to come has been written:

> Woe to him who seeks to please rather than to appal! Woe to him whose good name is more to him than goodness! Woe to him who, in this world, courts not dishonor! (*MD* 48)

Melville's courage does not fail him even when his words set him outside any society conceivable in his day, even when the sole church to which he can belong is one that can be found to be named and preached in his works only at the cost of his own dishonor.

The question, then, how there can be such a thing as a Catholic approach to *Moby-Dick* is acutely difficult. Here we have a novel whose principal character and narrator both assert the facelessness of God and disregard his primary commandment, a novel which denies all power to the Son, and which finds the Spirit only in an all-male homosexual communion, which recounts a compact with the Devil carried through with unwavering ruthlessness and as a conscious blasphemy, which disregards half the human race and most normal social relationships, and which shows the economic and social agreements it does depict being usurped and betrayed in the interests of a passionate pursuit of revenge which ends in annihilation. It is certainly a wicked book. Can it be read, as Melville asserted it had been written, without defilement? I am not sure. I fear maybe it strikes not the mask but the face. But perhaps nonetheless a case for it can be made. For all the apparent identity of the views of Ahab and Ishmael in respect of the fundamental theological issue—the facelessness of God—the two are at the end clearly distinguished. Like Goethe's *Faust*, *Moby-Dick* has two endings. The last chapter ends with a Mephistophelian vision of eternal emptiness such as we may assume Ahab to have attained now that he has struck through beyond the wall at last: the surf rolls back over the spot where the *Pequod* goes down as if creation had never been. At this point the fiction's aspiration to be authorless reaches its summit and in the same moment collapses. The only narrative viewpoint appropriate to these last sentences is that of God, the Creator, himself; the attempt to show nothingness founders on the necessity that it should be shown by someone to someone. Schopenhauer concludes *The World as Will and Representation* with a similar paradox, but unlike

Schopenhauer, Melville shows the deference towards reality of the poet. A second ending follows, an "Epilogue" which returns us to the viewpoint of Ishmael, now a survivor, for whom Ahab and the *Pequod* and its crew are the material of memory and a tale to be told. The artificiality of this second conclusion is apparent in its perfunctory brevity and its allusions to the sudden magical benignity of the sharks and seabirds which allows Ishmael to drift unharmed until he is picked up by the *Rachel*. This novel is not, after all, an authorless vision of nothingness but a weaving of words that come from a speaker and go to a listener and make up the endless web of mutual dependency that we know as language. The instrument of this reintegration of narrator and reader into a shared world is the *Rachel,* just as it was the encounter with the *Rachel* that definitively marked Ahab's separation of himself from everything that could be called common humanity and began his final race into destruction. Ahab's determination to meet faceless God and faceless Being "forehead to forehead" led him to ignore the pleas of Captain Gardiner of the *Rachel* to search for his son, another victim of Moby Dick. In life as in theology Ahab dispensed with the Son, through whom God's justice is present in limbs and lives not his, and that act of deicide is now reversed by the final words of the novel. Thanks to the humanity of the mourning *Rachel,* Ishmael, "another orphan"—for he too was abandoned by Ahab, left behind when he was thrown out of the whaleboat in the final chase—is adopted in the place of the missing son. Ishmael has chosen his name to indicate that his is the lesser inheritance, just as the biblical Ishmael was repudiated by his father, Abraham, and founded the lesser line of his descendants, the line which was not to include the Son of God. But that lesser inheritance is great enough, for it is the book *Moby-Dick.* In the place of the Son of God, denied throughout by Ahab and by every reflection of his consciousness, we have the words of Ishmael, creating and giving life and presence to every moment of Ahab's revolt and denial. God, after all, through His Son, creates sinners too and loves and sustains them even as they sin. The consciousness of Ishmael is an extraordinary creation, surpassing even Ahab and Moby Dick, and extraordinarily creative, for it encompasses them both. It begins as the mind and body of an "unlettered" and inexperienced seaman, in bed with Queequeg and learning the multiculturalism of the citizen of a free republic, and it grows ever more implausibly erudite and passionately speculative, verges on omniscience, translates itself into drama, and finally attenuates itself, in the last pages before the Epilogue, almost into nothingness. But throughout, as the image of the author of the fiction, it embodies that deference towards the real that the characters of the fiction—

including Ishmael—reject; just as the material of the narrative is largely a
hymn to the marvels and magnificence of the whale, even though the characters of the fiction seek only to kill and dismember it. A Catholic approach
to *Moby-Dick* can perhaps find in Ishmael the substitute expression of the
creating and loving, judging and forgiving presence of God in the world
which the characters of the fiction deny, and can thus read this book as a
commentary on the revelation to which so much of its vocabulary alludes.[13]
But it may also be that the whaling industry, which provides the book's all-
dominating image of the having and risking that separates modernity from
God, has entered too far into Ishmael's soul and that just as there is too
much about the life of the whale that it ignores—as if what really mattered
about a whale was the volume of its blubber to be chopped up with iron
spades—so there is too much about human life that it ignores as well.

A postscript: possibly the finest thing that Melville wrote apart from
Moby-Dick is the eighth sketch in the series of short tales about the Galápagos Islands published as a collection in 1856 under the title *The Encantadas;
or Enchanted Islands.* "Norfolk Isle and the Chola Widow"[14] tells the utterly
desolate story of Hunilla, a half-Spanish, half–Native American woman, ma-
rooned on one of these inhospitable volcanic islands with her husband and
brother who, shortly after her marriage, have decided to spend some months
there hunting the Galápagos tortoises for their valuable oil. Not long after
their arrival she sees her husband and brother drowned in the surf, and while
she is able to bury her husband under a makeshift cross her brother's body is
lost forever. The French whaler who had undertaken to return the party to
the mainland does not reappear. She suffers some other unnamed horror,
possibly at the hands of other visitors. After three years she is taken off by
the narrator's fellow crewmen and their sympathetic captain, though she has
to leave behind most of the pet dogs who have multiplied during her stay
and been her companions but now presumably must die of thirst. We last
see her riding into her hometown on a donkey which the generosity of the
crew has in part enabled her to buy. Her eyes are fixed on the cross on the
donkey's shoulders which in folklore dedicates the animal to Christ.

Three interrelated features of this story stand out. First, the depth of
sympathy with Hunilla's suffering, to the point where the narrative itself is
put in question. "Against my own purposes," the narrator says, as he comes
to the event he does not name, "a pause descends upon me here. One knows
not whether nature doth not impose some secrecy upon him who has been
privy to certain things. . . . In nature, as in law, it may be libelous to speak
some truths" (NI 267, 269). Throughout the story an attitude of unwavering

respect for Hunilla is preserved, for her pain, for her bravery, and for her reticence. At a certain point even to tell of her qualities would be a trespass. Ishmael knows little of this extreme delicacy required of those who would speak of the moral dignity of human life, and it may be that this story already presages the thirty-five years of silence that separate it from Melville's last prose work, *Billy Budd,* completed just before his death in 1891. Maybe Melville had learned what it might mean to reach the limits of writing. Second, there is in this story an altogether new understanding of Christ— not as the teacher of unmanly patience, but as the man on the cross, the place where God suffers. True, this Christ has no face. Neither the lopsided cross on the grave of Hunilla's husband nor the cross on the donkey's shoulders bears an image, and Hunilla's brass crucifix is "worn featureless, like an ancient graven knocker long plied in vain" (NI 272). She has prayed and knocked and it has not been opened to her, but the cross is still there, and so is she, and Melville perhaps knows that if Christ has a face it is hers. "Humanity, thou strong thing, I worship thee," the narrator writes, "not in the laureled victor, but in this vanquished one" (NI 268). So the third outstanding feature of the story of the Chola widow is that in it Melville has drawn a portrait of a brave and worthy woman. In all these three ways, especially perhaps in this last, Melville hints in this little sketch at what *Moby-Dick,* for all its colossal scope and ambition, fails to include.

CHAPTER 13

Faces (2): *Mansfield Park*

UNLIKE *MOBY-DICK, MANSFIELD PARK* (BEGUN IN 1811 AND FIRST published in 1814)[1] is not an obviously Faustian work. It is probably the least popular of Jane Austen's novels, no doubt because of the rather prim character of its heroine who has the misfortune—as far as readers are concerned—of being always right. That there are nonetheless points of contact with Goethe's world of reflection is shown by some remarkable parallels with his novel *Elective Affinities,* written just after he had completed *Faust: Part One* and published in 1809.[2] The parallels would deserve a study of their own, for which there is no space here, but it is worth mentioning some of them as an indication that the unusual character of this novel in Jane Austen's oeuvre is due to a deep understanding of the needs of the age rather than to a regrettable lapse into moralizing. Both novels concern the trial of virtue in a country house setting, both largely observe a unity of place, and both have heroines who come from penurious backgrounds and are from the beginning in a state of uncomfortable dependency on their benefactors. In both novels contemporary intellectual fashions—a vogue for landscape gardening and the aesthetic "improvement" of estates, for example, and in *Mansfield Park* the popularity of the German dramas of Goethe's adversary, Kotzebue—have an insidious influence on the society depicted and are at the very least a sign of indolence and irresponsibility. In both cases too, though more elaborately and extensively in *Elective Affinities,* the artificially altered landscape takes on a symbolic role, representing in space the moral transgressions of the characters. Above all, both novels are so structured as to present a steadily growing threat to the increasingly isolated heroine, who seems beset by ever subtler threats of corruption and ever more left to her own resources. This gradually intensifying structure is in both cases composed of two parts, the second presenting the problematic of the first in a yet more intractable form, so that an insistent theological undertone becomes apparent in both works, though the theology is very different.

In the case of *Mansfield Park* the first part, consisting of the first of the original three volumes and the first chapters of the second, introduces us to Fanny Price, daughter of an overprolific Lieutenant of Marines, to her four wealthy cousins, and to the establishment at Mansfield Park, the seat of Sir Thomas Bertram. It also introduces us to the beginnings of Fanny's affection for the younger son of the family, Edmund, an affection admitted to no one and scarcely even to herself, since the inequality of their worldly positions rules out any question of marriage—as Sir Thomas notes when first consenting to Fanny's being brought up in his house. The stern authority of Sir Thomas, a benevolent man but unable to make any outward show of affection, is felt in these early pages as an oppressive presence reinforcing Fanny's subordination to her aunts and her lack of confidence in her own worth. His departure for a year and more to attend to his plantations in the Caribbean, taking his elder son, Tom, with him, leaves the house without a guiding hand—much to the relief of his two daughters. The elder, Maria, is soon engaged to a harmless dolt, Mr. Rushworth, who is summed up in Edmund's judgment, thought, not spoken: "If this man had not twelve thousand a year, he would be a very stupid fellow" (*MP* 30). Also as soon as Sir Thomas has left, another and more seriously disturbing element arrives at Mansfield Park with Henry and Mary Crawford, the brother escorting his sister who has come to live with her relatives at the parsonage. Vivacious but crucially lacking in refined moral perception, the Crawfords are also culturally alien: although Henry has a country property he pays it little attention except in the shooting season, and like Mary he prefers to spend his time in London. Money talks to both of them far louder than nature. Mansfield Park is an old-fashioned agricultural estate. Mary shows no understanding of it and is struck with incredulity when money cannot hire her a horse and carriage during the harvest,[3] while Henry's interest in "improvement" (see *MP* 166–67) is aesthetic and theoretical rather than economic and practical. Although he professes to have a great eye for the "capabilities" (*MP* 64) of a place, he worked out his scheme for his own property not on the ground but while he was at school and university (Cambridge, incidentally, then notorious for its hunting fraternity, not the learned Oxford, attended by Edmund). His use of the term "capabilities" shows of course his pretension to emulate Lancelot Brown, employed to modernize the parklands of many of the great English families, most notably perhaps the Temples at Stowe in Buckinghamshire—but the Temples were Whigs, and it is more than clear that the Bertrams are Tories. The presence of the Crawfords subjects Fanny to a series of trials that are increasingly demanding: Mary Crawford at once begins to make advances to Edmund and usurps the pony on which Fanny, thanks to Edmund, has been learning to enjoy outdoor exercise. This is a purely private sorrow for Fanny, though it causes her to "struggle" for some days, we are told, "against discontent and envy" (*MP* 54), but she soon faces a more complex social dilemma. On a visit to the Rushworth estate Henry Crawford flirts outrageously with both the Bertram sisters, to the point that Mr. Rushworth is left deserted by his fiancée and at risk of a public humiliation which even he is capable of perceiving, and Mary Crawford renews her assault on Edmund. Suppressing her own disappointments, Fanny stays alone at her post while the party scatters around the park, and she is able to manage Rushworth's perplexed vanity so as to prevent a disaster. The third trial is more elaborate still. It forms the novel's famous centerpiece and for the first time shows the strong conscience that we have come to recognize in Fanny under deliberate attack from others. Young Tom returns from the West Indies ahead of his father and brings another new element into the company, an enthusiast for amateur theatricals. The idea for a private production of a drama of Kotzebue's is born and is enthusiastically supported by the Crawfords. Despite her curiosity about the theater, which she has never experienced, Fanny watches with alarm the development of a scheme which she is sure would not be approved by Sir Thomas. She has rightly sensed, moreover, not just that the plan is undignified but that the project is arousing and gratifying wrongful emotions: Henry Crawford and Maria Bertram spend an excessive amount of time rehearsing together, Rushworth is made to play an asinine count, and even Edmund is drawn in to play a pastor married off at the end to Mary Crawford. The persuasion of Edmund to take part is a special triumph for Mary Crawford: nonplussed when she first learned that he intends to become a clergyman, she has since been doing her best to belittle that profession without alienating him altogether. Not content with persuading Edmund to travesty his future vocation, the would-be players turn on Fanny: she too is needed, if only for a minor part, and although she stands firm for a while, she is inveigled into assisting with a private rehearsal, is surprised by a last-minute request just to read some lines, and is on the point of being entrapped when Sir Thomas's unexpected return puts an end to the whole project.

With the restoration of external authority, the first part of Fanny's testing is concluded. Order returns to Mansfield Park; Maria and Rushworth are married and leave; Edmund announces his intention to seek ordination in the near future. But this interval of calm is only preparing for Fanny the more serious trial which occupies the second half of the book. An underemployed Henry Crawford turns his attention to Fanny and out of sheer mischief forms the purpose of making her love him. Up to this point in the story we have been able to see Sir Thomas Bertram as the embodiment of moral authority: his return as a deus ex machina seems to have confirmed that role, and the terror he inspired in Fanny as a child could easily be interpreted as the source of her sense of right and wrong, as well as of her timorousness. Her pronounced moral sense would then be little more than submission to established social power. But in the second phase of the narrative Sir Thomas himself, his judgment and authority, is called into question, and he becomes Fanny's adversary and tempter. For to Sir Thomas Henry Crawford seems a most desirable match for his niece, who is fortunate to have the attentions of a man of such means, and he lends his support to the suitor. And to do him justice, Henry Crawford is soon the victim of his own stratagem and starts genuinely to pursue Fanny, and with a serious intent of marriage. Or at least he thinks his pursuit is genuine and his intent serious. In order to resist him Fanny has to believe not only that she knows better than Sir Thomas, but that she knows Henry Crawford better than he knows himself. She knows from what she has seen of him before Sir Thomas's return that he is a man of no "permanence" (*MP* 31) and that his behavior during the theatrical venture, and his recollection of that episode as the happiest time of his life, prove him to have "a corrupted mind" (*MP* 155).

But Jane Austen knows Fanny, and human nature, well enough to tell us that she would have been unable to resist the intensive courtship of "such a man as Crawford, in spite of there being some previous ill-opinion of him to be overcome, had not her affection been engaged elsewhere" (*MP* 159). Her unrequited love for the kindly Edmund, undeclared as it must be to anyone, sustains her throughout her confrontation with Sir Thomas—as Crawford makes himself ever more genuinely agreeable, uses his influence to be of service to her beloved brother, and finally declares himself in form. Her love sustains her even through the hardest trial of all, her effective banishment from Mansfield Park to her parents' home in Portsmouth, where

Sir Thomas hopes that an intensive course in the reality of poverty will bring her to her senses. All Fanny's supports are stripped away. The man whose voice was law has become her persecutor, she has to tell him "that he was wrong" and conceal her love from his suspicions (*MP* 213, 215); she has been expelled from the place that had brought order and a measure of consolation to her vulnerable existence; and when Edmund goes to London to join the Crawfords' circle for a while, she has to live in terror of the letter from him that will tell her of the engagement that will withdraw the last prop supporting her resolution "never, never, never" (*MP* 236) to say yes to the corrupted Mr. Crawford. Denuded of everything that has protected her, she is exposed to the final assault: Henry Crawford seeks her out in her exile in Portsmouth and in the guise of a reformed character—unrepulsed by her restricted surroundings, civil and genial to her nautical father, who smells of spirits, showing now, since months of absence have elapsed, a real persistence in a single course, showing too a change of heart towards his Norfolk estates to which he intends to return in order to save an honest tenant from being done out of his due by his manager (*MP* 280). When he leaves, Fanny reflects that he is "astonishingly more gentle and regardful of others than formerly" (*MP* 281). The dénouement, however, is swift. Henry Crawford does not return to a life of good works in Norfolk but stays in London and enters on an adulterous liaison with Maria Bertram, now Mrs. Rushworth, with whom he elopes. While he commits this act of social suicide, an illness of Edmund's brother Tom causes Mary Crawford to think that Edmund may soon be the heir to Mansfield Park and that she can perhaps overcome the rooted objections she has so far felt to being anything as dull as a parson's wife. Fanny reads her accurately at once: "she had . . . learnt to think nothing of consequence but money" (*MP* 296). But Edmund is horrified at the levity with which Mary Crawford treats her brother's transgression and breaks off his suit at the moment when she thinks she might yield to him. Mansfield Park is in mourning, but there are now no obstacles to the recognition of the manifest destiny of Edmund and Fanny. "Let other pens dwell on guilt and misery," Miss Austen breaks in (*MP* 312)—and in the final chapter she briskly distributes rewards and punishments all around and unites her lovers as the first worthy occupants of the parsonage that her story has seen.

The structure of *Mansfield Park,* then, is a relentless, single-minded—if two-stage—tightening of the focus on one point only: Fanny's resistance to the temptation represented by the intrusion of the Crawfords into Mansfield Park. The temptation, the testing, penetrates ever more layers of distraction and protection and comes ever closer to the core of her being. She has to overcome the temptation in the form, first, of pain to her comfort and self-esteem when the Crawfords first arrive; then as a challenge to show fortitude and self-denial in keeping a society together when the party visits Mr. Rushworth's estate; then as an unvarnished suggestion that she should do wrong during the theatrical episode. Then it speaks with the insinuating tones of impersonated love; then with the borrowed voice of social authority itself; then as the more than merely external pressure of the reduced circum- stances of life in Portsmouth—for the spiritual deprivation of her family is even more oppressive. And finally it speaks as a direct appeal to her sense of morality and the possibility of reform. Two related questions arise about this structure: what is the nature of the temptation? and what is the nature, the core, of Fanny's resistance?

As to the first question, we are clearly dealing with a struggle for power—a struggle which the book enables us to identify as, no doubt among other things, a struggle between social and economic "interests" (as Sir Thomas calls them) (*MP* 30) for the future of England (represented here by the future, bodily and spiritual, of Fanny Price). In the simplest contem- porary terms it is a struggle between Whig interests and Tory—between trade and finance, on the one hand, the "money" that alone is of conse- quence to Mary Crawford, and land, on the other. On the one hand, there is the busy, cruel, fashionable world of London where nothing lasts, cer- tainly not marriages, and for which the country is simply a place to which one retires occasionally for entertainment or to "improve" the "beauty" and "ornament" (*MP* 166) of one's properties. On the other hand, there is Mans- field Park, ordered and slow-moving, a place of serious husbandry, where Nature is acknowledged as a power in her own right: Edmund and Fanny even share an interest in the stars (*MP* 81), in a Nature beyond all human "improvement," while Mary Crawford sees "nature, inanimate nature, with little observation" (*MP* 58; cp. 142). On the one hand, there are tasteless modern German plays, which when the novel was being written had for over ten years been condemned by the English press as socially subversive and no better than French Jacobin tracts.[4] On the other hand, there are the inexhaustible riches of Shakespeare, eloquently declaimed by Mr. Crawford (though he admits he never read him much before) when he is seeking to impersonate the cause of virtue.

However, we have only to put the issue in terms of these simple oppo- sitions to realize that they are inadequate. For Mansfield Park itself is com- promised by its accommodations with the other party: how otherwise could it be so susceptible to the lure of the Crawfords? It is Sir Thomas's absence while seeing to his Caribbean ventures that permits them to establish their hold on his family. He allows the consideration of Rushworth's enormous wealth to override his judgment that the man is a dunce and his certain knowledge that his daughter does not love him (*MP* 138). It is an inability to give value to human feeling, as pronounced in its own way as the insensitivity of the Crawfords, added to that overvaluation of material advantage, that makes him try to impose his will on his niece. In their confrontation it becomes clear that the true resistance to the corrupting interests represented by the Crawfords lies, not in some countervailing political or economic or social party, but in Fanny. Her consistent integrity will in the end rescue even Sir Thomas from his compromises—the man who at one point seemed the embodiment of solidity and authority.

But what is it in Fanny that resists? Gradually the story strips away the contingent and secondary elements to reveal what is primary and essential to her opposition to the Crawfords. It is not just personal pique, for she rises above that in the pony episode. It is not just the timorous and diffident personality, for which Sir Thomas upbraids her, for her opposition to the theatricals is public and isolating. It is not mere passivity, for sensitive intervention is required to hold the party together during the visit to the Rushworth estates. It is not, obviously, the blind submission to Sir Thomas of Fanny's aunts. It is not even the fear of losing Mansfield Park, for that is taken from her when she is sent to Portsmouth. We can perhaps identify it negatively by the Crawfords' lack of it, a lack which leads them both to be characterized, at different points, as "evil" (*MP* 206, 309). When Edmund has seen through Mary Crawford, after hearing her blame her brother not for his adultery but for his making it so public through elopement, he tells Fanny, "[H]er is not a cruel nature. I do not consider her as meaning to wound my feelings. The evil lies yet deeper; in her total ignorance, unsuspiciousness of there being such feelings. . . . Her's are faults of principle, Fanny" (*MP* 309–10). When Fanny is trying to understand the repugnance she feels at Crawford's renewed assault once his good services to her brother have put her at a disadvantage, she discerns "a gross want of feeling and humanity where his own pleasure was concerned. And, alas! . . . no principle to supply as a duty what the heart was deficient in" (*MP* 223; cp. 215). When Sir Thomas has learnt his lesson, has rid his household of all association with the Crawfords and set his hopes on Edmund and Fanny, he is said to be "sick of ambitious and mercenary connections" and "prizing more and more the sterling good of principle and temper" (*MP* 320). "Principle" is what distinguishes Fanny from the Crawfords: principle, the first beginning of the moral life, so primary that Lévinas would call it beginningless, that is what the analytic structure of *Mansfield Park* finally isolates as the core of Fanny's resistance. That, in her own words to Henry Crawford, is "a better guide in ourselves, if we would attend to it, than any other person can be" (*MP* 280). It is principle that keeps her alone firm when everyone around her falls victim to delusion or compromise.

Or is it? One other element is not stripped away from Fanny in her experience of purgation and suffering, though she is in mortal terror that it may be: her love and hope for Edmund. That is the secret that she keeps from the searching gaze of Sir Thomas and the even more penetrating insight of her rival, Mary Crawford. That he has a "pre-engaged heart to attack" Henry Crawford has "no suspicion" (*MP* 221). Fanny's love is almost as private to her, almost as central to what she is, as her principle. Almost—but not quite. The presence of this hidden motive in Fanny's heart casts a slight air of ambiguity, a hint of calculation over her words and thoughts at times, which perhaps explains why some readers find her a prig and a hypocrite. It is all a matter of an "almost." The recital of his last interview with Mary Crawford leaves Edmund "so much affected, that Fanny, watching him with silent, but most tender concern, was almost sorry that the subject had been entered on at all" (*MP* 310). Is she "almost" sorry—rather than just "sorry"—because her compassion for Edmund is modified by principle, by the recognition that he has been saved from disaster and that articulating his feelings, painful though it may be to do so, will help to secure him against regret? Or is she "almost" sorry because her compassion is modified by her hidden motive, by the surely joyful thought that Mary Crawford's rivalry is at an end. We are, after all, told at the start of the conversation that Fanny listens "with . . . curiosity and concern . . . , . . . pain and . . . delight" (*MP* 308). How do we assess her decision to "add . . . to [Edmund's] knowledge of [Mary Crawford's] real character, by some hint of what share his brother's state of health [i.e., the likelihood that Tom might die and Edmund become the heir] might be supposed to have in her wish for a complete reconciliation" (*MP* 312)? Can we be sure that the interests of "reason" are here unalloyed by any other consideration? Fanny, we are told, felt "more than justified" in telling Edmund the truth—"more than" is another "almost." Was she *fully* justified, because she was acting on principle? Or was she justified—and something more as well? Gratified, perhaps? It is the last turn in the narrative before the author enters in her own person in the final chapter, and the question in our minds is left unresolved, just as the relationship between Edmund and Fanny is left by the last words of the chapter in a state of promise rather than finality: "Fanny's friendship was all that he had to cling to" (*MP* 312).

It seems that even a narrative as circumstantial and purposeful as *Mansfield Park* cannot disengage principle from the tangle of human motives and exhibit it in its pure state. If ever there was a novel that exerted itself to discern and formulate the primal command in human life, the original ethical modification of our being, this surely is it. And the conclusion is that it cannot be done. The limit cannot be transgressed that separates secular from sacred writing, though only the attempt to reach it, through that progressive tightening of the focus, produces the circumstantiality and the purposeful analysis. The final chapter, in which the author makes her bow to the audience and defines her work as "entertainment" (*MP* 320), contains a surprise as extraordinary in its way as the conclusion to Goethe's *Faust*, a sign of deference towards what cannot be uttered, achieved by the same device of the alternative ending. Jane Austen, in her distribution of summary justice to all her characters, includes in her account of Henry Crawford's fate a vision of what might have been, a vision of what might have happened had that last element of support been stripped away from Fanny and had she been obliged to renounce her love for Edmund. The course Henry Crawford had engaged in when visiting Fanny at Portsmouth was the "way of happiness." He had only to hold to it. The impersonation of reform might have become reform itself. "Would he have deserved more, there can be no doubt that more would have been obtained. . . . Would he have persevered, and uprightly, Fanny must have been his reward—and a reward very voluntarily bestowed—within a reasonable period from Edmund's marrying Mary." The view back from this rewriting of the story's end is quite dizzying. Were all those scenes and sufferings, was all that fearful firmness of purpose in the confrontation with Sir Thomas, the certainty of the corruption of Crawford's principles and the gross inhumanity of his feelings (*MP* 215, 223), the absolute assurance that she could never, never, never marry him only so much disguising—by Fanny, from Fanny—of one overriding motive: to leave herself free for Edmund? Was that all her principle amounted to? I think not. But I do think that Austen elaborates her alternative ending in order that we should ask these questions. What they amount to, I believe, is the final stage in that ever more focused questioning which gives the book its structure—and the question being asked, from the start of the book is, what is principle? We already know that it is not, for example, fear of authority or need for security. Now we discover that it is not a psychological factor, or a state of mind, and not a trait of character either, not "temper" as it is called, from which the book more than once distinguishes it. Principle is not a motive at all, in the sense in which love for Edmund is a motive. Principle is the awareness that, whatever one's motives or circumstances, life is to be lived as a duty, as subject to the Law, and not as a possession, to be either risked or consumed. The mental experiment shows that in the absence of that last supporting motive, the love for Edmund, the story of Fanny's principled life could, subject to two conditions, become a very different story, though her life would not for that be any less principled: it would become the story of how a girl of strong ethical sense but immature judgment learned to redirect her affections and reassess a man who, under her influence, was genuinely capable of reformation. The two conditions would be that Mary Crawford's distaste for a clerical marriage should be overcome; and that Henry should have done his duty by his deserving tenant and gone to Norfolk rather than stayed in London. The conditions have nothing to do with the purity of Fanny's principle: the events we have seen in the plot so far could be part of that different story, and yet we would not have to reinterpret them as evidence of her hypocrisy. The conditions depend on the behavior of people other than Fanny, and if they were fulfilled we would certainly have to reassess Fanny's judgment but not her moral integrity. But we only have to utter those words "if they were fulfilled" to see the fallacy in the mental experiment. For how could those conditions be fulfilled? Austen seems to be presenting them playfully as within the power of her authorial caprice, as if those changes could be brought about by a little more of the brisk tidying up that goes on in the rest of this final chapter. Thereby—deliberately, of course—she provokes us to object that the whole of her story so far has shown these conditions to be impossible. Fanny's judgment is right, as are her principles. She has judged, almost for as long as she has known them, that Henry is the sort of man who would neglect an important duty for the sake of his own pleasure and that Mary is the sort of person who has, as Edmund put it, "a total ignorance, an unsuspiciousness of there being such feelings" as those which lead him to wish to be a clergyman. We have believed that judgment to be right and not just to be determined by psychological motives, not just to proceed, for example, from Fanny's love for Edmund and consequent feelings of rivalry, as if, were that love to be thought away in a mental experiment, we should have to think away her assessment of the Crawfords as well. We know Fanny's assessment of the Crawfords' lack of ethical principle is right because we have evidence of it, evidence as direct as any secular narrative can provide, within the limitation that no secular narrative can directly represent the ethical imperative itself. Our objective evidence—as we might call it—of the rightness of Fanny's judgment of the Crawfords is their behavior in church.

The church is the central theme of *Mansfield Park*—not one theme among others, nor a quaint excrescence that gives the book a distinctive (or possibly more disagreeable) profile. The church is necessarily central because "principle" is central, and the church is principle made visible, principle given a name and a face, embodied in a particular time and place and social context. Let us cast our minds back to Part 1, in which I considered the relation of the Jewish Law to the original obligation of responsibility for the neighbor. Christ was the embodiment of the Law, its fulfillment in the flesh, and Christ's mystical, spiritual body was the church. And that means even the church of Jane Austen's early-nineteenth-century England, a prey to rationalism and neglect, to worldliness and indolence and all the maladies of establishment, that are shown with satirical ferocity in the progression of the Mansfield pastor Dr. Grant, brother-in-law of the Crawfords, from dinner to dinner, from a goose to a canonry to an apoplectic fit. The church may be in this novel like the chapel in the Rushworths' family seat—"left to the silence and stillness which reigned in it with few interruptions throughout the year" (*MP* 64)—but its stillness is that of the still center. It is tacitly present with us throughout in the issue that divides Edmund from Mary Crawford and unites him with Fanny: his resolve to become a clergyman.

It may be something of a canard that Austen claimed the subject of *Mansfield Park* was ordination,[5] but the idea gained currency only because it reflected a truth about the book. To be ordained is, in the most general sense, to accept a historically and institutionally defined station in life as a means of responding to the original ethical imperative, and Edmund makes it clear to Mary, as soon as she knows of his intention, that this is how he understands it. To her, who judges by London standards, by the standards of the world of money and ever-changing fashion, "[a] clergyman is nothing" (*MP* 66), and to want to be one is to be devoid of any comprehensible ambition. Edmund replies:

> I cannot call that situation nothing, which has the charge of all that is of the first importance to mankind, individually or collectively considered, temporally and eternally—which has the guardianship of religion and morals, and consequently of the manners which result from their influence. . . . The *manners* I speak of, might rather be

called *conduct,* perhaps, the result of good principles; the effect, in short, of those doctrines which it is [the clergy's] duty to teach and recommend. (*MP* 66)

To Edmund as to Fanny the "manners" to which this novel could seem to be devoted are the result of "principles," and thus are the visible practice of religion, with the guardianship of which the clergy are charged at ordination. When Sir Thomas, at the end of the story, reflects ruefully on the errors in his upbringing of his daughters, he makes the same equation of principle and religion:

He feared that principle, active principle, had been wanting, . . . that sense of duty which can alone suffice. They had been instructed theoretically in their religion, but never required to bring it into daily practice. (*MP* 314)

Edmund, by contrast, envisages his life as a clergyman as precisely a daily obligation (*MP* 170), not just delivering a sermon on Sundays, but living among his parishioners and giving them his "constant attention"—as, we are told, it is not possible to do in the large London parishes from which the Crawfords take their conception of the clerical state (*MP* 66). The Crawfords, however, see life not as a matter of a station to which one is ordained, a call that is heard, and which imposes a daily obligation of responsibility: the Crawfords, in their London way, see life as a game.

The conversation in which Edmund rejects Henry's plans for the "improvement" of his parsonage as incompatible with the duties of his state is interleaved with the progress of a game of cards in which Henry shows himself "pre-eminent in all the lively turns, quick resources, and playful impudence" that the game requires and that are characteristic of his way of living (*MP* 165). Tony Tanner has noticed the symbolic significance of Mary Crawford's play.[6] She stakes too much for the return that is on offer, just as in life she pays too much in the currency that really counts for the sake of victory in inessentials: "The game was her's, and only did not pay her for what she had given to secure it" (*MP* 166). But it is important also to notice the structural contrast with the surrounding conversation.[7] There is an alternative to the modern way of life, and it is represented by the church. Similarly there is a structural contrast throughout the book between acting and ordination, the actor who plays all roles and the clergyman who accepts the call to one. Edmund defends throughout the seriousness of the call to ordination, and it is, as Tanner also remarks,[8] the low point in his development when he briefly accepts the part of stage clergyman in Kotzebue's play. Henry Crawford sets out to make Fanny love him, as a game, and in the same spirit in which he plays cards. He sets out to act the part of the lover of a serious woman (and is then trumped and overtrumped by the seriousness of life: in the course of his playacting he discovers the real attraction of Fanny, and then loses her for real too). The summit of his deception—and it is self-deception also, for he is not devilish and is no Iago—is to reverse Edmund's transgression and play the part of clergyman in real life. He engages in serious discussion with Edmund about "liturgy" (*MP* 231)—the false note struck by that fashionably intellectual word warns us of his true intent—and about the qualities of a good sermon, even offering to preach himself, if only from time to time and before a London audience, all as part of his assault on Fanny's affections (*MP* 231). Fanny sees through him, as he realizes, when he condemns himself out of his own mouth, admitting that he could not play such a part "of a constancy." Constancy is of course the decisive distinction between acting and ordination, for roles cease but ordination goes on: constancy demonstrates principle.

Henry Crawford's final stratagem—with which, when his story ends, he is perhaps on the point of convincing himself as well as Fanny—is to play the part of the constant lover. The last scene in which we see him in this role, the last scene in which he is directly represented to us at all, shows him in Portsmouth accompanying the Price family to church. Whatever its defects, however slatternly the housekeeping and however poverty-stricken their accommodation, Fanny's family has two great merits that between them make it plausible that so powerful a sense of duty as hers could have been born there: first, Fanny's father, though overfond of the bottle, stays faithful to his wife; and, second, the whole family goes to church, regularly, and together. The Crawfords would seem to have lacked both these supports in their childhood. Henry Crawford, by joining the Prices for Sunday morning service, comes to the very heart and origin of Fanny's moral experience, and it is only at this point that she begins to waver. But we know that even here, even by entering the house of God, Henry Crawford cannot show himself to be a man of principle, without a break with his past more decisive than anything he hints at to Fanny. For we inevitably recall his first appearance in a place of worship, at the start of his relations with the Bertrams, the only other occasion when the narrative takes us inside a sacred building. In the Rushworth family chapel Mary Crawford made Fanny, we are told, "too angry for speech" (*MP* 62) when she painted a satirical picture of the agonies of tedium suffered in that place by previous generations of Rushworths and their servants, until the practice of morning and evening prayer conducted by a domestic chaplain was discontinued by the present Mr. Rushworth's father. "Every generation has its improvements," was Mary Crawford's comment (*MP* 62), as if we had not already learned to be suspicious of that word *improvement*. These improprieties in Mary's words, however, only pave the way for Henry's far greater impropriety in action. With Maria Bertram and Mr. Rushworth standing side by side, looking at the chapel's east end, it is suggested that if Edmund were ordained the marriage ceremony could be performed then and there. Henry Crawford chooses this moment, which is figuratively, therefore, or at least in travesty, a wedding, to "whisper . . . gallantries" to Rushworth's fiancée. He does not like to see her so close to the altar, he says, and if called on to give her away would do so with great reluctance (*MP* 63). The chapel is thus made a place not of marriage but of adultery, and this act of desecration both prefigures the development that is to come and inaugurates it. It is the beginning of the playacting that will end in real wrongdoing. When Henry Crawford enters the church in Portsmouth is he concluding that development with another act of desecration? The events that follow suggest that he is. The alternative ending allows that even then there was perhaps still hope for him.

In Fanny's world and circumstances the established Church of England is the socially and institutionally visible and audible presence of the call to principle, the call of the Law. The Crawfords' disrespect for the church, in word and deed, is not merely an offense against Fanny or Edmund's sense of propriety, as if it were a matter personal to them and the moral quality of what the Crawfords do or say were determined by Fanny or Edmund's motives for feeling or ignoring the offense. Rather the Crawfords' attitude, and the London world and way of life from which they have derived it, is shown by that disrespect for the church to be both socially and institutionally subversive. It is not after all true to say that the only opposition to the Crawfords shown in the novel lies in Fanny's principles. The opposition to the Crawfords is shown to lie in the church, for the Crawford way of life subverts the operation of a Law in whose nature it is to have such a social and institutional face. That face is turned to us in the novel's representation of the Church of England, in the profanation of it by the Crawfords but also in the acceptance of its order by Edmund and Fanny. Jane Austen thus resolves the fundamental problem posed for her by her desire to write a novel about the operation of "principle"—the problem, namely, that principle, the first origin and source of the ethical life, is unrepresentable by secular writing. For on the one hand she shows us the different responses of the Crawfords, Edmund, and Fanny to the appeal of principle, that speaks through the features of its social and institutional face, the church. And on the other hand she pointedly refrains from even attempting to communicate to us the appeal itself, to speak with its words or in its name. We are never introduced into a church in order to hear the words of a sermon or a service, for all the discussion of both that takes place between Edmund and Henry; we are never made privy to any prayers or devotions of Fanny, though her trials furnish ample occasion for both; nor are her thoughts, or indeed those of the Crawfords, stylized into struggles of conscience between virtue and vice, between the words of Scripture and the words of some tempter, for all the insistence throughout the novel on the need to turn religion into a matter of daily practice. Instead there is a conflict between two English social institutions, London and the Church, presented to us as a conflict between two evaluations of Edmund's decision to be ordained: Mary Crawford's— that it is an empty gesture, a nothing, which nonetheless stands in the way of a desirable and possibly profitable union—and Fanny Price's—that it is confirmation of a shared responsiveness to the unnameable Law which, if it cannot unite her to Edmund, must at least distance her from Henry Crawford, so long as he does not share it too. The church, and ordination to it, is therefore central to the novel, for it is what enables Jane Austen to present the social fabric of England, and its continuation in the "manners" and "conduct" of her characters, as mattering, as the battleground of "principle."

By the same token, the church is also the element in the novel's structure which enables Jane Austen to present it, and herself, its author, as the voice of a particular time and place, as accessible to the historical hermeneutic that applies to secular rather than sacred literature, to what is spoken rather than to what is written. The Church which is here the historically specific face of unrepresentable "principle" is the early-nineteenth-century church of rural England.[9] It is a modest affair, depicted unsparingly but without polemic, a church of unsung and largely unnoticed constancy in prayer and in its "attention" to its duties. Its character is suggested to us in the description of the Rushworth family chapel—"nothing awful[,] . . . nothing melancholy, nothing grand . . . no aisles, no arches, no inscriptions, no banners," just mahogany pews and crimson velvet cushions installed, we are told, in the time of James II (*MP* 61–62). There may, in other words, have been some overlavish expenditure, as was to be expected of that era, but there was clearly no compromise with that monarch's Catholicism; the Anglicanism of *Mansfield Park* is unshaken by Gothic revivalism, the Catholic resurgence of the period after 1800, or indeed by Methodism. It may seem a dry and sober affair—it certainly did to Mary Crawford—but it was, the novel tells us, true to the essential. We should also remember that this was the church that later in the nineteenth century first nurtured England's finest Catholic poet since Pope, for Gerard Manley Hopkins was as an Anglican a disciple not only of Pusey but also of George Herbert. The last stage of my investigation of the relation between sacred and secular literature requires us to consider in more detail some literary and cultural reflections of the relation between the Law of God and the church in England.

Rewards and Fairies (1):
The Idea of England

I HAVE BEEN CONSIDERING THE RELATION BETWEEN THE SACRED and the secular in literature of the modern period, the period since the Reformation. I have suggested that wagering—risking what one has in order to have more—is a characteristically modern attitude to living which has defined a characteristically modern form of secularity. Since the late medieval period this realm of having and risking has been opposed to the realm of the sacred, the realm of attentiveness to Being and to its primary modification, the Law. The mission of Christianity in this period—a mission which exploded into explicitness in the movement of Reformation—has been, as it always is, to find the word of reconciliation that will recover this new form of secularity for the sacred realm, to find the terms in which its redemption by Christ, already accomplished, can be articulated in human deeds and words and so made the potential object of faith. Secular literature—secular, since the Reformation, in this modern sense of secularity—necessarily, though often unwittingly, shares in that mission. For, to a degree determined by their place in the spectrum of writtenness, the genres of secular literature struggle too to find words that express why and how the world matters, why and how the world, as something that is possessed and risked, is also a revelation of what is and of what ought to be. I have also suggested that— partly perhaps because of the Reformation schism itself—the church has, to a considerable extent, failed in its mission. Attempts from deep within the realms of secularity to find the word of reconciliation have sometimes met with more obvious success and furnished true modern images of redemption.[1] But without a persuasive example from the church to follow, such attempts have more often gone astray, sometimes sadly, sometimes wildly, sometimes horribly. As a last stage in this investigation I want to pursue a particular secular theme, and its relation to its theological ground, through the whole of the modern period, though with particular reference to the twentieth century. Part 1 ended with some thoughts about the sacred land of Israel. The parallel secular theme with which I conclude this Part 3 is the idea of England: the ways in which English cultural productions reflect a changing conception of the relation between England and God. Inevitably, I shall venture rather beyond the bounds of literature, but the result, I hope, will be a proof by example that, at least when they have to define what matters, the written and the unwritten are continuous.

Rewards and Fairies is the title of the sequel volume to Rudyard Kipling's *Puck of Pook's Hill.* The two books, in which a rather earthy fairy, Puck, introduces two English children to fictitious but representative figures from the national past, together make up an imaginative, or imaginary, history of England which once had a prominent position on the bookshelf of every middle-class English nursery. The title comes from a seventeenth-century poem loudly intoned by Puck in a deep voice when the children first meet him.[2] He treats it as a motto for fairies in the modern world, a protest against the notion that they have disappeared, as if Kipling's books were a demonstration that the British Empire at its apogee has its fairies too. But the poem, known as *The Fairies' Farewell,* points in quite the opposite direction.

> Farewell, Rewards & *Faeries,*
> 　　Good Houswives now may say;
> For now foule Slutts in Daries
> 　　Doe fare as well as they;
> And though they sweepe theyr Hearths no less
> 　　Then Maydes were wont to doe,
> Yet who of late for Cleaneliness
> 　　Finds *six-pence* in her Shoe?
>
> Lament, lament, old Abbies,
> 　　The *Faries* lost Command:

They did but change Priests *Babies,*
   But some have changd your *Land;*
And all your Children sprung from thence
   Are now growne *Puritanes:*
Who live as *Changelings* ever since
   For love of your Demaines.

At Morning & at Evening both
   You merry were & glad,
So little Care of Sleepe or Sloth
   These Prettie ladies had.
When *Tom* came home from labour,
   Or *Ciss* to Milking rose,
Then merrily, merrily went theyre Tabor,
   And nimbly went theyre Toes.

Wittness those Rings & Roundelayes
   Of theirs, which yet remaine,
Were footed in Queene *Maries* dayes
   On many a Grassy Playne;
But, since of late *Elizabeth,*
   And later *Iames,* came in,
They never daunc'd on any heath
   As *when the Time hath bin*

By which wee note the *Faries*
   Were of the old Profession;
Theyre Songs were *Ave Maryes,*
   Theyre Daunces were *Procession.*
But now, alas, they all are dead,
   Or gone beyond the Seas,
Or Farther for Religion fled,
   Or elce they take theyre Ease . . .³

This poem is something rarer than fairies in the modern world: a light-hearted ballad written by a bishop, Richard Corbett (1582–1635), a High Churchman under Archbishop Laud. Though lighthearted and satirical, it contains some serious, even daring, cultural-historical reflection. Belief in

fairies, it says, has gone out with the Reformation: they last danced on English grass in Queen Mary's days, and Elizabeth and James finally banished
them. Fairies were clearly Catholics (ll. 33–34), a sentiment not noted by
Kipling, who had little sympathy for the Catholic church. But what is the
consequence of the loss of the fairies? Rewards have been lost too—the
gratuitous rewards for good and dutiful behavior that providence seemed to
bring, the good luck that attended virtue—you kept your fireplaces clean
and one day the fairies dropped sixpence in your shoe. In the modern, post-
Reformation England of the seventeenth century there is no such straightforward, unconsidered harmony between the nonhuman world and human
moral behavior. Instead, so the implication must run, virtue is its own reward, and if you get sixpence, that is your wages for the work you have
done, not a free gift from Dame Fortune. The ballad points to a connection
between England's national Reformation and a change in economic and
moral thinking. In the days of "the old Profession," the old creed, work and
leisure were equally the occasion of merriment (ll. 17–24): work was valuable in itself, therefore, not for the money it earned. The fairies in Corbett's
poem represent a natural principle of justice which ensures that what our
faith tells us is right and wrong about our everyday conduct, about the things
we daily do and make, receives its due reward and punishment in everyday
terms. The departure of the fairies therefore means that that link between
the sacred and the secular by way of natural justice, or natural law, is broken:
rewards can now be only either the wage for the labor performed or the
result of the exercise of naked power, by which, for example, the lands of
the abbeys have been usurped by Puritans. The new economy requires a
new and sterner theology. What is important about this *jeu d' esprit* is not its
idealized picture of the past but its awareness that the present is different,
and that the discontinuity affects not only beliefs about God but beliefs about
morality and money as well. That moral, economic, and indeed theological
dimension of the poem was ignored by Kipling when he commandeered it
for a purpose directly opposite to its intent. He suppressed what it really said
about fairies—that they were Catholic and they were gone—and by denying
the discontinuity made his own book into a statement about the continuity
through the ages of a thing called England, destined to be what in his own
day it had become: the heart of Empire. We now need to investigate how
this thing called England came into being and grew to a point where it
completely occluded in the consciousness of an intelligent and sensitive
twentieth-century writer a much more profound phenomenon: the radical
change brought about by the Reformation years.

Let us then first go back to the eve of the radical change—to a form of cultural production which reached its pinnacle in the late fifteenth century, which was essentially English, and which was known throughout Europe as such, for it was made, literally, from English substance, and yet to which the concept of England is wholly irrelevant.

The Victoria and Albert Museum in London has the world's best collection of medieval English alabaster carvings. Among the most popular themes of the carvings is the Trinity, and the museum has a particularly fine late-fifteenth-century example, with particularly well preserved coloring, of an interesting variant of the theme.[4] God the Father, his hands raised in blessing, looks down on God the Son, who is held between his knees and whose redeeming blood is being collected by angels in chalices—Holy Grails—as it flows from his hands and his feet. Those who see the panel for the first time will, however, naturally ask: where in this representation of the Trinity is the Holy Spirit? The answer, strictly speaking, is, in a hole. The Spirit has disappeared, for It was separately carved and secured by a dowel to the main panel from which presumably it protruded considerably. The dowel was inserted into a hole that can still be seen in the center of God the Father's chest, just above what looks like a basket of fruit hanging over the thorn-crowned head of the Savior. That little harvest is the distinguishing feature of this subgroup of Holy Trinities: the napkin, as the art historians call it, hanging from the Father's palms, contains only metaphorical fruit. The little human heads, as closer inspection reveals them to be, are representations of the souls of the blessed, of those saved by the sacrificial action depicted below them. In a particularly interesting subgroup of this variant of the Trinity theme, however, there is no dowel hole, for there never was a representation of the Spirit at all. Whether for practical or theological reasons the place of the Spirit was taken by the Souls of the redeemed. But perhaps we might say that in that case the Spirit was represented after all, represented in its effects or actions, in the many spirits of the redeemed, in the redemption enacted in human lives. Such an image, then, is the material manifestation of a public world of which it can clearly be said that God was not hidden in it; it is the material manifestation of the Spirit as present at every turn in a shared framework for living and thinking.

Hegel tells us, when talking of the Spirit, to distinguish between subjective, objective, and absolute Spirit, and first of all these alabasters are physical manifestations of God's operation in and as subjective Spirit. Although many panels were probably the central panel of an altarpiece, smaller representations of the Trinity were especially popular for personal and family devotion, and a number have been preserved in decorated portable wooden housings. Francis Cheetham's standard catalogue of English alabasters reproduces a painting of a fifteenth-century Flemish interior showing a Trinity mounted on a chimney breast over a fireplace, with a candle bracket in front of it.[5] Even as an altarpiece, however, an alabaster Trinity is an image of the divine mercy communicated to the individual who contemplates it. The image of the redeemed souls in the center of the panel, in the place assigned to the Spirit, and even, as we have seen, substituting for It altogether, is an image of the men and women who looked on the panel in the hope and trust that at this point on its surface they were looking into a mirror. The panel to a certain extent at least effectuated the grace that it represented, and to that extent it was a sacramental. The sacramental and specifically eucharistic role of the devotional alabasters is especially apparent in the most popular and widespread motif of all, at least in the late fifteenth century: the image of St. John the Baptist's severed head on a platter. It is of course St. John's essential function in the Christian tradition and its art to point to the Savior, just as his words "behold the Lamb of God" point to and introduce the moment of physical communion with the crucified and risen Lord in the Mass. These enormously popular miniatures are in one sense no doubt a part of a privatization of the sacrament, a withdrawal from its public celebration in the Mass and from the immediate consumption of the elements which few dared to approach with any frequency. But they are also part of a quite opposite process: the extension of the awareness of the sacramental reality into every moment and context of a secular life that is anyway, for its own secular and no doubt ultimately economic reasons, inexorably becoming more personal, private, and individualized. Armed with these relatively cheap and portable pointers towards Christ's permanent real presence in the world, the purchasers of these St. John's heads could hear "behold the Lamb of God" in any moment of their day, in any place where they could be at peace, or in any movement of their feelings, and they could find there the manifestation of the hidden God.

Which brings us to the world of objective spirit—the world of human society and institutions, including, crucially, their economic base. One of the most characteristic features of the English alabasters is that apart from the intrinsic attractiveness of the materials their aesthetic appeal is limited and their artistic quality is low. But, as I have said, the work was very popular, and not by any means only in England. Alabaster, crude and worked, was one of England's major exports in the fifteenth century. Panels and whole altarpieces have survived from places as far apart as Iceland and Dubrovnik,

Lisbon and Königsberg-Kaliningrad, and more than two thousand panels and figures are still preserved on the European continent. English alabasters were, in short, mass produced. Nottingham seems to have been the major center of the industry, with many alabastermen known by name over a period of a century and a half: the scale of production may be judged from a court action brought in 1491 by an image maker against his retailer for money owing on "fifty-eight heads of St John the Baptist, part of them in tabernacles and in niches."[6] Mass production also accounts in part for the relative cheapness of the later alabasters: heads of the Baptist were valued at as little as a shilling at a time when an artisan's daily wage was sixpence. The production of English alabasters, like the production of visual images today, whether on paper, celluloid, or digitalized disc, was an industry of major economic importance for numerous English communities, including some large towns, and even, given its export value, for the country as a whole.

And it was all done in the name of God. A medieval English alabaster panel is not only the concrete form of a subjective spiritual movement towards redemption—an expression of loving hope in God—it is also the concrete evidence of objective economic and social relations constructed out of that spiritual movement. It is an objective manifestation of the working of the Holy Spirit for it is evidence of social activity ordered towards God. We could go a step further, from the social into the cultural and historical sphere, and say that it is evidence of *English* activity ordered towards God. For let us be honest about England and English culture: what the English have always excelled at is the mass production of cheap and cheerful goods for the unsophisticated markets of the world: eighteenth-century Wedgwood, nineteenth-century printed cottons, twentieth-century pop music. English alabasters were the Brummagem ware of the fifteenth century. They were hugely successful because then as now the world needed its Brummagem ware. English art has always tended to the popular in a double sense; it has always had a strain of egalitarianism in it, a closeness to craft, industry, and commerce. What makes the difference between the medieval alabasters and what comes later in England is their unashamed and unreflective intimacy with the truths of the Christian religion, what Hegel calls absolute spirit.

The English alabasters are not simply the expressions and instruments of personal feelings and thoughts, nor are they simply the material currency or medium for widespread and large-scale social and economic relationships. They are both of those only in virtue of their also being representations of the truth about God revealed through a church which is itself part of the revelation. It is important to realize that the *orthodoxy* of these images is the key to their power. The images of John the Baptist are pointers to, images of, the Eucharist, and the many images of the saints and their lives which make up a very large part of the surviving alabasters are not detachable appendages to a tradition but pointers to the importance of tradition itself: these lives matter because they are part of the life of the church, part of the process of God's revelation on earth. Similarly the alabasters could be part of an economic network as wide as the continent of Europe because they spoke a language that was recognized across the continent. Their economic importance, their equivalence, that is, to the daily bread of those who produced them and those who bought them, was dependent on their being recognized by all parties as showing something absolutely true and ultimately important. When that ceased to be the case, when one of the parties denounced devotion to the saints as un-Christian, for example, the role of the images in the objective life of the Spirit—their economic value that is—was destroyed as well. Until that moment of sundering these objects were part of a world—more, they helped to constitute a world—in which God, though hidden in himself, was by grace revealed.

Let us turn by way of contrast to twentieth-century England and to the quintessence of twentieth-century English manhood, a Cambridge phenomenon, of course, the beautiful and brilliant but actually not very nice Rupert Brooke. At the very end of 1914, after he had returned from the expedition of Antwerp, on which he almost saw action, he wrote to Jacques Raverat:

> Did you hear of the British private who had been through the fighting from Mons to Ypres, and was asked what he thought of all his experiences? He said "What I don't like about this 'ere b___ Europe is all these b___ pictures of Jesus Christ and His relations, behind b___ bits of glawss." It seems to me to express perfectly that insularity and cheerful atheism which are the chief characteristics of my race. All the same, though myself cheerful, insular, and an atheist, I'm largely dissatisfied with the English just now. . . . I really think large numbers of male people don't want to die. Which is odd. I've been praying for a German raid.[7]

Clearly something has changed since England was the purveyor to Europe of cheap but charming and orthodoxly Trinitarian alabasters, and, as things were so different only four hundred years previously, Brooke is unlikely to be right in interpreting what he has heard as evidence of a permanent characteristic of his race. I do not, by the way, wish to enter on the question whether this story correctly represents the attitude of the early-twentieth-century English working class towards Europe, the Christian religion, and Christian art. It is enough for my purposes that Brooke, a member and icon of the officer class of English society, was pleased to think that it did. Whether the story is true or false, whether it is about uneducated Cockney privates or about Darwins and Cornfords and other joyfully indecorous bathers in Byron's Pool, something about England has changed fundamentally since the days of the alabasters for it to be possible to tell such a story, or invent it, if that is what happened, or repeat it, or enjoy it. What could it be?

In a sense what has changed are the gardens. Think, for example, of Stowe House, built at the midpoint of the period separating the alabasters from Rupert Brooke and a monument to the English Enlightenment. Stowe Gardens, together with a few other parallel creations, mostly of Capability Brown's, are by far the most significant and influential English contribution to European visual and plastic arts since the medieval alabasters. From them, and one or two other gardens like them, notably Claremont and Stourhead, an inspiration went out all over Europe to create landscapes in the English style, in which Nature, though "improved," as the Crawfords wished, seemingly had her way, falling of her own accord, and without artifice or regularity, into vistas from which the hand of Man was seemingly absent, but in which the occasional gentle emphasis of a well-placed structure suggested an Arcadian harmony of the human and the natural, as in a painting by Claude. Before I return to Rupert Brooke, let us consider the nature of the inspiration for this most English of arts, so English in fact that the national epithet has been attached not only to the style but also to individual examples of it, such as the "English garden," that is, park, in Munich.[8]

If we take first the subjective spirit moving in a major eighteenth-century landscape garden such as Stowe, it is at once clear that it has taken on a central and commanding role: "central" indeed is a crucial term, for the entire garden is constructed around its appearance to a single observer, who wanders through it and whose shifting viewpoint realizes the drama of the seen and the not-seen for which the script has been written by the designer. The success of a design, according to Pope, whose garden at Twickenham was as significant a contribution to European culture as his poetry, lies in "the contrasts, the management of surprises, and the concealment of the bounds"[9]—all of them terms (unlike, for example, "drainage" or "ecosystem" or "utility") which treat the garden as an object appearing, and appearing in constantly changing guises, to a single unchanging subject. And what is it that this all-important subject experiences in the garden, what is the object that it meets? It meets a landscape in which the distinction between garden and nature has been effaced. Thanks above all to the ha-ha—which Horace Walpole called "the capital stroke, the leading step to all that followed"[10]—the "bounds," as Pope required, are concealed and the garden flows without perceptible interruption into the terrain beyond it. And as a result that terrain too is incorporated into the garden: everything the eye can see is now part of an arrangement for its delight, for the arousal of emotions, whether tender or sublime. The garden is a hymn to subjective individualism, not an object that represents a source of redemption and consolation beyond the self but an object—an entire world—completely subordinated to the experiencing self and its need for self-enjoyment.

It is no accident that the creators of Stowe Gardens belonged to one of England's greatest dynasties of Whigs, whose affinity with Jane Austen's Crawfords would have been as apparent to her audience as their antipathy to her Bertrams. The spirit of Stowe Gardens is not just subjective Whiggery, sentimentalism and individualism, it is objective Whiggery too. The gardens express a myth—the myth that we are all independent subjects of experience and that to each of us the whole world is available as an object—and that myth has not just a psychological and emotional dimension but a social and political dimension too. The bounds that the ha-ha conceals are not just the bounds between subject and object, Nature and Art, they are also the bounds of property and the boundaries between social and economic functions. As it happens most if not all of the land one can see from the main lawn at Stowe belongs or belonged to the Temple family anyway, but at Stowe also the ultimate step in the concealment of objective bounds was taken in 1774 by Richard Grenville, Earl Temple. Having nine years previously built a triumphal arch to finish the vista from the house, he then remodeled the house itself, putting a neoclassical façade on its rear, so that it should fit in as the backdrop to the return view from the arch. This is surely the supreme act of mythmaking. For a garden like Stowe is not only one of the largest works of art in existence: it is also one of the most expensive. Unlike our Brummagem alabasters, such a toy can be afforded by very few individuals indeed. But as we have seen, the gardens are intended to create the illusion that the world, all the world, is there for the individual, any and every individual, to enjoy. That is the Whig myth, and it owes its power largely to its concealment of the reality that only for a few exceptionally wealthy and privileged people can the myth become a reality. And the economic power and political influence that made Cobham's family able to create Stowe had its real seat in the house, the one useful or functional part of the construction. That point of contact, or boundary wall, with reality was in 1774 concealed by the new rear façade, and with that the house itself, the real social and economic world, became subordinated to the garden and so part of the illusion that the garden creates. The illusion from then on was political: this landscape which stretches in an unbroken sweep from horizon to horizon and by implication beyond, and which therefore is synonymous with all England, is open to be experienced by any and every one, and the difference between work and wealth, between social sub- and superordination, which in reality prevents any but a few from being such all-important and omnipotent selves, is either concealed from view completely or reduced to a picturesque element in the total composition like the farm animals grazing beyond the ha-ha, the only visible evidence of the economic process of labor and production. The hollowness of the sociopolitical myth is revealed in the structures which crowd the gardens at Stowe and which even contemporaries found excessive. For although these suggest a human and social presence in the garden—they *look* like useful and purposeful constructions—they are, virtually all, uninhabitable or useless, they may not even provide shelter from the rain, only roofless or unwalled rooms where litter swirls, whether of paper or of leaves: hermitages that never saw a hermit, bridges over artificial lakes, temples never used for worship, even of Mammon. They are the fragmentary social furniture of an imaginary existence floating disjointedly in the medium of the garden like the components of the design on a willow-pattern plate.

But the buildings at Stowe not only reveal the deceitfulness of the garden myth in respect of social relations, they are also the expression, the deliberate expression, of what the garden designers understood to be truth. They are vessels of absolute Spirit in that they tell us, and were designed to tell us, what the Temples and English Whiggery thought was ultimately and absolutely true: they tell us to what God these gardens are the altar. The self, of course—the proliferation of temples is a deliberate play on the family name—but a self envisaged as integrating both the subjective illusion of omnipotence and the objective deceit about social and economic power relations. The God worshipped here is called Britain.[11] Sometimes it is called England, but Britain is the truer name because Britain is the name for England in imperial mode, setting out as Britannia to rule the waves, to create an empire that will be called British, not English, and to satisfy the illusion that the landscape that begins here, centered on one all-experiencing individual, extends over the horizon forever, never ceasing, however many invisible ha-has may be crossed into other climate zones or other time zones, to set wider still and wider its always concealed bounds, never ceasing to be the realm of the free, and never ceasing to be their property. "England" is this gentle pastoral landscape, this damp and temperate Claude Lorrain, the picturesque illusion; "Britain," its unseen but real projection across the world in slavers, traders, and ships of the line. Whether under its true name "Britain" or under its mythical name "England," however, Stowe knows no other God. The ideological culmination of Stowe's garden architecture, and the point at which it spills over into literature, is a British Pantheon built in an emphatically pagan setting: the Temple of British Worthies in the section of the garden laid out as the Elysian Fields along the waters of the River Styx. In this parody of an altarpiece—technically known as an exedra and modeled on a Roman wayside shrine—sixteen emanations of the Whig divinity are presented in bust and inscription, eight heroes of contemplation, eight of action. The allusions to antiquity in the structure and setting are not present out of some sentimental cult of the superiority to the modern world of Greece and Rome; rather they are being used simply to prevent any intrusion by the Christian God and so to head off any claims to divine status that might rival those of Britain. Antiquity is cultivated, not because it is superior to modernity, but because it is non-Christian. An unabashed naturalism prevails in all the literary and philosophical encomiums:[12] Bacon, Locke—"best of all Philosophers . . . [who] . . . refuted the slavish systems of usurp'd authority over the Rights, the Consciences or the Reason of Mankind"— and Newton—"whom the God of Nature made to Comprehend his Work"; Milton no doubt had to be present, but his genius is slyly said to have "equal'd a subject [God himself, of course] that carried him beyond the limits of the World"; Shakespeare's knowledge of the human heart is an easier topic. The heroes of action reflect the relations of this tribal deity to the world beyond his immediate bailiwick and include the adventurers Sir Walter Raleigh and Francis Drake, "who carried into unknown Seas and Nations the Knowledge and Glory of the English Name." Drake, it would seem, is one of the original missionaries of the British Empire. The most interesting monument of all is to the man who, according to this Whig theology, first put into practical effect the gospel of global trade, carried on under British auspices: Sir Thomas Gresham, "Who by the honourable Profession of Merchant having enrich'd himself and his country [the shamelessness is positively endearing], for carrying on the Commerce of the World, built the Royal Exchange." If we want to know how it came about that England gave up the continental trade in pious alabasters and defined itself, at least in the eyes of its intellectual elite, by its cheerful insular contempt for bloody Europe, with its bloody Christianity and bloody art, here is our answer. England, an important but secondary power in the medieval European order, was seduced (in the person of its monarch) by the prospect of nationhood and national autonomy, shook off its entanglement in mere Europe, a Christendom enmired in the worship of false gods, and turned instead to a wider world on which it could more easily impress its own divine image. England became Britain, the benevolent patron of the global market, "the commerce of the world," the source and center of the British Empire. Only the name of England remained, the myth of the little damp green lovable country at the origin of it all, the garden at the heart of the world and in the hearts of all of Britain's far-flung emissaries, the England in which all true-born Englishmen were at home, their heaven, their God. In Stowe Gardens, in the depths of Buckinghamshire's improved countryside, is the material, the sacramental realization of that myth, and at its heart is the material, the sacramental realization of its source: the lichen-covered bust of a banker.

For Rupert Brooke the picturesque myth of England has completely displaced any talk of the reality that is—or rather was—Britain and the British Empire. In the sonnet finished at Christmas 1914, which is surely his best-known poem, England is named six times, but there is no mention of Britain or of the British Empire, or indeed of the alien empires which disputed its global reach and with which it was engaged in a fight to the death. There is certainly no mention of that altogether other, postimperial, empire, the outgrowth of eighteenth-century Whiggery, and the true vessel of the gospel of global commerce which in the second half of the twentieth century was to inherit the spoils left on the empty battlefields of the first half, the United States (which, like Germany, Brooke had visited and enjoyed more than he cared to admit). But "The Soldier" is not a stupid poem; it is moving, as a poem must be which tries to think seriously about death and what its author died for, and theologically speaking it is of considerable interest. The process of replacing God by England—as the ultimate truth about human life which gives a transcendent validation to the historical contingency of the British Empire—a process which can be seen in full career in Stowe Gardens, has here almost reached its terminus. The hiddenness of God is here almost complete. Almost, but not quite. The term "England" in this poem acquires its transcendent power by pulling on clothes borrowed from the older theology, and the slightly ludicrous sense that they are a size or so too big for it betrays that they belong to someone else. In each mode of its presence in the poem the spirit can be identified as England—or rather England can be identified as the spirit—only by an uncomfortable catachresis. Inspiration, one might say, has become inflation.

The Soldier

If I should die, think only this of me:
    That there's some corner of a foreign field
That is for ever England. There shall be
    In that rich earth a richer dust concealed;
A dust whom England bore, shaped, made aware,
    Gave, once, her flowers to love, her ways to roam,
A body of England's, breathing English air,
    Washed by the rivers, blest by suns of home.

And think, this heart, all evil shed away,
    A pulse in the eternal mind, no less
        Gives somewhere back the thoughts by England given;
Her sights and sounds; dreams happy as her day;
    And laughter, learnt of friends; and gentleness,
        In hearts at peace, under an English heaven.[13]

Subjectively, the poem announces a complete identification—"think *only* this," it says—of the self and England. As a result the poem shows us oddly little of the poet's feelings about England: England is not so much the object of emotion as its source. The first-person pronoun is used only in the first line and is thereafter replaced by references to the activity of England: the octet shows us England making the poet's body, the sestet England making his heart (not "soul," for that, in opposition to "body," would be too obviously the old theology, nor "mind," for that severe Greco-German term is to be used in the next line for something, as the Temples put it, "beyond the Limits of the World," but "heart," an eighteenth-century English sentimentalist word, which may not mean anything very definite and leads to the confused and rather purposeless repetition in the last line but which on the way is so excellently reapplied in l. 10, "a pulse"). England, through its four elements, earth, air, sun, and water—the water of the rivers, l. 8, in which Brooke's circle bathed—has made this body in a process as natural and material as anything envisaged by Bacon or Locke or Newton, the British Worthies of Stowe. England too has given him his immaterial parts, his thoughts and perceptions and moral attitudes, all derived from the world which has nurtured him and which, with its flowers and paths (l. 6) and the laughter of daydreaming friends, outdoors and unoccupied (ll. 12–13), appears to be an Edwardian version of the boundless landscape garden projected by the leisured Whig self beyond the horizons visible from Stowe's South Lawn. The conceit in lines 2 and 3 is the nucleus of the entire sonnet: the assertion that even as a corpse he is England is carried through with a consistent materialism that probably few of the poem's readers, at the time of its first enormous fame or since, have shared. But at one point this systematic Anglo-Lucretianism wavers, and we become aware that the poet does not quite believe that he is simply the product of a shaping deity, a *Natura naturans,* which bears the name of England. There is a rather odd relative pronoun in line 5, "A dust whom England bore." Why "whom"? "Which" would have been more correct and natural after the common noun "dust," referring to an inanimate object. But of course the poet does not think of himself as an inanimate object, even though that is what he says he is—dust molded by England as Jeremiah's potter molds the clay. His use of "whom" is an admission that he does think of himself as a person in his own right, independently of this God who makes him, and *that,* independent, personality is left totally undefined by the poem. The pronoun makes us faintly aware that behind the poem is a young man striking an attitude, reciting a myth, but who he, who that "whom," might be, what his relation is with the real historical and international world that is about to kill him, he not merely does not tell us, he cannot tell us, and perhaps cannot even tell himself, so completely has he allowed the myth of England to take over his mind.

Absurdly, objective spirit appears in this poem as almost exclusively England: once again it is the "almost," the tiny exception or contradiction, that reveals the absurdity. In the poem taken as a whole England might seem to be the only human society, the only nation that exists. No other nation—not even any ancient nation—is presented in the poem as engaged in any kind of equal relation with England, either as a parallel case or as an ally, or even as an adversary. In a poem about war this is rather strange. (Well, in fact it is quite common, for most war poems are bad in this way, but that does not stop it from being strange.) England is not presented as a partner or component in an international system which is now in conflict. It has no enemy, no alien other or opposite. England is not even presented as the only place in the world that matters; it is presented as all but coterminous with the world. "All but"—there is of course an exception, an exception which is part of the poem's nucleus in those first two and a half lines that everyone remembers. All the world of this poem is England but for a tiny exception: one little piece of the world is alluded to that is not England, a "corner of a foreign field." And it is alluded to precisely in order to be colonized, to be turned into England after all: the only specific allusion to a non-English part of the world is colonial and imperialist. True, there is a condescending acknowledgment that abroad exists and is thought by its inhabitants to have value—its earth is "rich"—but the concession is made only for the sake of the rhetorical turn, for England's dust is then said to be "richer." And this turn produces an intolerable ambiguity. Either the dust is richer than the rich earth simply because it is dust of a human body—the poem then is overlooking that the soil of Europe, particularly of northern France and Flanders from which Brooke had just returned and where he wrote the poem, has been enriched since Attila by the bodies of the non-English victims of war—or the dust is richer because this dust is England, worth more than any foreign soil, however many human bodies have gone into its making. In either case the human worth and role of societies other than the English, which shape and animate non-English bodies, all the non-English varieties of objective spirit, are consigned to oblivion. This preposterous unrealism is possible because England itself, as here presented, is not objective spirit at all. The objective spiritual reality which is engaging in war and for which Brooke will die, which has made him and of which his thoughts are part, is not his mythical England but Britain and the British Empire. And that has no role in the poem except in that unacknowledged moment of imperial acquisition when reality is briefly revealed and the last little corner of foreignness in the world is appropriated for the myth. That last instinctive twitch or grab, the residual, dying, reflex clutch of empire, is the poem's one moment of realism, the one moment at which it touches the real world in which God works, and the source of its only and utterly memorable lines.

The sonnet does, of course, purport to have a theology. It does claim to rise to a vision of absolute spirit, "the eternal mind." But even at this culmination God is occluded, concealed by the ideological mask that is "England"—again, all but for one last, perhaps saving moment, one last remaining flicker of solar fire at the point of total eclipse. The one merit of the myth of divine England is that it cannot ultimately be taken completely seriously and the poem's last, perhaps saving, moment is a moment of at least possible humor. Just as the reader is adjured to think of Brooke's English body as performing a last imperial action, so in the sestet she, or more probably he, is told to think of Brooke's English heart as appropriating a corner of eternity. Only in a remote and indefinite "somewhere," but at least there, Englishness, the having been formed as a sentient, thinking, ethical being by *Deus-sive-Anglia,* has an eternal value, and, as in the octet of the sonnet, that process of Anglification is the only process in which Divinity is said to engage. Just as in the octet England is the sole acknowledged occupant of this world, so in the sestet she is the sole acknowledged occupant of the next, the world in which we give back to the spirit what we have received in the flesh. Despite a perfunctory reference to sweeping all evil away, however, Brooke expects what he gives back to be indistinguishable from what he has received, and in the afterlife England, its sights and sounds, the thoughts it has given—whether of Milton or of Sir Thomas Gresham presumably—and the happiness inspired by its landscape, and even, it seems, by its weather, are all preserved unchanged. Not even assumption into the eternal mind reveals an alternative to—let alone an improvement on—this English heaven. Except perhaps for those last words themselves. They are a witty conceit, like the corner of the field that is forever England with which the sonnet begins. At its end Brooke gives us that field's immaterial equivalent—a corner of heaven that is forever an English sky, overarching the leisured life of an Edwardian country house. In the moment of wit, by which the word *heaven* is transferred from its temporal to its eternal meaning, and in the possibly humorous, possibly self-deprecating indefinite article— "an English heaven," as if it is fleetingly acknowledged that this "heaven" is but a corner of all that eternally is—there is perhaps a saving recognition that England is a myth after all. Otherwise we would have to interpret the last gesture of the poem as colonizing heaven in the same way that it began with a gesture of colonizing the earth, and for not sharing in the smile that the last line has to raise, Brooke would become its object.

Rupert Brooke's sonnet just, but only just, leaves open the possibility that by recognizing "England" as a myth we may glimpse beyond it the reality that the myth, over the centuries, has grown up to obscure: the growth of the British Empire. That is: the growth in the islands of the Atlantic archipelago, once they had thrown off the shackles that bound them into European Christendom and into its economic, social, spiritual, and ecclesiastical order, of a political and military structure almost, but not quite, capable of providing the framework for the growing global market, the commerce of the world. Because that myth obscured the reality of the subjective personal and objective social life, it obscured the absolute truth as well. Those who choose not to see themselves or their fellows as they are will not see God either, however insistent or gentle his revelation. God, the God shown to us in Jesus Christ and his relations and pictured behind bloody bits of glass, was hidden from Britain by the shadow of empire. His place was taken by "England"; and the religion of this substitute deity functioned as false religion

always does, as an opiate deadening the senses to economic, social, and political reality. Since Brooke wrote his sonnet the reality concealed by the cult
of that mythical deity "England" has been swept away in a war of seventy-
five years' duration, the war that in turn destroyed the German, Austrian,
Turkish, Italian, Japanese, Belgian, Dutch, French, British, and finally, largely,
the Russian Empires. (The Chinese remains, for the present, but may be allowed to be a special case.) The energy that powered and sustained this most
destructive war in the history of humanity was no other than the energy that
had put together the empires in the first place, the power of world commerce, the relentless drive to the globalization of economic activity. Deprived
of the administrative and military structures that maintained and defended
their more and less worldwide economic blocs and gave political and cultural coherence not only to their colonial dependencies but also to the
metropolitan states themselves, the postimperial nations have faced a crisis of
identity—some since 1918, some since 1945, and since 1989 not only Russia
but also all those states, if states they can still be called, which had invested
their self-understanding, whether as free, socialist, or neutral, in the global
confrontation of the Cold War.

Separated now by the Seventy-five Years' War from Rupert Brooke's
Edwardian substitute religion we have woken up to reality, to a reality that
is completely changed. British culture, however, has kept pace with this
change and originated a cheap, or at any rate mass produced, and cheerful
icon of it that has once again achieved worldwide circulation and influence.
I mean the detective novel, in the broadest of senses, and it is from this genre
that I take my next and not quite last example. The detective novel has risen
as the empires have declined. After a long prehistory the defining moment
of the genre, its inauguration through the huge public success of Conan
Doyle, coincided with the apogee of the British Empire, and from about
1920 to about 1950, during the empire's sunset years, it enjoyed its golden
age. Indeed, the conventions of an entire subgenre—what Raymond
Chandler in his famous essay of 1950, "The Simple Art of Murder,"[14] calls
the English formula—require a setting in that period with its usually
country houses, its servants, and its dressing for dinner, in clear continuity
with the England celebrated by Rupert Brooke. However repellent in itself,
the social archaism was necessary for the genre, for it established the background of a moral order against which it was possible to measure two crucial deviations from it: the initial deviation represented by the crime itself
and behind the crime the corruption of motive that had made the criminal;
and, more subtly and significantly, the later deviation from the norm repre-

sented by the always somehow eccentric detective through whose intervention the order is restored. The detective represents as an individual the
values which his or her society at some level professes but which its institutions are—as the crime demonstrates—too corrupt, too weak, or too incom-
petent to put into effect. In the American context the detective will
represent attitudes or behavior that are felt to be part of the American way
of life, of the founding vision or even of the founding documents of the
nation, but that are negated or inadequately reflected in the nation's institutions, thanks to its explosive economic development. In the British context
the detective embodies in his or her own individualistic or eccentric way the
true values of the declining empire's ruling class, which in the book are
represented as betrayed either by degenerate members of the class or by its
well-meaning but hidebound official agents.

Around 1950, however, a new variant of the detective story began to
achieve popularity as the end of empire was publicly acknowledged and the
Cold War created a new framework for international relations that was both
highly formal and heavily moral. The spy story, which achieved its own
golden age in the years after the building of the Berlin Wall, at first maintained the fundamental moral structure of the detective novel. The free world
now was in the role of self-betraying repository of ultimate values, and the
spy was the eccentric loner who in his own unorthodox way restores what
the institutions have compromised, whether through excessive scrupulous-
ness or through treachery. In the earlier novels of Len Deighton, for example, the agent is still recognizable as a variant on Chandler's famous
definition of the detective—"down those mean streets a man must go who
is not himself mean, who is neither tarnished nor afraid." Tarnished and
afraid he may be, and deception and double dealing may be all around him,
but he remains the book's center of gravity by remaining truer than anybody else, if not to the British national interest, then to whatever England is
held ultimately to stand for. England may now be no more than a partner in
the Western Alliance, though it is probably the most, perhaps the only reliable partner in it and certainly provides the most reliable articulation of its
ideals, but it is still the England of Rupert Brooke's myth. Like the hero of
the detective story, the hero of the spy story may be, indeed must be, a solitary; his behavior may be morally questionable or downright illegal, but that
is shown to be less significant than his ultimate loyalty to the one clearly
good cause, and that in turn enables him to light a candle in the dark places
of the world, to show "honor," as Chandler has it, in those mean streets, and
so to achieve that redemption which Chandler also thinks essential to all

art. The answer to the question, who is the hero, the detective, the spy? is simply that he or she is the individual who has become the locus, perhaps the only visible locus, of the collective, social, national, perhaps even international belief about what is good. As the genre of the spy story grew older and more sophisticated, as espionage came to be treated as a job like any other and the rival secret services as little more than rival corporations, as double agency ceased to be synonymous with treachery and became just a psychological complication, so that individual locus of the good was lost and with it the rationale of the genre itself, which faded back into the novel of Graham Greene-land, from which it had in part arisen.

But in the mass culture of film English art combined with American resources to maintain the earliest conventions of the spy story genre and to create out of them a twentieth-century equivalent of the international commercial success of the medieval alabasters. The novels of Ian Fleming provided a formula which proved as irresistible as the small-format panel combining pure stone and rich decoration—the life of the individual, James Bond, in which every subjective need seemed to be fulfilled, indeed outrageously indulged; a totally clear and unproblematic objective social world, consisting simply of the national secret services and their enemies, whose roles were firmly fixed by the background or foreground presence of the Cold War confrontation; and an absolute good, never itself embodied in a specific character or institution but always implied behind immediate figures of authority, such as M or political ministers, namely, the England for which Bond worked. England provided the end to which all his personal indulgences were means, and thereby justified them; England provided his distinguishing identity among his fellow secret servicemen and the style with which he negotiated the social world, determining equally his taste in drink and his need to adjust his tie while driving a tank. This formula created by Fleming could be repeated, to the point of self-parody once the repetition could no more be left unacknowledged, long after Fleming's supply of story lines had dried up. Far more serious for the scriptwriters than the limited number of Fleming's novels was the end of the confrontation with the Soviet Union. Not simply because a simple structure of them and us was no longer available to provide the framework for secret service activity. The end of the Cold War in 1989 meant an end to the process of dissolution of the empires which had begun seventy-five years before, and so it meant the end even of the vestigial function of the myth of England. In the 1990s, at a time when England itself started to become publicly anxious about its identity, the Bond scriptwriters became increasingly embarrassed by the need to explain the controlling, absolute, function of Bond's Englishness. In 1995 they addressed the issue specifically in *GoldenEye,* a film which begins by contrasting an episode from the Cold War with the world after the collapse of the U.S.S.R. At the end the villain, a double dealer from that golden age of moral clarity, is dispatched by Bond, who drops him from a gantry suspended hundreds of feet above a concrete bowl. In their final exchange the villain, seeing his death in the eyes of his former colleague, asks, "For England, James?" and gets the reply "No—for me." At this moment, and in every sense, the myth of England falls away. But what does it leave behind? Who is Bond if he is not England? His only identity lay in his being the fulfillment of all subjective needs in the service of the good *as England;* his only identity was his Englishness. The answer furnished by later Bond films, already apparent well before 1995, was an answer for England too in its futile quest for an identity to replace the one that history had dropped. Bond has become the vehicle for all the top brands in the market, or rather for the brands that can pay most to have him accredit them as top. Bond is no longer the individual who embodies the absolute good as England; he is the individual who uses such and such a shaver, wears such and such a watch, drinks such and such a brand of whisky, and, of course, drives such and such a car and makes love to women who remove such and such garments for him. England too, we could say, has become simply a shop for internationally traded products on to which it can hope at best to affix some kind of national branding, seal of approval, or royal warranty.

Can we find God here too, after the demise of the God of Englishness who underpinned the deism of the Whigs, the atheism of the Edwardians, and the untheological belief in decency and honor of late-twentieth-century popular culture? God revealed in Jesus Christ ceased to be the shaping presence in England's public and cultural life in the sixteenth century, in the moment of Henry's breach with Rome, and his place was taken by God revealed in England. Despite Kipling's venture into retrospective colonization of the past, when England arrived the fairies said farewell. The end of Englishness has of course concerned the producers of England's high literary culture, its privileged secular scriptures, as well as the manufacturers of the more popular or less literary goods that I have been discussing here. England post-*GoldenEye,* post-1989, is, I believe, a concealed theme of a remarkable recent novel[15]—concealed, possibly, even from its exceptionally percipient author. Perhaps it is not so much concealed as absent, with a felt and paralyzing absence, for it is in the end the failure to bring out into the open England's twentieth-century transformation that prevents Ian McEwan's *Atonement* from achieving the goal that its title announces.

One of the ways in which *Atonement* comes close to being about the end of the idea of "England" is that it is in part a detective novel, a whodunit— and unfortunately, therefore, to discuss it is to reveal who done it. The criminal in *Atonement* (it might not be too much to call her the murderer) turns out, as postmodern fiction usually requires, to be the narrator. A three-part, third-person novel occupies most of the book. In the first part an omniscient narrative moves between the complex and precisely timetabled events of a single summer's day and night, and between the interlinked pools of consciousness that experience them, with all the subtlety and detached sympathy of Jane Austen. *Northanger Abbey* provides the epigraph, and the setting, in an upper-middle-class country house of the 1930s, is parodically related to the locale both of the golden age detective story and of the generic Austen novel. The parkland, we are told, retains some of its eighteenth-century features, including a decaying summerhouse of the kind where so many stories of the age of Sentiment came to a seemly or unseemly consummation, but the original Adam house has been replaced by a solid late Victorian baronial monstrosity: the industrial and imperial realization of a Whig dream, on which for a few sunset decades the inheritors of the idea of England continued to subsist. This is no Mansfield Park, however: the absent paternal authority never returns, not even to dispense justice at the novel's climax, but remains in London, where, as a higher civil servant, he plans for the decimation of the English people in the coming war and engages in long-term adultery. His youngest daughter, Briony Tallis, thirteen years old, is at the outset of a writer's career. With the jealous curiosity and insectlike objectivity of her age, she observes the sudden growth of sexual love between her older sister, Cecilia, and Robbie Turner, the former grammar school boy from the gardener's cottage on the estate who has been patronized by the Tallises and allowed to grow up with the family. Both Cecilia and Robbie have just come down from Cambridge, where they read English and Robbie picked up Dr. Leavis's interest in D. H. Lawrence but not his concern for the moral mission of literature. An unusually intense and sultry heat wave undoes such slight conventional bonds as this hollow society recognizes. During the night, Cecilia and Robbie make love in the underused library, while a brute from the right drawer in the class structure, for whom Robbie is simply an offensive upstart, rapes Briony's provocative fifteen-year-old cousin in the darkness of the park. Briony, unaware of most of what is going on in the boring adult world, allows her writerly imagination to run away with her, and when the police and the doctors arrive she claims to have seen Robbie commit the assault. An incriminatory Lawrentian letter seems to bear out her belief that Robbie is a "sex maniac." The true assailant goes on to marry his victim and to make a fortune out of supplying artificial chocolate to the troops during the war, while Robbie, convicted and imprisoned, is released early on condition that he serves in the British Expeditionary Force.

Part 2 tells of Robbie's retreat with two other fleeing soldiers to the Dunkirk beaches, of random death and dismemberment, and of the pity and the callousness of war. Throughout he is sustained by the hope—nurtured by letters from Cecilia, who has broken off her relations with her family and trained as a nurse and has promised to wait for him—that he will return to England, clear his name, and live with her in love. In part 3 the focus moves to Briony, who, oppressed by guilt, is now following her older sister's example and training at the same hospital. As the wounded and dying, evacuated from France, begin to arrive, her experience of their appalling injuries and desperate emotional needs is juxtaposed with her literary ambitions. A virtuoso parody of a letter from Cyril Connolly, patronizingly rejecting a novella based on the moment when she first understood both the love between Cecilia and Robbie and her own vocation as a writer, is a comic highlight in a work whose tone is increasingly somber. Briony at last resolves to call on Cecilia in her dowdy flat in Balham where Robbie is visiting her on leave. Briony offers to retract her evidence: her offer is accepted, though she does not expect and does not receive forgiveness. But as she leaves she feels free to begin on her real act of "atonement"—a redrafting of her novella that will tell the whole truth about her crime.

At this point, when the novel appears to have ended, a postscript from Briony herself, dated 1999, springs its well-prepared surprise. It is a wry, nononsense retrospect, not unlike Gwen Raverat's *Period Piece,* and Briony also resembles Gwen Raverat in having been briefly married to a Frenchman, one of the war victims she nursed in hospital. Now a celebrated novelist, she fills in her family's later story while recounting a grand reunion held at the old house to celebrate her seventy-seventh birthday. The house, though, has been sold and converted into a hotel, the park into a golf course; the lake, on the bank of which the rape occurred, has been filled in; the summerhouse has gone; in its place there is a bench and a litter basket. The past is buried, and with it the crime, which forms no part of the family's genial and—by comparison with the neurotic and secretive world of the 1930s—uninhibited recollections. For it is now confirmed for us that the previous three parts of the book are Briony's redrafted novel, in which fact and fiction have intermingled. Her crime was real enough but not the consoling conclusion to her story: Robbie died of septicemia on the Dunkirk beaches, never reunited with Cecilia, who was killed shortly afterwards in an air raid and has disappeared from the family's collective memory. The truth of what happened is presumably still known to the rapist, now an almost nonagenarian peer, plutocrat, and patron of the arts, and to his wife, lean, tanned, stylishly dressed, and wearing high heels at eighty. But England's libel laws ensure that the truth will not be told, and Briony's novel will not be published, until after they have died and are beyond the reach of justice. Since Briony has just been diagnosed as suffering from a fatal degenerative disease, that will in all probability be well after her own death.

For fifty-nine years, then, Briony has been seeking to make amends for her part in the destruction of the love, and lives, of Robbie and Cecilia. Is her novel the atonement she said it was in the last lines of part 3? In the postscript she admits that it is not. Insofar as it is fact, it must remain unpublished and of no practical effect in the world of law courts and reputations. Insofar as it is fiction, it cannot say or do anything of consequence to mend the terrible harm of which it speaks, for as fiction it can as easily end with the reunited lovers sailing into the setting sun as with the "bleakest realism" (*A* 371) that shows squalid, pointless, and unfulfilled deaths in Dunkirk and Balham:

> The problem these fifty-nine years has been this: how can a novelist achieve atonement when, with her absolute power of deciding outcomes, she is also God? There is no one, no entity or higher form that she can appeal to, or be reconciled with, or that can forgive her. There is nothing outside her. In her imagination she has set the limits and the terms. No atonement for God, or novelists, even if they are atheists. (*A* 371)

Briony, it seems, has discovered the emptiness of the literary ambition that overcame her in the moment when she saw the awakening of the sexual attraction between Robbie and Cecilia:

> [S]he could write a scene . . . and she could include a hidden observer like herself. . . . She could write the scene three times over from three points of view. . . . She need not judge. . . . Only in a story could you enter these different minds and show how they had an equal value. That was the only moral a story need have. (*A* 40)

She has discovered that the author cannot do without a moral when she is a part of the story herself. She needs a forgiveness for her crime that she cannot find if her crime is only an episode in a story told by an evenhanded omniscient and omnipotent narrator who does not judge. In the world as Briony imagined it to be, a world in which the author's imagination alone sets the limits and the terms for any story, there can be no forgiveness for any sin of the author (especially not for her original sin of violating the privacy and integrity of her characters by inventing them). But the world as Briony imagines it is not the world as it is. Authors are not God and do not create the world about which they tell their stories, nor do they set the limit which requires that any human story is subject to the Law and has to be told in moral terms. At best they are faithful scribes—describing and transcribing the world that God has made and called and bought again when it was lost—and their contribution to God's atonement for their sins is the fidelity of their transcription, which imitates, and so shares in, his love.

Briony's impasse, her inability to choose between two ends for her story, reveals, as double endings do, the author's manipulating presence. But the author revealed is a false author, with a false conception of authorship. In the novel's last lines a hint appears of another and truer author, and so perhaps of a truer relation between this story and the created world. The feminine pronouns which emphasize that Briony imagines the novelist as female remind us that this book was written by a man and that its author is not to be identified with the woman who has, at the end, revealed herself to be its narrator. The man by whom this book was written is a part of the story that the book tells insofar as the book is about the social and cultural, political, economic, and world-historical network of meanings that we call England between the 1930s and 1999. As an expression of England's self-knowledge at the end of that period, however, *Atonement* could hardly be more bleak.

England's physical substance, represented by the house, has passed out of the hands of manufacturing magnates through those of public officials into the grasp of the self-sustaining service industries of postmodern society. Where fortunes were once made out of cast and worked metal (the Tallis patriarch traded in locks and bolts), they are now made out of fake chocolate. The social establishment is built on crimes of violence, lust, and treachery. The courts, the police, the medical profession may not be corrupt, but they provide no forum or instrument for attaining truth. Literature, deprived of its last voices of seriousness—Lawrence and Leavis, the latter reduced to an ignored, distant, and semicomic shade—has no more effect on anyone's life than the utterly ineffectual and absurd English church. How could it, when Briony's aesthetic prevails? Subjective spirit, in *Atonement,* has been evacuated: all the selves in parts 1 to 3 turn out to be fictions of the hidden observer, and she in turn is fictionalized by the novel's conclusion. In the objective realm too the spirit of England has been detached from all substance. Briony's perspective excludes England's international and imperial role from her picture of the ruling class of the 1930s. She is aware of a continuity with the first great conflict of 1914–18 (*A* 23–24) but her narrative of the retreat to Dunkirk knows nothing of the greater slaughters and huger crimes occurring or impending farther east and gives no explanation, superficial or profound, for the involvement of English society in these world-making events. As in Brooke's sonnet, or his letter to Raverat, we are on the outermost margin of England, venturing only into the corner of a foreign field in order to bring it back home as part of an English story. As a consequence Briony can offer no account of the social and economic processes (by now international, indeed global) that have dissolved the physical and human milieu in which she grew up but have brought the surviving members of her family together in prosperity at the end of the 1990s. Briony may give a far subtler picture of the hollowness of a society that has forgotten the wrongdoing and suffering on which it is based, but James Bond gives us a clearer, truer picture of the forces that have made it what it is.

As for absolute spirit, Briony's narrative is no more capable than Brooke's sonnet of relating to an eternal mind that is anything other than an ideological mask: Brooke looks out into God-as-England, Briony into God-as-the-novelist, and in both cases what passes for an inescapable absolute is a theologizing disguise and evasion of the writer's real historical situation—the imperial *Endkampf* in Brooke's case, in Briony's the postimperial, postmodern, global market. Can we, in this ultimate case, distinguish between Briony's perspective and McEwan's? I rather think we cannot. To have access to a truth beyond Briony's limitations we need more than the hint that there is something, and someone, "outside her." We need an atmosphere of discourse, as Lévinas might say, that will breathe life into the immobile statue; we need a spirit common to the historically determinate author and to our historically determinate selves, so that he can show us his face. We need a church that, like the Georgian Anglican church in *Mansfield Park,* can be both realistically represented within the narrative and recognized by the narrative's readers as the channel and home in their own lives of the Law that the narrative cannot represent. But in *Atonement* the Norman parish church near the Tallis estate is "presided over" only by a "supremely undemanding being" who is of less significance to Robbie than a ghost (*A* 93). As he struggles to the French beaches across fields crowded with demoralized soldiers, Robbie notices in passing amid the slaughtered horses and the bonfires of clothing, destroyed lest it be of use to the enemy, amid the artillerymen smashing their guns and disabling their motor vehicles, a "chaplain and his clerk dousing cases of prayer books and bibles with petrol" (*A* 243). It is a comic *coup-de-théâtre,* properly left uncommented, for this immolation of English religion, meaningless outside England, symbolizes the absence from the novel of any higher discourse to link the imperial age that is ending at Dunkirk to the wider story of humanity, or to link the world of the narrative to the world of its readers. It is an acknowledgment both that McEwan shares with Briony the "amorality" for which, we are told, her fiction is known (*A* 41) and that neither of them can say what it now means to be English.

How is God revealed now in the public and cultural world of what once was England? Now as always the answer has to be, as it was for Jane Austen: in the church. That answer is nowadays more clearly given in popular writing than in more sophisticated narratives. It is a curious, and in its way heartening, fact about the global market, the worldwide dominion of having and risking in which we now live, that one of its most successful cultural commodities has been an attempt, serious in its way, to create a literary symbol of the church through an engagement with the historical fate, in the twentieth century, of the idea of England—J. R. R. Tolkien's *The Lord of the Rings.*

CHAPTER 15

Rewards and Fairies (2):
The Lord of the Rings

THERE IS SOMETHING EMBARRASSING ABOUT DISCUSSING *THE LORD of the Rings* in an academic context. It is so obviously not real literature. "He doesn't really belong to literature or the arts" said Tolkien's biographer, Humphrey Carpenter, "but more to the category of people who do things with model railways in their garden sheds."[1] That catches well *The Lord of the Rings* as it usually appears to serious readers. Emotionally and narratively impoverished, its plot a repetitive alternation of discomfort and snugness,[2] gender stereotyped to the point where women are largely absent, morally simplistic to the point where the bad guys are virtually all dehumanized, carelessly, even badly written—the charges are familiar, and they are also largely true. And then there is the most damning charge of all: look at the fans. But in the eighteenth century *Robinson Crusoe* had a similar mass appeal to an audience well beyond the professionally literary classes, and the sixteenth-century chapbooks about Doctor Faust would deserve slating on all the critical counts I have just listed. Perhaps *The Lord of the Rings* is a late-modern equivalent of those early-modern myths of Crusoe and Faustus. It is in fact a prime example of that familiar product, English Brummagem ware, and like its predecessors—alabasters, James Bond, the poetry of Rupert Brooke—it has found a mass market. That success must not be underestimated. A book that has several times been voted the best book of the twentieth century and whose worldwide sales (50 million by 1997, before the current surge) are outclassed only by the partially derivative Harry Potter and by the Bible, deserves some attention. Perhaps it deserves more—recognition, for example, as at least in some respects a great book. And the reasons for its greatness lie, I believe, in its idiosyncratic (but, experience has shown, immensely appealing) delineation of the boundary between the sacred and the secular and in what it has to say about England.

First of all, let me be clear that I am talking about the book, *The Lord of the Rings,* not the fantasy world, the parallel universe, mythology, and philology that Tolkien over the years built up in Carpenter's garden shed. Since his death more and more of those compulsive jottings have been turned by the publishers into fodder for the fans, but they only obscure the achievement. I will reluctantly allow that the appendices to the third volume of *The Lord of the Rings*—the first hint to the public of that vast model railway—may be included as part of that book: the appendix giving the true or at any rate further story is after all a feature of modernist fiction from *Lolita* to *Atonement.* (The self-reflection caused when Tolkien's parallel philology enters the text of *The Lord of the Rings* bears more than a passing resemblance to the effects favored by Nabokov: the eighty chapters and few blank pages of the book Frodo presents to Sam at the end[3] correspond to the eighty-one chapters of *The Hobbit* and *The Lord of the Rings* combined, and the portentousness of certain passages should, as with Thomas Mann, be attributed not simply to Tolkien but also to the epic and would-be epic narrators of his invented sources.) And it must be allowed that in one respect Tolkien's fantasizing has genuine literary merit, however eccentric: the absolute internal consistency of his invented languages and nomenclatures, and their "translation" into forms related to English, is the work of a philologist of genius and gives his imaginary world a concealed structural stability comparable to the multilingual underpinning of *Finnegan's Wake.* Essentially, though, Tolkien's literary achievement, whatever it is, begins with the words "When Mr Bilbo Baggins of Bag End" and ends with the words " 'Well, I'm back,' he said." And the reason I exclude the *Silmarillion* and all the rest is the same reason I do not think that in *The Lord of the Rings* itself it is the heroic narrative as such that should be the focus of our attention, the derring-do of kings and elf-lords and armies, which naturally attracts the filmmaker and which gives rise to those tiresome passages that read like Victorian translations of Homer or extracts from the Book of Mormon. The reason is there in those opening and closing words and in one of the less noticed literary refinements of *The Lord of the Rings*—its deliberate structural parallels with Tolkien's first book *The Hobbit, or: There and Back*

Again. What marks out *The Lord of the Rings* from the obsessively methodical daydreaming that formed its materials, and what gives its narrative a unique character that deserves to be called literary, is the intersection within it of the world of heroic fantasy and the world of the hobbits—not the epic, let them even be pseudoepic, events, but the hobbits' perspective on them. The title Frodo gives to the book which is supposedly the source of the narrative that we read is *The Downfall of the Lord of the Rings and the Return of the King (as seen by the Little People . . .),* and nearly all of the narrative, apart from a chapter or two in the second volume, has a hobbit observer at least implicitly present. My daughter, Mary, a brave defender of the *Silmarillion,* tells me that Tolkien—understandably—disagreed with those who did not want to know more about the many names and events from the history of Middle Earth that are mentioned in *The Lord of the Rings* but only partially explained. But I think those who wish to be left in ignorance are right, and why they are right has to do with hobbits. We therefore, clearly, have to ask ourselves what hobbits are.

In one sense it is perfectly obvious what hobbits are: they are in the first instance people like Tolkien, who himself said in a letter, "I am . . . a Hobbit (in all but size)."[4] They are middle-class, middle-aged, mid-twentieth-century English men who have, or would like to have, nothing very much to do but enjoy food, beer, pipe smoking, talking to each other, long walks in the country, hot baths, and domesticity (i.e., the company of women) insofar as it does not interfere with any of their other pleasures. They are also of course the people by whom such people would like to be surrounded: the country folk of preindustrial England. These share the tasks of their masters, as far as class differences allow, and engage in "unmechanized" agriculture and traditional crafts. They do not, however, live in a wholly undatable Arcadia: they belong to the rural world of the late nineteenth or early twentieth century; they have post offices, though they do not have banks or paper currency; they have a watch but not a police force; they eat potatoes and smoke tobacco and drink tea but have no knowledge of coffee; an allusion to a firework passing overhead like an express train does not seem out of place, but a mill powered by a steam engine is a violation. The hobbits, then, are Tolkien's vision, or fantasy, of the people of England—that is obvious enough, and Tolkien says as much. "The hobbits are just rustic English people [and] the Shire is based on rural England. . . . After all the book is English, and by an Englishman."[5] "I lived for my early years in 'the Shire' in a pre-mechanical age"; "any corner of that county [Worcestershire] . . .

is in an indefinable way 'home' to me, as no other part of the world is" (*TMM* 153–55, xiii). Having myself grown up in Worcestershire, I know what he means, and long before I knew that the author was a fellow countryman I recognized in his book the topography of those "counties upon the West Marches" in which alone a "Westmidlander" (*TMM* 154) can be "at home." His book was in an indefinable way a picture of home to me.

But let us nevertheless try to define it. In what sense of "England" are the hobbits English? Is it the England of *Puck of Pook's Hill* and *Rewards and Fairies?* Kipling's Puck, with his hairy feet, has some physical resemblance to a hobbit, though he is as long-lived as a Tolkien elf, and Tolkien alludes to Puck's magic of oak and ash and thorn in a song at the end of his first book about Bilbo's adventures. Puck revives for a modern pair of children the English past that has been buried in their local landscape. But that English past turns out to be heavy with a British future. It is peopled with freebooting adventurers who explore the trade routes that are to come, Roman soldiers who foreshadow another army flung far to the margins of the world, churchmen who reflect the need for a national Reformation. The England in which this past is infused is the England of Whiggish, picturesque illusion, the England that is "home" for the empire builders abroad, the England of Rupert Brooke. And that is quite certainly not the England of the Shire. Tolkien wrote in 1943, "I love England (not Great Britain and certainly not the British Commonwealth (grr!))" (*TMM* 135)—the "(grr!)" being perhaps directed as much at the hypocritical new name as at the imperial reality continuing underneath it. Equally, however, the Shire is not another early-twentieth-century England that plainly influenced Tolkien: the England of Kenneth Grahame. *The Wind in the Willows* also covers with a rich glow of nostalgia a still just premechanical countryside on which motor cars are a dangerous intrusion, though railways are as established a feature of village life as post offices in the Shire. *The Wind in the Willows* is also a book in which a significant place is given to the romance of food and drink and long walks in masculine company for the leisured classes, who are, if not exactly rich themselves, friends of the rich who live in the stately homes such as Toad Hall. There is much living underground in tunnels, and the animal status of the principal characters does not prevent them from having relations with the human world, albeit relations in which their difference is politely acknowledged. Being an animal in this book, then, is not unlike being a hobbit, and the protective seclusion of the River Bank is perhaps a foreshadowing of the Shire. However, there is more to Grahame's England than the River Bank. There are, for instance, the railways and the canals and the comically antiquated social institutions which condemn and imprison Toad and seem to have strayed in from a Gilbert and Sullivan opera. And this England differs fundamentally from Tolkien's Shire, for what Grahame calls England has no outside to it, no foreign relations. Other countries just do not exist. Grahame's England is pretty close to being the English heaven in the last line of Brooke's sonnet: it too, like Pook's Hill, is in the end the picturesque illusion that keeps out of sight the reality that is Britain and Empire. Like Brooke's England too, Grahame's needs no God: as Brooke toys with Spinozist pantheism so Grahame, in the chapter "The Piper at the Gates of Dawn"[6] toys with Pan, an implausibly Mediterranean import set up to paganize the English countryside, rather like a piece of statuary performing the same function at Stowe.

Tolkien's Catholicism, naturally, prevents him from sharing in this Edwardian substitute religion, and prevents him from going down the road that leads to it. In 1953, just before his first volume was published, he wrote, "*The Lord of the Rings* is of course a fundamentally religious and Catholic work, unconsciously so at first, but consciously in the revision" (*TMM* 100). It was unconsciously religious and Catholic, I believe, because its entire imaginative structure was determined by its author's Catholicism. That was the Catholicism of an English Catholic, in an age when a strain of anti-Catholicism ran, more or less unacknowledged, through all English institutions, and when it was not irrational for Tolkien to see his mother as literally a martyr to her faith, driven to an early grave by the hostility of her family to her conversion. It was therefore impossible for Tolkien to build into his work a conception of England that had its origins in the breach with Rome, in the establishment of a trading and industrial nation theologically sufficient unto itself, and in the development of a worldwide empire to give political shape to the global market it had done so much to create. The Shire could not possibly lie under, or have any part in, Brooke's English heaven. It is the ultimate source of such literary strength and prophetic power as *The Lord of the Rings* has that it is built on a conception of England that is not just an alternative to the imperial myth but is directly opposed to it. That is what the book is about and why it provides the beginnings of an answer to the question: what is England after the end of the imperial myth? what is England after Bond? Part of the reason for the book's worldwide success must be that in the global market virtually every national tradition has its local variant of that question.

Tolkien's Shire is England, but it is not the England of Kenneth Grahame and Rupert Brooke, for all the superficial similarities. It is not the mythical England of the Great Britain project, of the four-and-a-half-centuries long imperial adventure, because, unlike Grahame's England, the Shire has an outside, and, unlike Brooke's England, it does not ignore the rest of the foreign world apart from a corner that it colonizes. On the contrary, the Shire itself is only a corner of the field, and the collision between the Little People and the Big People, the impact of each on the other, is Tolkien's theme. If most of the inhabitants of the Shire do not ever comprehend their involvement, passive and active, in a greater history, that does not make them unlike their English originals: after saying that the hobbits "are just rustic English people" Tolkien went on to tell his interviewer that they were "made small in size because it reflects the generally small reach of their imagination." The contrast between the full-sized societies and the hobbits—the "halflings," as they become as speech grows nobler in the more epic reaches of history—is therefore a constant reminder throughout the tale that it is chronicling the intersection of different imaginative worlds, of the Shire and Middle Earth, of England and a bigger story. Four hobbits—five if we include Bilbo—create that intersection by passing the boundaries of the Shire and observing or participating in an epic action which is significant to us as readers not in itself but because it contrasts with or threatens or, eventually, damages the Shire. They meet societies that are recognizable as like their own but larger—grander and older, or more wild and violent, materially and culturally wealthier, or used to different conditions of life. They meet representatives, good and evil, of a half-seen spiritual world. They meet also principles of Nature, some almost untouchable by the doings of human or humanlike society, some threatened by them to the point of extinction. They travel in a great variety of landscapes, variously different from what they have known at home—bleak northern moors, high mountain valleys, several distinctly different forests, rich grasslands, rivers large and small, a complex ancient city, industrial wasteland and lava desert—and these, together with the sense of distances traversed and distance from home, are among the indisputable literary pleasures of the book. All of this world outside the Shire is something that the hobbits are not but something they nonetheless belong to—something that Tolkien's England is not, but something it belongs to. By contrast with Grahame's England, there is a world outside; by contrast with Brooke's England, the world outside is belonged to, not colonized.

Above all, it turns out that the hobbits belong to the world outside the Shire because they have a responsibility in it and for it. Quite unexpectedly and improbably it turns out that the Shire contains a power that can precipitate the ruination of the world beyond and within its borders, of the great multiplicity that the hobbits are not, and of the hobbits themselves. It contains the Ring. That is as unexpected and improbable, we might say, as that an offshore agricultural island on the margins of Christendom, happily producing cheap alabasters for wealthier and more sophisticated markets in continental cities, talking its own little Germanic dialect and contributing the occasional scholar or poet to the universal Latin culture, should turn out to contain the power that would give the world mechanization, industry, global trade, empire, and the new Latin—American English. If the Shire is Tolkien's England, it is an England that is not only a part of Europe, but an England that rejects the temptation to secular modernity to which the real England succumbed when at the time of the Reformation it set off on the road that led to nationalism, capitalism, imperialism, and, eventually, the economic and political subordination of Europe and everywhere else to the English-speaking United States. That temptation is represented in Tolkien's story by the Ring, the Ring made by an emanation of the Devil, which is able to lay nature waste, enslave the world's population, and empty our lives of substance, reducing us to ghosts as we seek its power for ourselves. It would, I think, trespass on the integrity of Tolkien's vision to attempt to identify the Ring, by way of allegory, with some specific factor in the change that came over England at the end of England's Catholic period—individualism, Protestantism, capitalism, nationalism, or any of the other elements in modernity that I have mentioned. That the Ring stands in the closest relationship to that change, however, is guaranteed for us by two facts: the Shire, which above all else in the story is threatened by the Ring, is England; and it is an England which has not gone down the route chosen in the sixteenth century by the historical England—it is an England which, by rejecting the Ring, rejects that historical choice, both for itself and for the world to which it belongs.

Middle Earth, the world to which the Shire belongs, rejects the Ring by leaving it in the hands of the hobbits; the hobbits reject it, both in the person of Sam, Frodo's gardener and batman, the representative of the qualities and limitations of the Shire, at their most admirable, and principally of course in the quest of Frodo himself, the Ringbearer, the representative of Shire and Middle Earth alike, through whom runs the intersection of Tolkien's England with the world outside it. Sam's rejection of the Ring, in the name of the Shire alone, so to speak, is brisk and straightforward: like all the principal characters in the tale he has to be tempted with fantasies of power, tempted in the manner most apt to his best qualities, but his temptation does not last long:

> [D]eep down in him lived still unconquered his plain hobbit-sense: he knew in the core of his heart that he was not large enough to bear such a burden [Tolkien's England, we might gloss this decisive reference to the littleness of the Little People, is *not* the world], even if such visions were not a mere cheat to betray him. The one small garden of a free gardener was all his need and due, not a garden swollen to a realm; his own hands to use, not the hands of others to command. (*LR* iii, 177)

The case of Frodo is more complex. His quest is the main strand in the narrative, the quest to destroy the Ring in the place of its first making. From the start Frodo's character has been presented as divided, and to this division correspond two different aspects of his quest. On the one hand, Frodo, even more than Sam, is the appointed and destined representative of the Shire, and this quest is presented to us as the moment when the Shire enters history, when the halflings stand forth   the moment when their special virtues of stamina, decency, humor, realism, and above all a capacity for being overlooked do more for Middle Earth than the counsels of the wise and the courage of the strong. It is understandable that in a book largely written during the Second World War, and completed shortly before the Festival of Britain in 1951, this theme—we might call it: little England saves the world—should have seemed like a commentary on recent events. But such an interpretation—at least if it is thought to imply that Tolkien's book celebrates what in 1951 was held to be British culture and a British victory in the recent war—is plainly impossible and not just because Tolkien himself rejected it.[7] If the book showed the destruction of the Ring as corresponding to the finest hour of an outnumbered and outgunned faithful few, it would be a contribution to the triumphalist British—we might call it Churchillian—myth of the great twentieth-century conflict, not a critique of it. And a critique it must be, for a historical parallel to the success of Frodo's quest could only be, not the triumph of Britain, but its self-immolation—the dissolution of the empire and of everything built on the act over four centuries old by which England ceased to be Catholic and became Britain, a willed rejection of all the features of modernity that made mid-twentieth-century British society possible. Some of those features of modernity were indeed stripped away from Britain in the great cataclysm, and there may be some more still to go. Tolkien, thanks to his marginal position as a Catholic in British society, may have been able to sense this process earlier than many, and to have provided a metaphor for it is part of the prophetic achievement of his book. It is, however, an eschatological metaphor, a sign of what shall or should be, or what should have been, not simply of what was and is in our own time. Some of the work of modernity may have been undone in the great crisis of the twentieth century, but much remains intact. The imperialism and nationalism, perhaps even the Protestantism, may have gone, but the commercialization and mechanization have only grown in intensity, and Catholicism is unrestored. Tolkien's metaphor is appropriately ambiguous. The success of Frodo's quest cannot be treated simply as the triumph of the hobbit virtues, the triumph of Englishness—not just because in the mid-twentieth century that did not happen, or happened only partially, but because the success of Frodo's mission is a salvation which only a Catholic view of life can explain. To interpret the quest, and its end, without reference to Tolkien's Catholicism is to lose a whole dimension of its significance. It is also to lose sight of the second half of Frodo's divided character.

For Frodo is not just the representative of the Shire: he is the figure in which the Shire and the world the Shire belongs to intersect. He is the hobbit who more than any others—there are others—belongs to the wider world: he is the friend of wizards and elves; he has an urge to follow his uncle Bilbo and travel beyond the boundaries of the Shire; his knowledge and understanding of the deeper past and the wider present may be sketchy, but they are enough for him to grasp what is required of him—to be the member of the Little People who has the central role in the big action. And because he has that wider scope, in thought and deed, he is exposed, as Sam is not, to the temptation of the Ring, the temptation to think that he is large enough to bear its burden. Tolkien understands that as soon as his England steps on to a wider stage, as soon as it recognizes that it belongs to a wider world, it will be subject to the temptation to become Britain. Frodo, the chosen representative of Tolkien's England, succumbs to the temptation. His quest is not only the moment when the Little People play their part in history, it is also the moment when they fail. Frodo cannot in the end resist the temptation to try to be big. Perhaps no one can, certainly not anyone in the historical and fallen world to which all the characters in the epic belong (apart from the mysteriously sequestered Tom Bombadil, over whom alone the Ring has no power). Frodo fails, but his quest succeeds. The success is due not to any virtue of his own, not to his possessing in an eminent or any particular degree the qualities attributed to the folk of the Shire; it is not a triumph of innate goodness or plain common sense or a Churchillian refusal to give in. All the supports, all the personal and moral resources fall away in the final temptation, and the success, the eucatastrophe as Tolkien called it, the poignant reversal of fortune towards the good, is brought about by powers quite different from those which have ruled in the individualistic, secular fictions of the modern era that we know as "novels." True, the hobbits' courage and perseverance and devotion to each other have brought them to the point where the destruction of the Ring is possible, but their quest succeeds only thanks to the operation of an intention deeper than their conscious minds and wills: that intention may operate through them and their conscious choices, but it operates also through the unknown and, by them, unintended consequences of what they and others have done. It operates, that is, on the thoroughly Catholic principles of the necessity, but not sufficiency, of good works for salvation and of the communion of saints. The hobbits are on their own in the desolation of Mordor, but the acts and gifts and influences of others have combined to bring them there and even give them some measure of protection. But more important still is that because of the pity shown by Frodo and by Sam, and earlier by Gandalf and Aragorn, in sparing him, the former hobbit Gollum is enabled both to be there too and, by his own conscious but very different choice, to carry out the Ringbearer's intention when the Ringbearer is no longer able to do so. Rejection of the temptation represented by the Ring cannot, it seems, be the matter of an unaided decision of the will, let alone the individual will, in full awareness of the nature and consequences of its actions. None of us is large enough for that. It requires the collective and collaborative willingness of many—perhaps distant from each other in space and time—to do all that they can for what is good and right, despite their knowledge of the inadequacy of what they do, and with no more support or validation of it than the faith that it will be joined to other work, of which they have little or no knowledge, so as to achieve the purpose of which they all seem to fall short. "'Why did [the Ring] come to me? Why was I chosen?'" Frodo asks, and Gandalf replies, "'Such questions cannot be answered. . . . You may be sure that it was not for any merit that others do not possess: not for power or wisdom, at any rate. But you have been chosen, and you must therefore use such strength and heart and wits as you have.'" (*LR* i, 70) And when

Frodo's strength and heart and wits give out, his good deeds and those of others come to his aid; even evil deeds and intentions are turned to good, and an unseen and incalculable plan is brought to completion.

When Tolkien said that "*The Lord of the Rings* is . . . a fundamentally religious and Catholic work," I think he must particularly have had in mind this group of themes—the calling of the individual, the communion of saints, and the relation of grace and works. They, rather than the invented mythology and cosmology out of which it is carved, structure many aspects of the book; they help to define the boundary, which in all works of fantasy is dangerously fluid, between secular fiction and sacred meaning; and they are the ultimate source of the book's ability to speak to a very large audience about some of the greatest issues of our time.

The combination of a sense of personal vocation and a belief in the joint or collective nature of faith, in the indispensability of the church and of the love of Christians for one another, is a characteristic feature of the Catholic ethos. Catholics are alone with God together, and the sense of being solitaries engaged in a common venture permeates *The Lord of the Rings*. It provides the first volume with its theme and its title: the Ringbearer is surrounded and supported by a Fellowship. The members of the Fellowship in turn are representatives of individual communities, differently affected by the impending crisis, with their own roles and expectations, but linked in solidarity by a common cause. A similar pattern determines most of the episodes in the narrative: individual groups, with destinies as distinct as those of the Shire and the kingdom of Gondor, are encountered and lend support, of varying extent and out of varying degrees of benevolence and self-interest—whether it is the initially suspicious horsemen of Rohan, the doomed and marginally humanoid Ents and their herds of trees, or the ghostly armies on the Path of the Dead. All these groups, while fulfilling their own fate, also acknowledge, with more or less reluctance, their own common obligation to an overriding call. Now the understanding of Christianity as a way for different individuals to live together in the company of the transcendent partly explains the prominence of the practice of the Imitation of Christ in Catholic devotion, particularly in the Catholicism in which Tolkien grew up. Christianity is a way of living—individually and collectively living—a good life, rather than a conceptual structure or a historical or theological drama. Tolkien's book, consequently—this is one of the things that it must mean to say that it is fundamentally a Catholic work—shows us ways of living rather than dramatizations or allegorizations of theological principles. Tolkien himself said that the Incarnation and Redemption were far too high a theme for him to dare to attempt to depict it (*TMM* 110)—in that he was following, admittedly from a considerable distance, the example of Dante—and so the lives of his characters provide, not analogies to the life of Christ, but examples of attempts to imitate him. Since he yields to temptation, Frodo plainly cannot be an analogy of Christ, nor, even, can Gandalf, whose sufferings are not expiatory. (Tolkien told a friend of mine that Gandalf was "not Christ, but an angel.")[8] Yet both of these figures undergo sufferings that clearly reflect those of Christ.

Technically, we should probably say that they are types of Christ's sufferings, not reflections but foreshadowings. The events of *The Lord of the Rings* are located within the broad scheme of biblical chronology insofar as they occur on this earth—the moon and the constellations are those known to us now, for example—after the Fall but before the Redemption (*TMM* 110). This setting in a world that does not yet know the Christian, or even the Jewish, revelation has the singular advantage that it also, as it were, prefigures a world so secularized that it has largely forgotten them: the archaic, or archaizing, features of the book are the metaphors for its ultramodernity. The hobbits find themselves wandering through a landscape, both natural and human, that, metaphorically at least, is post-Christian. It is a landscape heavy with a past meaning, now largely forgotten but not entirely so: it still lingers on here and there in the mind. Old memories, now faded or effaced, are suddenly and unexpectedly revived by meetings with ancient powers or those who preserve in some secluded refuge the names or habits or languages of another time. To this process the hobbits are essential: it is their limited experience, their littleness in time, that makes memory defective or the past past at all. Thanks to the perspective provided by the hobbits, *The Lord of the Rings* repeatedly conveys the startling transition from unawareness of the past, or a sense only of its strangeness and difference, to recognition of it as one's own past, or even as one's own present, as closer and more immediate than had been thought. Or conversely, there are glimpses, behind a lively and familiar present, of previously unknown depths and layers of other times and places and contexts—as when Frodo realizes that his kindly host Elrond, a skilled healer, has personal memories of vast battles that ended previous ages of the world and are now among hobbits at most the matter of legend, or when magic provides him with an unexplained sighting of his lifelong friend Gandalf wandering, probably far away and long ago, on some unidentified mission. The variety of these encounters with the past is remarkable: at one extreme there are relics of wholly alien and forgotten cultures, primitive, silent, and enigmatic, on the verge of nonentity:

> At each turn of the road there were great standing stones that had been carved in the likeness of men, huge and clumsy-limbed, squatting cross-legged with their stumpy arms folded on fat bellies. Some in the wearing of the years had lost all features save the dark holes of their eyes that still stared sadly at the passers-by. . . . Merry gazed at them with wonder and a feeling almost of pity as they loomed up mournfully in the dusk. (*LR* iii, 67)

At the other extreme there is the surprise of meeting a piece of well-loved family history and discovering that it is not all words and embroidery: the hobbits, unaware that they have followed the route taken by Bilbo on the journey recounted in Tolkien's first book, come across the trolls turned to stone in an early adventure of Bilbo's, one of them now with a bird's nest behind his petrified ear (*LR* i, 218). But the main type of such vivified memories is the emergence out of the landscape or some ancient artifact or even some person, of an aspect, new to the hobbits, of the greater story to which theirs belongs, as the Shire belongs to Middle Earth. Always the unexpected strand of the story emerges in contrast to the barrenness, or the ruinousness, or simply the ordinariness of the context in which it is found. The green mounds of the Barrow Downs or the crumbling, grass-grown stone ring on the summit of Weathertop have almost returned into the earth from which they were taken, like many a Bronze Age feature of the English landscape. The hobbits' experience of them, however, brings flashes of recollection of the ancient wars during which they were made—a night-time assault on a fort, a long watch against peril from the North (*LR* i, 154, 197)—and, in an arc which spans the whole book from the first volume to the third, the enemy whose victims have been buried a thousand years is gradually revealed as their own principal visible adversary, the first of the Ringwraiths who is brought low on the field of battle by a knife taken from one of the barrows. Again, when the Fellowship of the Ring is traveling south in small boats down the Great River, they pass on either side two massive images that mark the old northern boundary of the realm of Gondor, now much reduced since the days of its foundation by emissaries from the western kingdom of Númenor:

> Upon great pedestals founded in the deep waters stood two great
> kings of stone: still with blurred eyes and crannied brows they
> frowned upon the North . . . , the silent wardens of a long-vanished
> kingdom. Awe and fear fell upon Frodo . . . as the boats whirled by,
> frail and fleeting as little leaves, under the enduring shadow of the
> sentinels of Númenor. (*LR* i, 409)

But in the same moment, Aragorn, the leader of the party, proudly steering
the tiny boat along the rushing waters, reminds them and us that, contrary
to all appearances, these are his ancestors and the king is returning to his
kingdom. That too is a part of the meaning of the events in which Frodo is
involved, cowed though he is by the enormity of his task and dwarfed
though they all may be by the memory of an earlier and greater time. Such
moments, when a past larger than anything the Little People have known
hitherto is infused into their present, need not be only fearsome or awe-
inspiring. The one allusion in *The Lord of the Rings* to a religious ritual
occurs when Frodo and Sam, on enemy territory, have fallen in with a
raiding party led by Faramir, heir to the Stewardship of Gondor. Before a
simple meal of bread and wine, salt meats and cheese and dried fruits, the
whole party turns west for a moment of silence. Frodo and Sam have to be
told by Faramir what to do. "'We look towards Númenor that was,'" he explains, "'and beyond to Elvenhome that is, and to that which is beyond Elvenhome and will ever be. Have you no such custom at meat?' 'No,' said
Frodo, feeling strangely rustic and untutored" (*LR* ii, 285). For the representatives of the Shire all these entries into the communion of the saints, all
these recollections of earlier ages, revelations of unexpected continuities,
placings of daily life in larger and more lasting contexts, are so many encounters with their own boundaries and marginality and littleness. That
makes them analogies of any encounter between a reduced present and a
more meaningful past, whether in Tolkien's Middle Earth or in our own
world. The Shire, like Middle Earth in its state of decline, and indeed like
modern England, is defined by what it has forgotten, and the hobbits' great
expedition into the world to which the Shire belongs is a reawakening that
will redefine the home from which they started. That is part of the explanation, I think, for the extraordinary mass appeal of this book: it captures
the experience of coming after meaning, after the fairies' farewell, the experience of inhabiting a world in which a great story was once present but is
now accessible only in shards of illumination and memory, moments of

communion with saints; yet it is a world in which life has to be lived and a task has to be performed, it is a post-Christian world in which Christ still has to be imitated.

The episode on the Barrow Downs is perhaps the moment at which the hobbits finally pass beyond the boundaries of the Shire out into a landscape where immediate revelations of the greater meaning become possible. It is marked by the distribution among the party of weapons—the equipment of epic, and so potentially a sign that the narrative is about to stray into areas where the principle of reticence will be abandoned and only bombast can result. But Tolkien is careful to keep to the hobbits' perspective, which makes this a moment on the boundary and so itself a moment of revelation: they feel awkward with these unfamiliar objects under their jackets. "Fighting had not before occurred to any of them as one of the adventures in which their flight would land them" (*LR* i, 157). A converse moment occurs near the end of the third volume when they come back through this same transitional territory bringing with them the signs of the greater world:

> The hobbits suddenly realized that people had looked at them in amazement not out of surprise at their return so much as in wonder at their gear. They themselves had become so used to warfare . . . that they had quite forgotten that the bright mail peeping from under their cloaks . . . would seem outlandish in their own country. (*LR* iii, 272)

The hobbits are returning to the Shire with news of the Return of the King. The eschatological reference is clearly deliberate, and Tolkien manages it with care. The images of an ideal fulfillment are restricted and are largely images of the healing of wounds. For *The Lord of the Rings* is not just the story of hobbits venturing out to discover the greater world to which the Shire belongs. It is also the story of the greater world breaking in on the Shire, potentially with annihilating consequences. The Black Riders are at their most uncanny when their footfall is heard on a summer evening in the lanes and woodlands of the Shire, and the desolation wrought by the Ring is at its least fabulous and metaphorical in the lock-ups, rationing, intimidation, and protoindustrial vandalism inflicted on the hobbits by malevolent bullies, the jetsam cast up by the last ripples of the far-distant storm. The healing of that hurt—rather than the splendor of coronations and princely weddings—turns out to be the culmination of the hobbits' story, the purpose, as Gandalf tells them, for which they have been trained. When that work has been done—and it is theirs to do, without any assistance from external powers—the one sign of completion, apart from an *annus mirabilis* of fertility, is the planting in the Shire of a fairy tree. It is a sign of the full reintegration of the Shire into the world beyond its borders, a sign to silence all the scoffers and unbelievers we heard gossiping in the inn at the very start of the story. The political and constitutional outcome of the reintegration, the settling of the place of the Shire in the returned King's kingdom, is, by contrast, the subject of only one or two hints in the narrative proper and is reserved for the appendices. The appendices, however, only make explicit what the entire structure of the story anyway suggests— that, as Tolkien put it, "the progress of the tale ends in [something] like the establishment of an effective Holy Roman Empire with its seat in Rome" (*TMM* 136). By the same token, the planting of the fairy tree, which puts the Shire under the special protection of an Elf Queen, is something like the return of England, Mary's dowry, to the Roman faith. The ultimate answer to our question, what are the hobbits? must then be that they are, at least by the end of the book, the representatives of a Catholic England which has resisted the temptation to secular modernity, in particular to Britishness, and has accepted its place within Christendom.

But, as I have said, Tolkien manages his eschatology with care. That fulfillment, for which in his day the English Catholic church prayed every week in a special Prayer for England, lies on, perhaps even beyond, the margins of his conclusion, unless we advance into his appendices. *The Lord of the Rings,* like other books I have considered in this study, has two endings, not one. Beyond the golden age at which its conclusion seems to hint, lies a decline into our own era. The dominant note in the last pages of the book (prolonged but not eliminated in the appendices) is elegiac, a pensiveness and sense of loss that is not the fulfillment of prayer but an invitation to it. It is literally a fairies' farewell and leaves us, as readers, with what our hobbit representatives have so often seen: a vision of the glory that has departed. Our sobering experience of emerging from the book's imaginary world is reflected in the narrative by the impossibility, for the characters most intimate with life's transcendent ground, of remaining in it either— since it is well on the way to becoming the fairy-less and secularized world that we, the readers, normally inhabit. The conclusion to *The Lord of the Rings* springs a last surprise in that, for all the allusions to *The Hobbit,* it proves not to have the same comfortable and circular structure as the earlier book: it is not a story of there and back again. It is Frodo who sets out from Bag End, just like Bilbo in *The Hobbit,* but it is Sam who in the last line says, "Well, I'm back." The divided character, the character who achieved the reconciliation and reintegration of the two worlds that intersected in him, has no place in the new world he has brought into being, for he is too marked, too deeply wounded, by the division he has healed. Those who win great victories pass away like those they have defeated, for they too belong to the time of conflict, not to the time of peace that they have made possible. Frodo loses the Ring and he loses the Shire, though he has saved it for others. "'It is gone for ever,'" he says, half in a dream, when the memory of his burden returns to haunt him, "'and now all is dark and empty'" (*LR* iii, 304). It is one of the book's genuinely great moments. For Frodo there are no rewards: the change of the times that he has lived through and helped to bring about leaves him, like the contemporaries of Richard Corbett, not more but less at one with his surroundings. Not for him or us as readers a happily ever after, enjoying "the Shire . . . for years and years" (*LR* iii, 309), as Sam expected. Frodo joins the wizards and the Elven kings and queens as they pass through the woods of his homeland westwards towards the ocean, in the direction of Faramir's prayer, and is soon, like Corbett's fairies, gone with them "beyond the seas." Our last moment on the boundary between the Shire and the world beyond—whether that means the moment when the narrative reaches out beyond the westernmost shore of Middle Earth or the moment when we close the book—is another moment of revelation, a revelation of bereavement.

In the end *The Lord of the Rings* is after all a lament for the passing of the imperial era, specifically of the Whig project for a global Great Britain, not because that was an admirable project—on the contrary, it was for Tolkien the work of the Devil—but because that project could be opposed by an image of England that was sustained by the hope of the country's eventual transformation back into Mary's dowry, so that, in the words of Robert Lowell, "the world shall come to Walsingham."[9] The passing of the diabolical project—in a conflict with a more devilish power still—meant the passing also of the hope, just as the rejection of the temptation of the Ring in the conflict with the Dark Lord meant an end to the immediate presence in the world of the magical and Elvish powers that had resisted him. Much that was good perished in the conflicts of the twentieth century as well as much that was evil. The secular modernity with which we now have to struggle is no longer a product of merely national ambitions (though to those who have not learnt the lessons of the last century it may all seem to emanate from a single great Satan in the United States). Hopes expressed in merely national terms can therefore no longer sustain us. If we ask what England is now—now after *GoldenEye*—the answer is, a story. England is now the story of the good and bad things that people did in England's name, and of the hopes that they had for it. Wherever we live in the global market it can be that for us, and even if we live in England it cannot, except by way of illusion, be any more. Our identity, our duty, our past and our hopes, insofar as we are not deceiving ourselves, come now from the global market and its greater meanings. Such a moment of transformation, when what was an urgent necessity, a life-and-death struggle of the spirit to express and fulfill the Law, becomes a finished story, "a symbol perfected in death,"[10] is made imminently, though not quite, present at the end of *The Lord of the Rings* when Frodo gives Sam his book of eighty chapters, leaving him to write the last.

Whatever its shortcomings, *The Lord of the Rings* has a touch of greatness. Any book must have a touch of greatness that has been so successful for so long. It has deserved the popularity it has achieved because it has been able to provide symbols of some of the decisive public experiences of the twentieth century as many, indeed most, of that century's major narratives have not. The alliance of its dark forces with the powers of mechanization, authoritarian discipline, mass society, and environmental despoliation has provided an imaginative vocabulary, however schematic, for generations of dissenters. It has dared to depict war as necessary, the temptations both of power and of fear, and disagreement and distrust between allies even when they face a common enemy. These are not themes that have lost topicality with the lapse of time. More subtle is its portrayal of the experience of coming after a period in which a unified system of life and belief held sway, of stumbling across survivals or memories of past meanings. Most significant of all, because most deeply felt, is its depiction of the experience of historical change—of the transition from one age to another and of the cost to those who are called on to live through such a crisis. That experience has been virtually universal in the twentieth century, though Tolkien mediates it to his wider audience through the specific experience of the England that he knew and his specific hopes for the England for which he prayed. England and the English experiences of the temptation to modernity, of the identity conferred by conflict, and the loss of identity in historical transition are made into a symbol for the benefit of the world. And of that symbolic England the representatives are the hobbits.

The perspective provided by the hobbits, the perspective of the Little on the Big, is essential to the structure of the book. In this study I have argued that works of secular literature can give us access to the realm of sacred literature, can provide a commentary on what is commanded by the

Law that is not simply a book but is fulfilled in Jesus Christ as a person. But I have also argued that works of secular literature can do this only insofar as they incorporate in themselves a recognition of the boundary separating them from the sacred, from the utterance of the Law, and a recognition of the forgiveness brought by knowledge of the Law in its fullness. No doubt *The Lord of the Rings* is not—quite—real literature. Like alabasters and Rupert Brooke and James Bond, it emerges from and, wittingly or not, is addressed to a public and collective need: it belongs to popular and therefore necessarily commercial culture. But still it contains that structural element of the boundary, the principle of reticence, that brings us up to the frontier of the Law and, by not uttering the Law, the command "Thou shalt," establishes its right to be regarded as about it. By not telling us what it is in the uttermost West on which Faramir's eyes are set during his grace before meals, by telling us little even about the realms that lie between it and the viewpoint of the untutored hobbits, though telling us more as we get closer to them, so that we know more about Númenor than we do about Elvenhome, more about Faramir's land of Gondor than we do about Númenor, and considerably more about Sam and Frodo than about Faramir, Tolkien creates an analogue of a secular world imbued with a sacred presence that may be largely unknown but is, in varying degrees, in principle knowable, and was certainly better known in the past than it is now. That structured perspective is absent from the working papers in which Tolkien elaborated his fantasy world, and so the analogy with the real world is lost. But in *The Lord of the Rings* itself he has written a piece of popular literature that, in the spirit of G. K. Chesterton, reclaims the myth of England for Catholicism and uses that myth both to represent a more general twentieth-century experience of historical uprooting and to give new sense to the old tradition of the ascetic life lived in imitation of Christ and in the communion of saints. The act of deference, or reticence, by which Tolkien maintains the distance of his text from the original source of the command to asceticism qualifies his book after all for a place among works of literature— secular literature, that is, which can be read as commentary precisely because it knows, and shows, that it cannot be read as Bible.

1. "Literature as the 'Site' of Theology"

1. I am grateful to Janette Gray, who is preparing a study of Chenu's theological anthropology, for information on this point.

2. Marie-Dominique Chenu, "La littérature comme 'lieu' de la théologie," *Revue des sciences philosophiques et théologiques* 53 (1969): 70–80, henceforth "La littérature."

3. Matthias Joseph Scheeben, "so far the greatest German theologian since the age of Romanticism." Hans-Urs von Balthasar, *Herrlichkeit: Eine theologische Ästhetik. 1.Bd. Schau der Gestalt* (Einsiedeln: Johannes Verlag, 1963), pp. 98–110.

4. See Brian Wicker, *Culture and Liturgy* (London: Sheed and Ward, 1963), and *Culture and Theology: A Sketch for a Contemporary Christianity* (London: Sheed and Ward, 1966); the journal *Second Spring;* John Milbank, *Theology and Social Theory: Beyond Secular Reason* (Oxford: Blackwell, 1990).

5. See, for example, Northrop Frye, *The Great Code: The Bible and Literature* (London: Routledge, 1982), illuminatingly confronted with other approaches by Kevin Hart, "The Poetics of the Negative," *Reading the Text: Biblical Criticism and Literary Theory,* ed. Stephen Prickett (Oxford: Blackwell, 1991), pp. 281–340; and the survey volume by Stephen Prickett and Robert Barnes, *The Bible,* Landmarks in World Literature (Cambridge: Cambridge University Press, 1991).

6. Blaise Pascal, *Pensées et Opuscules,* ed. Léon Brunschvicg (Paris: Hachette, 1966) (Brunschvicg *minor* edition), No. 421; henceforth *P* with the number of the relevant *pensée.*

7. George Steiner, *Real Presences* (Chicago: University of Chicago Press, 1991), pp. 215–16.

8. One of the many ways in which this quest can fail will be if too crude a correspondence is established between the religious and the literary, or at too superficial a level. It could, for example, be too crude to say that a work espouses atheism or promiscuity and is therefore bad (it might appear to do both but could prove on finer analysis to be animated by true love of God and neighbor), and it

would almost certainly be too superficial to conclude that a *work* was bad because *some characters in it* were atheists or promiscuous (they might after all just be the villains).

9. Thomas Aquinas, *Summa Theologica,* Ia, q.1, art. 8.

10. Jean Calvin, *Institution de la religion chrétienne* (Geneva: Labor et Fides, 1967), I, 6, p. 36.

11. Ibid., I, 7, pp. 40, 38, 41.

12. See also Calvin, *Institution,* IV, 9.

13. *Die symbolischen Bücher der evangelisch-lutherischen Kirche, deutsch und lateinisch,* ed. J. T. Müller (Gütersloh: Bertelsmann, 1900), p. 518.

14. William Chillingworth, *The Religion of Protestants a Safe Way to Salvation* (Oxford: John Clarke, 1638), p. 375 (ch. 6, §56). I was very fortunate that at this point my text could profit from the assistance of the late John Cochrane O'Neill, a far-sighted scholar, a devout man, and a dear friend, to whom I also owe the description of the Reformed chapel in Göttingen.

15. Samuel Taylor Coleridge, *Confessions of an Inquiring Spirit* , ed. H. St. J. Hart, Library of Modern Religious Thought (London: Adam and Charles Black, 1956), Letter IV, p. 58; Letter VII, p. 77. Hart (p. 8) refers us to Lessing's fragmentary drafts of "Bibliolatrie," a part of his polemic against Hauptpastor Goeze (*Werke,* ed. K. Lachmann and F. Muncker [Stuttgart: Göschen, 1886–1924], 16, pp. 470–76). Lessing makes it clear that the term is his own coinage and (as usual) while denying the implication that it is parallel to the term "idolatry," admits that it is "ambiguous," and so allows the implication to stand. The text was published in Lessing's *Theologischer Nachlaß* in 1784 and republished in his collected works in 1793 and must have been known to Coleridge. Coleridge cites Chillingworth's formula (effectively, as the English equivalent to "bibliolatrie") in Letter VI, p. 76. We might say that the identification of the *sola scriptura* principle as bibliolatry was the point at which the English intellectual tradition began to engage with the new biblical hermeneutics elaborated in Germany over the previous two generations.

16. See, for example, Leslie Stephen, *History of English Thought in the Eighteenth Century* (London: Hart-Davis, 1962) ch. ii, §9, vol. 1, pp. 69–71.

17. Cited by Stephen, *English Thought,* ch. vii, §19, vol. 1, p. 307.

18. Nicholas Boyle, "Lessing, Biblical Criticism and the Origins of German Classical Culture," *German Life and Letters* 34 (1981): 196–213.

19. Karl S. Guthke, *Der Blick in die Fremde: Das Ich und das andere in der Literatur* (Tübingen: Francke, 2000).

20. Karl Barth, *Die protestantische Theologie im 19. Jahrhundert* (Zurich: Zollikon, 1947), p. 302.

21. Johann Gottfried Herder, *Vom Geist der ebräischen Poesie*, in *Schriften zum Alten Testament*, ed. Rudolf Smend (= *Werke*, ed. Günter Arnold et al., 5; Bibliothek deutscher Klassiker, 93) (Frankfurt: Deutscher Klassiker Verlag, 1993), 661–1308, p. 663; henceforth *GEP*.

2.   History and Hermeneutics (1): Herder

1. For the following argument, see in particular *Über den Ursprung der Sprache* in *Frühe Schriften 1764–1772*, ed, Ulrich Gaier (= *Werke*, ed. Günter Arnold et al.; 1; Bibliothek deutscher Klassiker, 1) (Frankfurt: Deutscher Klassiker Verlag, 1985), pp. 695–810; *Shakespeare* in *Schriften Zur Ästhetik und Literatur 1767–1781*, ed. Gunter E. Grimm (= *Werke*, ed. Günter Arnold et al., 2; Bibliothek deutscher Klassiker, 95) (Frankfurt: Deutscher Klassiker Verlag, 1993), pp. 498–521 (henceforth *S*); *Auch eine Philosophie der Geschichte zur Bildung der Menschheit* in *Schriften zur Philosophie, Literatur, Kunst und Altertum 1774–1787*, ed. Jürgen Brummack and Martin Bollacher (= *Werke*, ed. Günter Arnold et al., 4; Bibliothek deutscher Klassiker, 105) (Frankfurt: Deutscher Klassiker Verlag, 1994), pp. 9–107 (henceforth *AP*).

2. See Marcus Walsh, "Biblical Scholarship and Literary Criticism," in *The Cambridge History of Literary Criticism, vol 4: The Eighteenth Century*, ed. H. B. Nisbet and Clive Rawson (Cambridge: Cambridge University Press, 1997), pp. 758–77, esp. pp. 766–71.

3. Goethe, conversation with Eckermann, 9 November 1824.

4. J. C. O'Neill, *The Bible's Authority: A Portrait Gallery of Thinkers from Lessing to Bultmann* (Edinburgh: T. and T. Clark, 1991), pp. 39–53, esp. pp. 40–41, 46–47.

5. Herder, *Adrastea (Auswahl)*, ed. Günter Arnold (= *Werke*, ed. Günter Arnold et al., 10; Bibliothek deutscher Klassiker, 170) (Frankfurt: Deutscher Klassiker Verlag, 2000), p. 658.

6. *GEP* 923–24, but cp. in the same volume (*Schriften zum Alten Testament*: note 21 to ch. 1 above), pp. 305, 496. The argument of *Die älteste Urkunde des Menschengeschlechts* is that Moses was (merely) the collector of the material in Genesis 1–11 and specifically did not write Genesis 1, which Herder thinks the direct voice of God (ibid., p. 495).

7. *The Jerusalem Bible* (London: Darton, Longman and Todd, 1966), "Introduction to the Pentateuch," p. 8.

8. *The New Jerome Biblical Commentary*, ed. Raymond E. Brown, S. S., et al. (London: Geoffrey Chapman, 1991), p. 330.

9. Albert Schweitzer, *The Quest of the Historical Jesus,* ed. John Bowden (London: SCM, 2000), p. 35.

10. *The Documents of Vatican II,* ed. Walter M. Abbott, S.J., and Joseph Gallagher (London: Geoffrey Chapman, 1966), "Dogmatic Constitution on Divine Revelation" (henceforth DR), pp. 107–132, §6.

11. Nicholas Boyle, " 'Art,' Literature, Theology: Learning from Germany," in *Higher Learning and Catholic Traditions,* ed. Robert E. Sullivan (Notre Dame: University of Notre Dame Press, 2001), pp. 87–111.

3.   History and Hermeneutics (2): Schleiermacher

1. F. D. Schleiermacher, *Hermeneutik und Kritik,* ed. Manfred Frank (Frankfurt am Main: Suhrkamp, 1977); henceforth *H.*

2. *H* 89; and see Frank's footnote, p. 100.

3. Friedrich Ast; see Hans W. Frei, *The Eclipse of Biblical Narrative: A Study in Eighteenth- and Nineteenth-Century Hermeneutics* (New Haven: Yale University Press, 1974), p. 300.

4. The phrase seems to have been invented in 1910 by Albert Schweitzer's English translator, W. Montgomery, to render "Leben-Jesu-Forschung," a concept unfamiliar, presumably, to either an academic or a general public in England at the time.

5. The following exposition is based mainly on Schleiermacher's *Über die Religion: Reden an die Gebildeten unter ihren Verächtern,* ed. Hans-Joachim Rothert, Philosophische Bibliothek Bd. 255 (Hamburg: Meiners, 1958).

6. See my "Lessing" (note 18 to ch. 1 above).

7. Soame Jenyns, *A View of the Internal Evidence of the Christian Religion* (London: J. Dodsley, 1776), pp. 131–33.

8. Ernst Troeltsch, "Die Krise des Historismus," *Neue Rundschau* 33.1 (1922).

9. According to Hayden White, philosophy of history after Hegel did not (except for Marx) take "historical consciousness beyond the point where [Hegel] had left it." *Metahistory: The Historical Imagination in Nineteenth-Century Europe* (Baltimore: Johns Hopkins University Press, 1973), p. 40.

4.   Revelation and Reason: Hegel

1. G. W. F. Hegel, *Werke in 20 Bänden,* ed. E. Moldenhauer and K. M. Michel (Frankfurt am Main: Suhrkamp, 1970), xvi, p. 36; henceforth *W.*

2. Georg Christoph Lichtenberg, *Schriften und Briefe,* ed. W. Promies (Munich: Hanser, 1967–92), i, p. 394 (E215).

3. Cp. *W* xvii, 292: "Es ist die Endlichkeit, die Christus angenommen hat."

4. "It has been observed with truth as well as with propriety, that the conquests of Rome prepared and facilitated those of Christianity." Gibbon, *The Decline and Fall of the Roman Empire* (Chicago: Encyclopaedia Britannica, 1952), i, Ch. 15, 201. Hegel seems to have read Gibbon in Berne in 1794: H. S. Harris, *Hegel's Development: Towards the Sunlight, 1770–1801* (Oxford: Clarendon, 1972), p. 157.

5. On the significance of the mediating role of Rome for Christianity and for European culture generally, see Rémi Brague, *Europe, la voie romaine* (Paris: Critérion, 1992); English translation by Samuel Lester: *Eccentric Culture: A Theory of Western Civilization* (South Bend: St. Augustine's Press, 2002).

6. See, for example, Deborah Sawyer, "Identity and the Other: The Emergence of Christianity," *New Blackfriars* 75.878 (January 1994): 39–51.

7. In the early fragment known as "Der Geist des Christentums und sein Schicksal," *W* i, 274–418, pp. 277–80.

5.   Revelation and Realism: Frei and Ricoeur

1. Frei, *The Eclipse of Biblical Narrative* (note 3 to ch. 3 above).

2. Erich Auerbach, *Mimesis: The Representation of Reality in Western Literature,* trans. Willard Trask (Princeton: Princeton University Press, 1953; originally Bern: Francke, 1946); "Figura," in Erich Auerbach, *Scenes from the Drama of European Literature* (New York: Meridian, 1959), pp. 11–76.

3. But note the criticism by James Fodor, *Christian Hermeneutics: Paul Ricoeur and the Refiguring of Theology* (Oxford: Clarendon, 1995), p. 285: "On the whole, then, Frei's attempts to read biblical narrative less as history and more as literary creations analogous to prose realism is ultimately unsuccessful. The analogy is fundamentally unsound."

4. Hans-Georg Gadamer, *Wahrheit und Methode: Grundzüge einer philosphischen Hermeneutik,* 4th ed. (Tübingen: J. C. B. Mohr (Paul Siebeck) 1975); henceforth *WM.*

5. Implausibly, both because Schleiermacher was not a fountainhead but only the channel through which a post-Kantian response to the joint Deist-historicist critique of Christian revelation was passed on to the nineteenth century and, above all, because Schleiermacher distanced himself from the conflation of art and religion which was essential to the self-definition of Romanticism. See note 8 to ch. 8 below.

6. Instead we find Gadamer following Dilthey and explaining the birth of Protestant hermeneutics as a response to the Council of Trent's defense of "tradition" (WM 162–63). It may well be that the Formula of Concord was influenced, among other things, by the need to reply to Trent, but the critique of tradition was already fully developed in Calvin's *Institutes* of 1536.

7. Paul Ricoeur, "Herméneutique de l'idée de Révélation," in Paul Ricoeur et al., *La Révélation,* Publications des facultés universitaires Saint-Louis, 7 (Brussels: Facultés Universitaires Saint-Louis, 1977), pp. 15–54 (henceforth HR); English translation by D. Pellauer, "Toward a Hermeneutic of the Idea of Revelation," *Harvard Theological Review* 70.1–2 (January–April 1977): 1–37 (hereafter TH).

8. Kant, *Die Religion innerhalb der Grenzen der bloßen Vernunft* 4, 2: *Theorie-Werkausgabe,* ed. W. Weischedel (Frankfurt am Main: Suhrkamp, 1968), viii, pp. 838–89.

9. "The parable . . . is the conjunction of a *narrative form* and a *metaphorical process.* Later I shall add a third decisive trait[,] . . . 'limit-expressions[,]' . . . linked to the character of extravagance of the parables of Jesus." Paul Ricoeur, "Biblical Hermeneutics" *Semeia* 4 (1975): pp. 27–148, pp. 30, 75.

10. As Kevin Hart notes, rather more critically: "The Poetics of the Negative" (note 5 to ch. 1 above), p. 305.

11. In adopting the phrase in 1968, Ricoeur attributed it to Éric Weil. See "Freedom in the Light of Hope," in Paul Ricoeur, *Essays on Biblical Interpretation,* ed. Lewis S. Mudge (London: SPCK, 1981), pp. 155–82, p. 166: "Dialectic in the Kantian sense is to my mind the part of Kantianism which not only survives the Hegelian critique but which triumphs over the whole of Hegelianism," p. 167. See also Lewis S. Mudge, "Paul Ricoeur on Biblical Interpretation," ibid., pp. 1–40, pp. 33–36; and Fodor, *Christian Hermeneutics,* p. 259. In 1975 Ricoeur called his use of the phrase "ironical": "Biblical Hermeneutics," p. 142.

12. Hegel, *W* xvii, pp. 286–87.

13. *Catechism of the Catholic Church* (London: Geoffrey Chapman, 1994), p. 30, art. 108.

6.   Lévinas (1): Beyond Bibliolatry?

1. Emmanuel Lévinas, "La Révélation dans la tradition juive," in *La Révélation* (see note 7 to ch. 5), pp. 55–77 (henceforth R); also in *L'au-delà du verset: Lectures et discours Talmudiques* (Paris: Minuit, 1982), pp. 158–81. English translation in *The Lévinas Reader,* ed. Sean Hand (Oxford: Blackwell, 1999), pp. 190–210 (henceforth *LR*).

2. In the plenary discussion, Ricoeur began with a conciliatory suggestion that this difference was not a "discordance profonde" but "une simple nuance" (*La Révélation*, p. 210). Lévinas, however, insisted on the priority of the prescriptive over (particularly) the narrative element in the Bible, seeing in it the guarantee of the transcendence of Revelation, its "extrinsécité radicale" (p. 213), which alone can dethrone the pretensions of the ego. Ricoeur then agreed to leave the matter as no longer "un débat purement théorique" but a question of "l'engagement de chacun dans sa tradition" (p. 226). He acknowledged that his own position might owe something to his need to overcome "une certaine fermeture moralisante" in Protestantism. But if Jesus is the fulfillment of the Law, and so (as I suggest below) the foundation of the moral existence—as called, lost, and bought again—of every human subject, maybe the conflict between the prescriptive and the narrative, and between the religious traditions that give them different priorities, is more apparent than real, at least "theoretically."

3. *La Révélation*, p. 213.

4. Luke Timothy Johnson, "Renewing Catholic Biblical Scholarship," *Priests and People*, August–September 2002, pp. 297–301, p. 301.

5. Asked by Paul Tihon why, "and in virtue of what prescription," the writing of the Torah and the oral law had ceased, Lévinas answered that the persecution and dispersal of the Jewish community had made it necessary to commit tradition to writing: "Je ne crois pas qu'il faille y chercher une signification métaphysique" (p. 230). (It might have been more difficult to deny the event *hermeneutic* significance.) He declined, that is, to insert the Law, oral or written, into a history which the Law itself might inform or describe. Yet that seems to me precisely what his own notion of the "confluence" of the sacred texts requires.

6. "[T]he face to face, the commandment, is never mediated and cannot be learnt. . . . [D]ifficult liberty cannot be tried and tested." Gillian Rose, *Judaism and Modernity: Philosophical Essays* (Oxford: Blackwell, 1993), p. 221.

7. Pascal, *P* 740.

7.   Lévinas (2): Two Branches of Judaism

1. N. T. Wright, "Jesus' Self-Understanding," in *The Incarnation: An Interdisciplinary Symposium on the Incarnation of the Son of God,* ed. Stephen T. Davis, Daniel Kendall, S.J., and Gerald O'Collins, S.J. (Oxford: Oxford University Press, 2002), pp. 47–61, p. 56.

2. St. Luke, who emphasizes the Temple-based piety that surrounds Jesus throughout his life, transfers it to the trial of Stephen.

3. Eph 2:20–22, 1 Pt 2:5, Rv 11:1–2, but cp. already 1 Cor 3:11.

4. Even the concept of the possible destruction of the Temple need not have been an anachronism unavailable to him: in A.D. 28, if John 2:20 is to be trusted, the Temple was felt to have been so completely rebuilt by Herod the Great that it was said to be only forty-six years old. Within living memory one Temple had been replaced by another, and what had happened at least twice in Israel's history could certainly be imagined as happening again.

5. Emil Fackenheim, *The Jewish Return into History: Reflections in the Age of Auschwitz and a New Jerusalem* (New York: Schocken, 1978), p. xii: "[T]he Holocaust and the rise of a Jewish state after two thousand years of Jewish statelessness. So immense are these two events, and so close are we to them, that it is reasonable to doubt that thought can grasp them. . . . Two duties are conferred on us. One is to confront the Holocaust honestly. . . . The other is to recognize the centrality of Israel in contemporary Jewish life." Fackenheim's book concentrates on the first of these duties and on the second only in relation to the first. That is understandable, but it has the consequence that a complementary aspect of the second task is entirely overlooked—recognizing the absence of Israel from the two thousand years of Jewish statelessness and the effect of that absence on the formation of Jewish identity and Jewish religion.

6. I take the phrase "New Testament Judaism" from the writings of David Daube, whose use of it was "a deliberate act": *New Testament Judaism: Collected Works of David Daube, Volume 2,* ed. Calum Carmichael, Studies in Comparative Legal History (Berkeley: Robbins Collection, 2000), p. xvi.

8.   The Spectrum of Writtenness

1. "If it is the Spirit that sanctifies, then every authentic book is a Bible" (*Pollen,* 102), Novalis, *Schriften,* ed. H.-J. Mähl and R. Samuel (Darmstadt: Wissenschaftliche Buchgesellschaft, 1999), 2, p. 275. On 7 November 1798 Novalis wrote to Friedrich Schlegel, who was planning to write a Bible himself, that the Bible was "the Ideal of any and every book. The theory of the Bible, once elaborated, yields the theory of all writing or word-formation—which at the same time provides the symbolic, indirect, rule for the construction of the creating spirit" (*Schriften* 1, 673).

2. Johnson, "Renewing Catholic Bible Scholarship" (note 4 to ch. 6 above).

3. To be fair, Ricoeur claims that "this de-psychologizing of interpretation does not imply that the notion of authorial meaning has lost all significance." That, he goes on, would be "the fallacy of the absolute text: the fallacy of hypostasising

the text as an authorless entity. . . . [A] text remains a discourse told by somebody, said by someone to someone else about something." Paul Ricoeur, *Interpretation Theory: Discourse and the Surplus of Meaning* (Fort Worth: Texas Christian University Press, 1976), p. 30. But Ricoeur gives no reason for not pursuing the process of depsychologizing to its logical conclusion, nor for regarding such a conclusion as a reductio ad absurdum—as veneration of sacred books in more than one religious tradition shows it is not. More important, the concession to Schleiermacher does nothing to reestablish a generic difference between the Bible and secular writing (maybe Ricoeur was persuaded to make the concession by disagreeable memories of *sola scriptura*). The task Ricoeur does not address is to define *how far* the hermeneutic of authorship applies (to which works, or which aspects of which works) and *how far* the depsychologized hermeneutic of the text.

   4. Friedrich Hölderlin, *Patmos,* line 225, *Sämtliche Werke und Briefe 1. Gedichte,* ed. Jochen Schmidt, Bibliothek deutscher Klassiker 80 (Frankfurt am Main: Deutscher Klassiker Verlag, 1992), p. 365.

   5. HR 39. I assume here that what Ricoeur calls "fonction référentielle" includes what a biblical exegete such as Frei would call "sensus litteralis." The distinction between sense and reference (which for Frege is a matter of proper names) is difficult to maintain once one starts dealing with utterances longer than a single sentence.

   6. See my "'Art,' Literature, Theology," (note 15 to ch. 2 above).

   7. Lichtenberg, *Schriften* (note 2 to ch. 4 above) 1, p. 706 (J357).

   8. See Andrew Bowie, *From Romanticism to Critical Theory: The Philosophy of German Literary Theory* (London: Routledge, 1997). For our purposes, however, Bowie elides a crucial distinction by following Gadamer in categorizing Schleiermacher's hermeneutics as Romantic. For all his close personal connections with the early Romantic circle, Schleiermacher retained a certain intellectual distance: what he called religion had to remain autonomous and was not to be subsumed under the heading of "art" (see ch. 3 above). This is the conclusion of Gunter Scholtz, "Schleiermacher und die Kunstreligion," in *200 Jahre "Reden über die Religion,"* Akten des 1. Internationalen Kongresses der Schleiermacher-Gesellschaft Halle 14–17. März 1999, ed. Ulrich Barth and Claus-Dieter Osthövener (Berlin: de Gruyter, 2000), pp. 515–33, p. 531: "[Schleiermacher's] Zeitgenossen aus dem Romantikerkreis aber vollziehen eine andere Bewegung." For the young Friedrich Schlegel and his circle there always existed at least the possibility of an immediate relation between the Ideal and the text (that was why he thought one man could write a Bible), whereas for Schleiermacher that relation had to be mediated through history.

   9. For the development of the German culture of print, see Albert Ward, *Book Production, Fiction, and the German Reading Public, 1740–1800* (Oxford: Clarendon,

1974); Nicholas Boyle, "Das Lesedrama: Versuch einer Ehrenrettung," in *Kontroversen, alte und neue,* Akten des VII. Internationalen Germanisten-Kongresses Göttingen 1985, Bd 7 (1986): 59–68.

10. I am not saying that familiarity cannot be revelation too, though it is perhaps one of the rarer sources of revelation in literature—and that is not because it can be found only in multivolume epics, for reading Emily Dickinson can get you there in a few lines. Rather it is because literary forms mainly presuppose at least the pretence of having something new to say, something, as the dominant modern form has it, novel.

11. *Aristotle on the Art of Poetry.* A revised text with critical introduction, translation and commentary by Ingram Bywater (Oxford: Clarendon, 1909), ch. 9, p. 27.

12. Developing Roman Jakobson's remark that poetry is "reference split in two," Ricoeur claims that in metaphorical statements, such as Baudelaire's "La nature est un temple," "the 'is' is both a literal 'is not' and a metaphorical 'is like.' The ambiguity, the splitting, is thus extended from sense to reference and across the latter to the 'is' of metaphorical truth. Poetic language does not say literally what things are, but what they are like." "Biblical Hermeneutics," pp. 84, 88, virtually unchanged from the equivalent passage in *La Métaphore vive* (Paris: Seuil, 1975), pp. 311–12. See the critique of this view by Janet Martin Soskice, *Metaphor and Religious Language* (Oxford: Clarendon, 1985), pp. 86–90.

9.   A Catholic Approach to Literature

1. Kant, *Kritik der Urteilskraft,* "Analytik des Schönen," 1, §5, in *Werke,* ed. Weischedel, 10, p. 288.

2. Inaugurated of course by Friedrich Schiller, *Über die ästhetische Erziehung des Menschen* (1795). See the bilingual edition, *On the Aesthetic Education of Man in a Series of Letters,* ed. and trans. E. M Wilkinson and L. Willoughby (Oxford: Clarendon, 1967).

3. Hayden White, *Metahistory* (note 8 to ch. 3 above), esp. pp. 1–42, 88–94; Paul Ricoeur, *Temps et récit 1* (Paris: Seuil, 1983), on Hayden White, pp. 228–39. There is a shorter treatment of the "act of narrating common to historians and storytellers, playwrights, novelists" in "The Narrative Function" in Paul Ricoeur, *Hermeneutics and the Human Sciences: Essays on Language, Action and Interpretation,* ed. John B. Thompson (Cambridge: Cambridge University Press, 1981), pp. 274–96.

4. See note 12 to ch. 8 above.

5. *Aristotle on the Art of Poetry,* ch. 4, pp. 9–11.

6. Gilbert Keith Chesterton, *The Victorian Age in Literature,* Home University Library (London: Thornton Butterworth, 1938), p. 119 (first published 1913).

7. Friedrich Nietzsche, *Werke in drei Bänden,* ed. Karl Schlechta (Munich: Hanser, 1954–56), vol. 1, p. 40 (*Die Geburt der Tragödie,* §5); cp. J. P. Stern, *A Study of Nietzsche* (Cambridge: Cambridge University Press, 1979), pp. 171–201.

8. Charles Dickens, *Oliver Twist, or, The Parish Boy's Progress,* ed. Philip Horne (London: Penguin, 2002), p. 449. Coffee and ham: pp. 66, 69.

9. I am grateful to Rosemary Boyle for this example.

10. Similarly, Wittgenstein comments in the *Tractatus* that scientific writing tells us not what is but how things are (what is, or is not, the case)—that is, he adds, nothing of any importance. *Tractatus Logico-Philosophicus,* trans. D. F. Pears and B. F. McGuinness (London: Routledge, 1966), 6.41, 6.52.

11. Kant, *Kritik der Urteilskraft,* "Die Dialektik der ästhetischen Urteilskraft," §59, "Von der Schönheit als Symbol der Sittlichkeit," in *Werke,* ed. Weischedel, 10, pp. 458–63 .

12. Peter Spufford, *Power and Profit: The Merchant in Medieval Europe* (London: Thames & Hudson, 2002).

10.   Wagers (1): Pascal's *Pensées*

1. *P* 77, Brunschvicg *minor* edition (note 6 to ch. 1 above). Information about the structure of the projected *Apology* is taken from the edition by Louis Lafuma: *Pascal: Oeuvres complètes* (Paris: Seuil, 1963).

2. B. Pascal, *Pensées,* ed. L. Lafuma (Paris: Luxembourg, 1951), vol. 3, pp. 149, 152.

3. Alexander Waugh, *God* (London: Review, 2002), p. 288; Per Lønning, *Cet effrayant pari: Une 'pensée' pascalienne et ses critiques* (Paris: Vrin, 1980); cp. Alexandre Koyré's dismissively laconic references to Pascal: *From the Closed World to the Infinite Universe* (Baltimore: Johns Hopkins University Press, 1957), 43; *Metaphysics and Measurement: Essays in Scientific Revolution* (London: Chapman and Hall, 1968), p. 20.

4. Lucien Goldmann, *Le dieu caché: Etude sur la vision tragique dans les Pensées de Pascal et dans le théâtre de Racine* (Paris: Gallimard, 1955), esp. pp. 315–37.

5. For the full title of this section see Lafuma, ed., *Pensées,* (note 2 above) vol. 1, p. 131; vol. 2, p. 39.

6. Notably *P* 204, 236–38 (= Lafuma nos. 159, 158, 153, 154). References to the themes "cachot" (*P* 200, 218 = Lafuma 163, 164) and "désaveu de la raison" (*P* 267, 272 = Lafuma 188, 182) and to the capacity of reason to deal with the infinite (*P* 72, 430 = Lafuma 199, 149) also seem related.

7. *P* 17. The aphorism was of considerable importance to Nietzsche, who based on it a part of his currently influential essay, *Über Wahrheit und Lüge im außermoralischen Sinn, Werke,* ed. Schlechta (note 7 to ch. 9 above), vol. 3, p. 320. Nietzsche, however, did not see the connection with the argument of the wager.

8. Brunschvicg *minor* edition, pp. 146–62. See also P. Courcelle, *L'Entretien de Pascal et de Sacy: Ses sources et ses énigmes* (Paris: Vrin, 1960).

9. The term originates in a phrase of Montaigne's ("ce petit caveau où tu es logé." *Essais* II, 12, Montaigne, *Oeuvres complètes,* ed. A. Thibaudet and M. Rat [Paris: Pléiade, 1967], p. 504). It is retained by Pascal through six versions of a sentence in *P* 72 (pp. 348–49) and is developed into a foreshadowing of the wager in *P* 200; cp. 237, 199. It furnishes the title of *P* 218.

10. Brunschvicg situates the remark as if it were preparatory for the wager fragment, but in Lafuma's ordering (201) it has to be subsequent to the argument from probability (it appears in chapter 15).

11. Lichtenberg, *Schriften und Briefe* (note 2 to ch. 4 above), i, p. 254 (D 161).

12. I should perhaps make it explicit that by "the Law" I always mean also, if the context allows, the fulfillment of the Law in the person of Jesus Christ.

13. Nicholas Boyle, *Who Are We Now? Christian Humanism and the Global Market from Hegel to Heaney* (Notre Dame: University of Notre Dame Press; Edinburgh: T.&T. Clark, 1998).

14. Goldmann, *Le Dieu caché,* pp. 336–37.

11.   Wagers (2): Goethe's *Faust*

1. Christopher Marlowe, *Doctor Faustus,* ed. Keith Walker (Edinburgh: Oliver & Boyd, 1973), henceforth *MF;* here I.i, 70–97.

2. Line references are given to Johann Wolfgang von Goethe, *Faust,* ed. Erich Trunz (*Goethes Werke,* ed. Erich Trunz, 3) (Hamburger Ausgabe) (Munich: C. H. Beck, 1988); henceforth *F.*

3. Matthew Bell, "Faust's Pendular Atheism and the British Tradition of Religious Melancholy," in *Goethe and the English-speaking World: Essays from the Cambridge Symposium for His 250th Anniversary,* ed. Nicholas Boyle and John Guthrie (Rochester: Camden House, 2002), pp. 71–83.

4. Georg Lukács, "Fauststudien," in *Goethe und seine Zeit* (Bern: Francke, 1947), pp. 127–207.

5. If one thinks there is only one ending one will probably want to ask Patrick Sherry's question: "was the poet taking evil seriously enough?" Patrick Sherry, *Images of Redemption: Art, Literature, and Salvation* (London: T.&T. Clark, 2003), pp. 187, 177–79.

12.   Faces (1): *Moby-Dick*

1. *LR* 45 ("Time and the Other"), pp. 82–84 ("Ethics as First Philosophy"). See also *Totalité et Infini: Essai sur l'extériorité,* Phaenomenologica 8 (The Hague: Nijhoff, 1961), IIIB, "Visage et éthique," pp. 168–95.

2. *Totalité et Infini,* 50.

3. Bernhard Waldenfels, "Lévinas and the Face of the Other," in *The Cambridge Companion to Lévinas,* ed. Simon Critchley and Robert Bernasconi (Cambridge: Cambridge University Press, 2002), pp. 63–81, p. 68. But Lévinas says, "Autrui n'est pas l'incarnation de Dieu, mais précisément par son visage, où il [=Autrui] est désincarné, la manifestation de la hauteur où Dieu se révèle." *Totalité et Infini,* p. 51.

4. *Poems and Prose of Gerard Manley Hopkins,* selected with an introduction and notes by W. H. Gardner (Harmondsworth: Penguin, 1963), p. 51.

5. Quoted by Charles Olson, *Call me Ishmael* (London: Jonathan Cape, 1967), p. 53 (first published 1947). I am particularly grateful to Richard Francis for guiding me through the Melville labyrinth.

6. Olson, *Call me Ishmael,* 52; *Moby-Dick,* ed. Harrison Hayford, Hershel Parker, and G. Thomas Tanselle, Writings of Herman Melville, Northwestern-Newberry Edition, vol. 6 (Evanston and Chicago: Northwestern University Press and the Newberry Library, 1988), p. 489 (henceforth *MD*).

7. Olson, *Call me Ishmael,* 21.

8. Ibid., 23; and see *MD* 849.

9. The anonymous expurgator of the first English edition omitted the second of these phrases and the suggestive lines at the start of chapter 11 (*MD* 53, 933).

10. Graham Ward, *True Religion* (Oxford: Blackwell, 2003), pp. 106–14, p. 110.

11. Charles Bruce Gordon, C.S.C., *"Uses of 'Supernatural' in England in the Late Sixteenth and Early Seventeenth Centuries"* (Ph.D. dissertation, Cambridge University, 1998), pp. 36–44 and *passim,* esp. pp. 226–32. The association of homosexuality and paganism through the comparison of Queequeg to Socrates has been noted by

T. Walter Herbert Jr., "Calvinist Earthquake: *Moby-Dick* and Religious Tradition," in *New Essays on Moby-Dick,* ed. Richard H. Brodhead (Cambridge: Cambridge University Press, 1986), pp. 109–40, pp. 118–19. See also the reference to the novel's "masculinism" in the editor's introduction, pp. 9–10.

12. "[T]he caress does not know what it seeks. . . . It is like a game[,] . . . absolutely without project or plan[,] . . .with something . . . always other, always inaccessible, and always still to come. . . . The caress is the anticipation of this pure future . . . without content" (*LR* 51). Ishmael's squeeze of the hand might seem to have this eschatological quality—as his reference to angels suggests—but it is contaminated after all by a "project or plan," as the whole crew is contaminated by Ahab's supreme and monomaniac project. The plan is that the crew should squeeze themselves into each other, and Lévinas stresses that he wishes to "contest the idea that the relationship with the other is fusion." On the contrary, fusion eliminates the other and establishes a relationship of power, the only relationship that interests Ahab. Squeezing is not caressing, it is more like grasping, and "[p]ossessing, knowing, and grasping are synonyms of power" (*LR* 51). The counterproject to Ahab's is therefore no counter at all.

13. Lawrence Buell, by reading the novel in the light of Ricoeur's HR, came to a somewhat similar conclusion, namely, that *Moby-Dick* "verges on revelation" which, if "revelation" means revealing what a sacred text reveals rather than what Ricoeur thinks any text reveals, is all that I believe any secular scripture can ever do ("*Moby-Dick* as Sacred Text," in *New Essays on Moby-Dick,* pp. 53–72, p. 68). In Buell's view Ahab speaks with the voice of Ricoeur's (false) prophet, and on his words Ishmael provides a commentary in the mode of historical narrative (pp. 64–66): Ishmael exposes "the arbitrariness of all particular readings of the divine . . . in a narrative pattern in which all speculation about the divine is abruptly displaced by the revelation of that which might actually be a mark of the divine [i.e., Moby-Dick]. Yet then again, it might not" (pp. 67–68). He illuminatingly suggests that Melville is attempting to rise to the challenge presented by Emerson in his controversial graduation *Address* of 1838 to "'acquaint men at first hand with Deity'" (pp. 56–59, 67) (we have seen that Ahab's hand, in striking through the mask, is trying to do just that). But he does not elaborate the consequence—that the theological dilemmas posed by *Moby-Dick* derive from a definitive rejection of Trinitarianism (cp. Melville's story, "The Lightning-Rod Man," in *The Piazza Tales* of 1856, *Billy Budd and Other Tales by Herman Melville* [New York: New American Library, 1961], pp. 224–31). Buell may be right that Melville is a post-Calvinist (p. 69), but it should not be forgotten that Calvin's God was triune, and that difficulties with Calvin's Father need also therefore to be understood as difficulties with Calvin's Son.

14. "Norfolk Isle and the Chola Widow," in *Billy Budd and Other Tales,* pp. 261–74; henceforth NI.

13.   Faces (2): *Mansfield Park*

1. Jane Austen, *Mansfield Park* (Norton Critical Edition), ed. Claudia L. Johnson (New York: Norton, 1998); henceforth *MP.*

2. Goethe, *Die Wahlverwandtschaften,* in *Goethes Werke,* ed. Erich Trunz, 6 (see note 2 to ch. 11 above).

3. Tony Tanner, *Jane Austen* (London: Macmillan, 1986), p. 150.

4. Marilyn Butler, *Jane Austen and the War of Ideas* (Oxford: Clarendon, 1987), pp. 92–93, 114–17, 232–34; the campaign against German drama may be dated from the first publication of *The Anti-Jacobin* in 1797: Catherine Waltraud Proescholdt-Obermann, *Goethe and His British Critics: The Reception of Goethe's Works in British Periodicals, 1779–1855* (Frankfurt am Main: Lang, 1992), pp. 96–104.

5. Butler, *Jane Austen,* 236n. The punctuation of Austen's letter to her sister Cassandra of 29 January [1813] is, however, best left unamended, for its ambiguity surely reflects the associative flow of the writer's consciousness. She might not wish to reduce the subject of her new book to a single word, but getting the details of ordination procedures right has a high priority for her.

6. Tanner, *Jane Austen,* p. 158.

7. Throughout the scene there is a contrast between the details of the game and the topic of the conversation, which culminates in Mary Crawford's reflection, "It was time to have done with cards if sermons prevailed" (*MP* 170–71).

8. Tanner, *Jane Austen,* p. 164.

9. Austen's religious position is identified as "Georgian Anglicanism" and "the *via media* of mainstream Anglicanism" in Michael Giffin, *Jane Austen and Religion: Salvation and Society in Georgian England* (London: Palgrave Macmillan, 2002), pp. 24–25, but Giffin does not refer to the Rushworths' chapel or to Henry Crawford's behavior in it.

14.   Rewards and Fairies (1): The Idea of England

1. Sherry, *Images of Redemption* (note 5 to ch. 11), e.g., p. 116.

2. Rudyard Kipling, *Puck of Pook's Hill* (London: Macmillan, 1906), pp. 9–10.

3. "A Proper New Ballad intituled The Faeryes Farewell," in *The Poems of Richard Corbett,* ed. J. A. W. Bennett and H. R. Trevor-Roper (Oxford: Clarendon, 1955), pp. 49–52, here pp. 49–51.

4. Francis Cheetham, *English Medieval Alabasters* (Oxford: Phaidon and Christie's, 1984), pp. 38, 302. Examples without the Spirit: pp. 300, 303.

5. Cheetham, *Alabasters,* 30.

6. Ibid.

7. *The Collected Poems of Rupert Brooke: With a Memoir* (London: Sidgwick & Jackson, 1933), p. cxxxiv.

8. The style, however, is meaningless when detached from its social, economic, and religious context. The Munich "garden" leaves a sense of emptiness and pointlessness because it was not laid out in relation to a house. As a public, or rather state, celebration of detached subjectivity it does of course have its own relevance to the German culture from which it really sprang.

9. Joseph Spence, *Anecdotes, Observations and Characters of Books and Men . . . ,* ed. Bonamy Dobrée (London: Centaur Press, 1964) (Sec. VII, 1742–43), p. 159. Pope here alludes to his own *Epistle IV,* ll. 55–56.

10. Horace Walpole, *The History of the Modern Taste in Gardening,* with an introduction by John Dixon Hunt (New York: Ursus, 1995), p. 42.

11. "The fundamental assumption of a link between the English landscape garden and the British Constitution, which others had implied before him, underlies all of Walpole's discussion." Ibid., p. 8.

12. The text of the inscriptions is available on the excellent Web site http://panther.bsc.edu/~jtatter/stowe.html.

13. Brooke, *Collected Poems,* 148.

14. *The Second Chandler Omnibus* (London: Hamish Hamilton, 1973), pp. 3–15, p. 3.

15. Ian McEwan, *Atonement* (London: Vintage, 2002); henceforth *A.*

15.   Rewards and Fairies (2): *The Lord of the Rings*

1. Joseph Pearce, *Tolkien: Man and Myth* (London: HarperCollins, 1999) (henceforth *TMM*), p. 133, citing Carpenter's contribution to a BBC program, *Bookshelf,* on 22 November 1991, collected in an unpublished manuscript by Patrick Curry.

2. Jenny Turner, "Reasons for Liking Tolkien," *London Review of Books* 23.22 (15 November 2001): 15–24.

3. J. R. R. Tolkien, *The Lord of the Rings* (London: Allen & Unwin, 1954–55), iii, 307; henceforth *LR*.

4. Humphrey Carpenter, *J. R. R. Tolkien: A Biography* (London: Allen & Unwin, 1977), p. 176.

5. Ibid.

6. Kenneth Grahame, *The Wind in the Willows,* 28th ed. (London: Methuen, 1928), pp. 144–62, pp. 154–56.

7. See the foreword added to the second edition of *The Lord of the Rings* in 1966, vol.1, pp. 6–7.

8. The late J. A. W. Bennett, who also told me that he thought Tolkien the only man he had known who was clearly a genius.

9. Robert Lowell, "The Quaker Graveyard in Nantucket," vi, in *Poems, 1938–1949* (London: Faber, 1964), p. 23.

10. T. S. Eliot, *Little Gidding,* iii, in *The Complete Poems and Plays of T. S. Eliot* (London: Faber, 1969), p. 196.

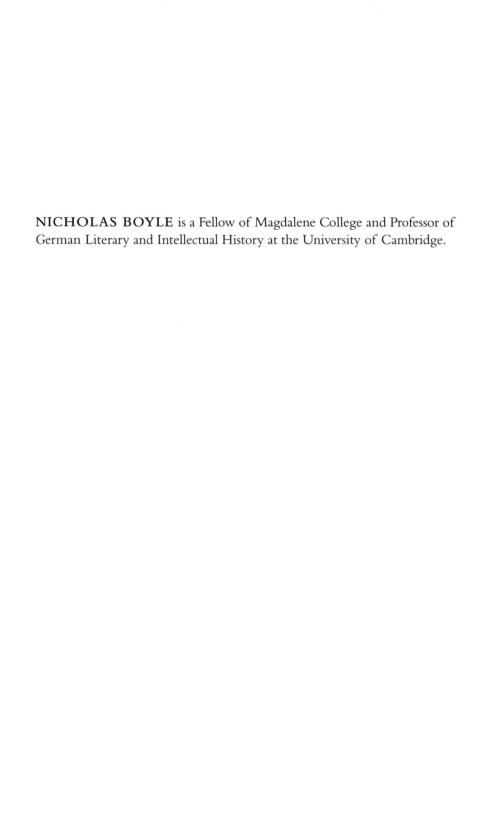

NICHOLAS BOYLE is a Fellow of Magdalene College and Professor of German Literary and Intellectual History at the University of Cambridge.